KU-485-355

Brian Moynahan

Airport International
revised edition

Pan Original Pan Books
in association with Macmillan London

First published 1978 by Pan Books Ltd,
Cavaye Place, London SW10 9PG
and simultaneously by Macmillan London Ltd
8th printing 1980
This revised edition published 1983 by Pan Books Ltd
in association with Macmillan London Ltd
© Brian Moynahan 1978, 1983
ISBN 0 330 26605 5
Phototypeset by Input Typesetting Ltd, London SW19 8DR
Printed and bound in Great Britain by
Cox & Wyman Ltd, Reading

Contents

For Priscilla

Acknowledgements I should like to thank the following for their help with this book: British Airways, Middle East Airlines, Pakistan International Airlines, Cathay Pacific, Malaysian Singapore Airlines (now MAS and SIA), KLM and Qantas. I am particularly indebted to British Caledonian Airways, and to John Delahaye and Captain Adrian Ross. Many airlines take the view that the less their passengers know about flying, the better. The above are notable exceptions, enabling me to ride on flight decks and 'fly' simulators round the world. It would not be possible to list all the pilots, cabin staff, air traffic controllers, baggage handlers and others connected with the airline world who gave me interviews. Several informants would in any case prefer anonymity, for obvious reasons. I am however deeply indebted to Captain Fred Insole, 747 captain and member of the Air Safety Group, who was kind enough to read the manuscript. Any errors that persist are mine.

Notes Useful conversion factors for those readers interested (and equipped with pocket calculators or formidable mathematical brains): multiply knots by 1.1515 to get miles per hour; 8 pounds or 3.65 kilos equal one gallon of jet fuel; multiply imperial gallons by 1.2 to get US gallons.

Airport International

Bestseller – the first edition:
- sold over 170,000 as a Pan paperback
- was published simultaneously in hardback by Macmillan
- was serialized in the *Daily Mail*
- sold in a successful US edition
- translated into several European languages
- extracts appeared in magazines worldwide

Brian Moynahan was educated at Sherborne and at Cambridge where he got a double first in history. In 1964 he became a foreign correspondent for the *Sunday Times* travelling to over fifty countries and flying with seventy-four different airlines, reporting on affairs such as Ulster and Vietnam. Having become an air travel addict he can now fly light aircraft himself and is learning to fly a helicopter. He now works as Paris correspondent for the *Sunday Times* and as well as numerous articles for the paper he has also contributed to several other magazines and papers and appeared on television and radio.

He is married with two children.

Prologue

My first flight was from Paris to Portsmouth in 1959. The pilot arrived late, with the stewardess. He wore a reefer jacket, blue serge trousers and Wellington boots. The stewardess wore laddered stockings and mirror sunglasses. They both went into the cockpit without a word.

When the English coast loomed up the stewardess appeared in the cabin. She was still wearing sunglasses, but her lipstick was smudged. 'Southend, anyone for Southend?' she shouted. The boy in front of me put up his hand.

The ageing DC3 abruptly landed. The boy was bundled out on to the grass field and we took off again. The stewardess went back into the cockpit. As we circled Portsmouth Harbour, I reflected that there was more to this flying business than met the eye.

Experience has proved me right. There is much knowledge to be mined from the brave new world of air travel. It is breeding new species: men who scare away birds, who pour whisky down drains, who balance turbine blades, who smuggle rare birds in shoeboxes. There are new airports, too: Paris's eerie and space-like Charles de Gaulle, or Dallas/Fort Worth with its Texan vastness and its claim to be the airport of the future. There are airports which are almost choked with traffic, like Chicago's O'Hare, Majorca's Palma or Tokyo's Haneda; and there are deserted airports like Tanzania's Kilimanjaro, lying beneath the snows of that great mountain waiting for the tourist boom that never came.

But the greatest of them all is London's Heathrow. It handled more than 230,000 international flights in 1980. Its closest rival, Frankfurt Rhein-Main, managed only 130,000. Heathrow's lead in international passengers is similar, its eighteen million being way ahead of New York JFK's twelve million. It is interesting to note that Palma de Majorca's San Juan makes the world top ten in international passengers, along with Heathrow, JFK, Frankfurt, Amsterdam, Rome, Zurich, Copenhagen, Paris Charles de Gaulle and San Francisco International. That Majorca should be ahead of such giants as Tokyo shows the extraordinary growth of package holidays in Europe.

Heathrow can serve as representative of all these airports, and exhibits the problems common to all – from overcrowded airspace to overstretched ground facilities to a runaway crime rate. It is the focal point of the great air routes between Europe and North America in one direction, and between Europe and the Gulf of Iran, Africa and Asia in the other. It seethes with all the denizens of this strange world, rich and poor, honest and dishonest. It is the Airport International *par excellence*.

The first edition of this book was greeted with a storm of protest at Heathrow. Airport shop stewards, taxi drivers and the British Airports Authority, which owns the complex, protested at the detail given of the dishonest side of the airport. Heathrow, they said, if it does not actually smell of roses, smells of nothing worse than jet fuel.

The period between the two editions has, alas, proved that the first edition was all too accurate. For what has happened? Since then, Heathrow has witnessed the world's most bizarre airport strike: baggage loaders struck because so many of their colleagues had been suspended on suspicion of theft that those remaining felt themselves grossly overworked.

That scarcely smacks of honesty. The original edition detailed, for the first time, how passengers could best avoid the traps that lie in wait for them at international airports, from pirate taxis to stolen luggage. I have expanded on this, and have included fresh material from New York's JFK.

The fares jungle has become denser since the first edition. It has been calculated that up to twenty-eight different fares can be charged to passengers on a single 747 flying from London to Los Angeles. New information is included. So are league tables of the world's most popular and unpopular airlines and airports, based on polls of experienced travellers.

The new information should enable the reader to have a sporting chance of obtaining something that has become in ever shorter supply: a pleasant flight.

Brian Moynahan
London 1981

Part One
Airport

1 Airport International

Heathrow handles more than 28 million passengers, international and domestic, a year. Traffic controllers and the pilots of seventy-five airlines worked their way through 275,000 take-offs and landings in 1980. It is a city in its own right, employing 56,900 people full time, the working population of Newcastle. Like all the great airports, it dates back only to the last days of the war.

The first runway – still annoyingly out of line with the prevailing winds – was built on the flat, marshy land near Staines in 1944. It was an historic site. One of the most important Anglo-Saxon temples is buried under the Number Two Terminal. The water for the fountains for Wolsey's great palace at Hampton Court comes from the Longford river which runs along the south side, and poses a considerable security problem. The hamlet of Heathrow is under the main car park.

The last wolf in England was killed on the southwest perimeter. The area was a favourite haunt of highwaymen, waiting for the rich gentlemen and packed coaches moving down the Bath Road. This famous coaching road marks the northern perimeter of the airfield. Dick Turpin plied his trade here. Lamps and false tracks were used to tempt traffic off the road and into a marshy area close to the main entrance tunnel, where the horses would bog down and robbery was easy.

Travellers did not feel safe until they were well past Heathrow and into Staines, under the protection of the troops barracked at Windsor.*

Two families of gypsies have lived between the main runways, in caravans in a little copse, the home of badgers and hedgehogs, reached by a lane choked with tyres and gutted cars. The holding point for aircraft taking off to the east, towards London, is only two hundred yards away. 'Look at one of they,' says the senior

---

* A special squad of troops is still stationed at Windsor, to protect travellers from terrorists and hijackers at Heathrow.

Romany, pointing at the jets. 'Now they would make a lot of scrap.'

The hare and the rabbit snaring is excellent by the runways. When the jets are not flying, foxes bark incessantly. The riding school ponies and the pigs from the smallholding by Runway 10 Left add to the rural noise. The drainage ponds on the west side had the best perch fishing for miles around until the number of permitted anglers among airport staff was restricted. Someone slipped in pike for vengeance. Tomatoes and mushrooms flourish, and hay is harvested from the grass between the runways.

It is a curious, flat area of small rivers, ponds, gravel pits, orchards and decaying smallholdings. It was excellent hunting country. Lord Grantley Berkeley said after a run right across the present airport: 'It was a devilish good run, but the asparagus beds were heavy and the grass was up to one's hocks.'

Close to the airport, shaken by every aircraft that takes off, is St Mary's Church at Harmondsworth. It has a first edition of the Authorized Bible. Richard Cox, whose Orange Pippins grew in orchards on the airfield, is buried in the churchyard. One of the greatest timber buildings in Europe is there: a massive tithe barn dating from the Normans.

Colnbrook, another of the airport villages, was one of the great centres of the coaching age. It was the lunch stop for stage coaches heading west from London, and the last changing point for horses coming towards London. The great inns still stand – Elizabeth I stayed at the Hart whilst travelling as a teenage prisoner to Hampton Court.

On the southern perimeter is Stanwell. The local school was built by Baron Knyvet, the magistrate who discovered Guy Fawkes in the cellars of Parliament.

The airport has ghosts. A Saxon prince haunts the ponds, where he drowned, and a highwayman clatters through the concrete of the cargo sheds, tricorn-hatted with a black horse.

The runways are the heart of any airport. Heathrow has three. Two of them are 12,000 feet long and capable of handling any type of aircraft. The third is only 7,700 feet and must take the traffic on the few days when south-westerly gales are blowing.

They are regularly washed with detergent and giant scrubbing machines clear the oil from jet exhausts. Burst tyres on take-off can cause crashes – an East African Airways VC10 had a fatal crash at Addis Ababa after debris left lying on the runway punctured a tyre. The runways are continually checked by a patrol in a special vacuum cleaner truck. It sucks up the screws, bolts and other pieces of metal that can fall on a runway. The patrol also checks the runway lights, which have to take the thump of jets landing 260 tons at 160 mph on them. The lighting systems are crucial, and a big airport like Heathrow has over 500 miles of cables.

Besides aircraft, an airport has a bewildering supply of vehicles. There are yellow runway patrol and 'Follow Me' marshalling vans; snow clearance trains with plough blades, brushes and blowers; aircraft tugs that can pull a loaded Jumbo; special fuel bowsers which can carry up to 20,000 imperial gallons or 90,000 litres; high lift catering trucks and trucks with steps.

Every airport has its own large fire services, with trucks that have the emphasis on a 'quick KO' – knocking out the fire with a vast amount of foam for a minute or so whilst the passengers and crew get out. There are fleets of 'quick dash trucks' carrying oxygen masks, ladders, axes, first aid and cutting equipment. Large tractors are kept as rescue vehicles to pull out aircraft that get bogged down off the runways.

There are special bird-scaring jeeps. Birds can cause crashes if they are ingested into the engines and break the turbine blades, particularly on take-off. Heathrow has twenty-one men involved in keeping it free from birds. Their Land-Rover has a loud hailer that sends out bird distress calls when a flock is sighted. Cassette recordings of the shrieks of birds of prey, hawks and falcons, also frighten them off.

About 100 big fireworks are used most days at Heathrow, sending out a cloud of silver stars as well as a bang to unnerve the birds. The Bird Unit members are sent on special courses along the Essex coast to increase their knowledge of the birds and their habits. When there are gales round the coast, the gulls arrive. In one night 300 gulls were killed, damaging seven aircraft.

The Royal Navy keeps falcons at Lossiemouth in Morayshire, Scotland, where training against bird strikes is carried out. At Copenhagen's Saltholm airport, ornithologists deal with the eggs. In Canada there are ornithological forecasts to warn pilots. These are based on radar sightings (radar can spot large flocks of birds), migration patterns and the weather.

The problem is considerable. There are some 2,000 bird strikes a year in the US, and they can be killers. An Electra airliner hit a flock of starlings during take-off at Boston, an airport plagued by birds, and crashed, killing 61 of the 72 on board. A United Airlines Viscount hit a swan 6,500 feet above Maryland. The bird lodged in the elevator controls, forcing to plane into an uncontrollable dive. All aboard died. The captain of an Indian Airlines DC3 was killed when a vulture smashed through the cockpit windscreen, the co-pilot safely landing the plane. Modern windscreens will withstand impact with a 4-lb bird at 470 mph.

Ninety per cent of bird strikes are below 1,500 feet, except during migration when there is dense bird traffic between 1,500 and 2,000 feet. One particular danger is that vibration from jet engines at airports brings worms to the surface, attracting birds. However, geese have been sighted above 15,000 feet. The airports with the highest bird-strike rates in the UK are Belfast Aldergrove, Cardiff, Edinburgh, Glasgow and Luton. The rates for Heathrow, Gatwick and Manchester are among the lowest. Gulls are involved in about half the incidents. An average of fourteen engines and two windscreens a year have to be changed in Britain after bird strikes.

The bigger the aircraft, the more likely is a hit. A 747 averages ten hits per 10,000 hours, a 707 only 1.5.

At least at Heathrow there is no need for anti-snake patrols. In Kuala Lumpur, and at Manaus in the Brazilian Amazon, they have to make sure snakes do not crawl up into the aircraft. A light plane pilot in Malaysia found a cobra coming out of his instrument panel in flight. Fortunately the soothing heat and steady note of the engine kept it too soporific to attack.

An airport is as complicated to run as most cities. Heathrow has its own quantity surveyor, domestic and foul drainage water supervisor, electrical and mechanical engineer, and security chief.

The taxiways are so complex, with turn-off points and crossovers, that there is a special A to Z taxiway guide for pilots, who were getting lost between the runways and the terminals. In fog they still do, although it is possible for a ground controller to talk a pilot from a runway on to a stand by using the airport radar. It is so accurate that the aircraft type can be recognized from the screen. The controller normally guides the aircraft in fog with green lights along the taxiways. The captain simply keeps his nosewheel along the lights.

Using radar in an emergency, the controller can tell the pilot to turn left or right, speed up or stop, making sure that he gets safely past other aircraft. The system is also used for vehicles in thick fog. In one crash in the US the wrecked aircraft could only be seen on radar, and the rescue services were painstakingly directed out to it one by one on radar.

More than 23,000 people work in the huge maintenance areas on the east side. Much of the work on instruments is done in special dust-free rooms, with filtered air and nylon overalls designed to trap fabric particles.

The engine testing areas are surrounded by banks of earth and baffer boards. Maintenance men work through the night to get planes back on line. Airports are sleepless places. They never close. Indeed, it is technically illegal for them to do so. Although they can advise a pilot not to land because of fog or snow, they cannot stop him; the decision is his.

The fuel facilities have to cope with a demand of two million gallons a day. Tankers are slow and ponderous for machines as thirsty as the Jumbo, which can swallow 40,000 gallons, so there is an underground network of fuel pipes, running from a tank on the west side to hydrants on the aprons. With these, 500 gallons a minute can be pumped into an aircraft's tanks from each hydrant. Where JFK was storing 600,000 gallons in 1948, it now has 25 million gallons in a special tank farm.

The cargo area on the south side is a miniature airport of its own. The freighters never come near the passenger terminals. There are special customs posts for cargo and enough storage to cope with half a million tons a year at Heathrow and JFK, and over 400,000 tons at Frankfurt and Orly. A typical load on one 707 freighter flying from Heathrow to Chicago: two poodles, eight plastic bags of eels, a box of radioactive Thorium-X, 5,000 Swiss umbrellas, 500 assorted boxes of goods for a department store, one ton of German cuckoo clocks, six tons of Dutch blankets and £500,000 worth of precious stones.

The cargo area is the most exclusive on the airport. This is where the Queen flies from, a bleak-looking shed spruced up with carpets and flowers, and a dirty concrete apron used by tubby freight aircraft.

The private aircraft also live on the cargo side. The sleek executive jets are kept there by the big corporations. There are the house colours of de Beers, RTZ, Beechams and Sir Charles Forte. A visiting Convair turbojet has 'Capitalist Tool' written on it, the jokey property of an American business magazine, *Forbes*.

Special groundstaff look after the 18,500 passengers who disembark on the south side every year. They have their own strong views on the famous: 'Katherine Hepburn, she's everyone's favourite. And Elizabeth Taylor. She went to Italy once and she took so much along with her that the aircraft had to make a second trip back to pick up her luggage.' And on the infamous: 'Yul Brynner, the chief skinhead, comes in a miserable chartered Dove, with *propellers*, and acts as if he owns the place. And Sinatra. Tries to insist that the Customs and Immigration go out to him. Maybe he's all right, but his bodyguards are the most unpleasant people I've ever come across.'

All but State visitors have to clear Customs and Immigration on the north side. Royal flights have special codes to get immediate priority. The Queen is called Kitty Hawk; Prince Philip is Kitty Rainbow. Others are simply 'Ascots'. There is little fuss for royalty, and little special security. Airport staff are in awe of American Presidential visits. Two special Hercules transports carry bullet-proof Lincolns. A Starlifter, the world's largest plane, brings seven helicopters and a posse of seventy secret servicemen with radio receivers in the earpieces of their dark glasses, pistols under their armpits, and badges on their lapels so they will not shoot each other.

The airport has special Government reception rooms for VVIPs and VIPs, Very Very and the merely Very Important People. These are different from airline hospitality lounges, which are for the CIP, the Commercially Important People. The VIPs get strictly graded welcomes. There are eighteen varieties starting with foreign royalty and working down through Presidents and Prime Ministers to the lowest rating, Ambassadors to the Court of St James. This means that, although the Haitian Ambassador in London is a VIP, the US Ambassador in Moscow is not. The

Foreign Office has its own delicate social hierarchy. There are orchids for Presidents' wives, rare bouquets for Foreign Ministers, roses for Ambassadors. The red carpet is only unrolled on the tarmac for Heads of State.

Special staff look after the protocol, and manage the government-provided conference rooms. These have all telex and television facilities, the scene of many dramatic interviews with returning hijack hostages or errant film stars. The prompt boards, left stacked up by the door, also bear dumb witness to the unending stream of platitudinous politicians. 'Like it or not this *is* a changing world. We live *in* a changing world. We are on a collision course with the future. Think about it.' 'At this present moment in time, we must pull *together* in order to overcome these difficulties, which *all* countries and not just our own are currently facing.' The emphases are italicized.

The Important People are told in advance what films will be on their flight. Extra swift, personal service eases them through Immigration. Discreet security may be provided by RAF aircraft for the VVIPs.

The terminals are intensely complex. Routes through the building have to be organized carefully so that streams going in different directions do not mix. They must ensure that the dishonest cannot jump ticket, passport and baggage-checks. The passenger has to pass through a number of stages in the right order and at speed. In terms of control and routing, catching a plane is the most complicated journey most people will make.

During the rebuilding of Cairo airport, the chaos was so bad that I met a man who had failed to get his plane to the Philippines three times. He had been to Geneva twice in error, and once to Beirut. He had also fractured his toe when a basin in the (rebuilt) loo collapsed on it. In contrast, the design at Dallas/Fort Worth is so sophisticated that the average distance from car to entrance terminal is normally 100 yards and never more than 300 yards. From the terminal entrance to the plane is 120 feet – passengers on a 747 have to walk twice that distance simply to get to the back of the plane, and a half-mile walk is necessary at many airports to get to the aircraft.

The Queen's Building, next to Heathrow's Terminal Two, is the flight-crew core of the airport. This is the BA pilots' building.

Their smoke-filled rest rooms, briefing rooms and company offices are here. This is where they get their medical checks. Eyesight is tested for long sight, near sight and muscle balance. Peripheral vision must be clear or there will be problems with cabin pressures. Reflexes are tested with a hammer, the heart and lungs listened to through a stethoscope.

There is an electrocardiogram every six months for older pilots, chest expansion is measured, blood pressure and pulse rate examined. For the lucky pilot, there is a piece of buff paper with FIT stamped on it. For the unlucky, a career is over.

The Medical Unit is centred here, looking carefully for incoming infectious diseases. Each terminal has its staff who can give vaccinations and injections when necessary, and who dole out yellow cards to intercontinental passengers that warn of tropical diseases.

The airport chapel is built underground in a vaulted shell like a crypt. It has a circular nave extending outwards into three apses, each with its own altar so that three services for different denominations can be held simultaneously. It has two full-time chaplains. There is a prayer board where passengers have pinned up their hopes on scraps of paper. 'Jeanette come back safely, we love you.' 'Lord keep the Russian Orthodox Church safe.' 'Please God don't let my old father find out nor any one of my family or work people and please keep it out of the papers God please.' What desperation is behind that girlish trembling script?

150 air traffic controllers work round the clock in the nearby Control Tower to bring the aircraft in. The air in the tower is cool, the calm icy, the controllers in shirtsleeves. The curtains are drawn against the sun, the lights are green-shaded so that eyesight adapts to the instruments. The only conversations are the controllers' instructions and the pilots' acknowledgements as they repeat them.

An aircraft passes through up to four controllers during the landing sequence. The first controller guides the aircraft in along the airways from an Air Traffic Control Centre. The airways stretch out like thin interlocking fingers, from 5,000 to 30,000 feet high and up to ten miles wide.

The London ATCC guides the aircraft to one of the holding points for Heathrow, the famous 'stacks' over Bovingdon (for aircraft from Northern Europe and America), Epsom (the main stack for aircraft from Southern Europe, the Mediterranean and the Channel Islands), Biggin Hill (Central Europe) and Ongar (Northeast and East), twelve and twenty miles out from the airport. Here the aircraft circle with 1,000 feet of vertical space between them, waiting their turn to land.

Then an approach controller takes the aircraft off the stacks. He steers them on radar towards their landing runway, keeping a three- to four-mile interval between them and the aircraft in front and behind. A distance of six miles is kept free behind a Jumbo, which creates so much wash, or wake, in the air that it can fling smaller aircraft out of control. The wake can also send birds spinning into the ground.

Approach control finally establishes the plane on its landing path. At a few airports, such as Hong Kong and Bermuda, an aerodrome controller can check it down on Precision Approach Radar. The set has two screens. One shows if the aircraft is on the centreline for the runway: if not, he will steer it left or right. The other shows if it is on the correct glide path, descending at the correct angle so that it will be at 200 feet at the runway threshold. The controller orders it up or down.

Normally, the pilot uses the instrument landing system, where an instrument in his cockpit tells him if he is on the right approach to the runway.

After the landing, a ground movement controller takes over to talk the planes through taxiing. He also gives them permission to start engines, and gives priorities. Many pilots accuse certain airports of blatant nationalism in giving their own airline priority over others, so that it keeps to schedules and others don't. Worst in this respect is Tokyo, which also gives the best cruising heights to Japan Air Lines, forcing others to fly at lower, slower and more expensive heights. Canada has a reputation for helping Air Canada. The ground movement controller also controls all the vehicles on the airport, from the bird scarers to the big grass-cutting machines.

Further from the centre of the airport is the police station. It has five cells, a huge picture-board of world terrorists and hijackers, fourteen golden labradors for sniffing out drugs, and 300 policemen.

Next door are the main Customs House and the Queen's Warehouse, where impounded and seized goods are stored. There is a special animal hostel run by the RSPCA, further out along the northern perimeter.

The catering kitchens are alive round the clock, producing 30 million meals a year, consuming cattle by the herd and sheep by the flock. The Airmail Unit is close by, with a security truck to take any suspicious parcels to the decompression chamber on the other side of the airport.

The slightest breeze along the airport starts the senses. The sharp tang of hay and dung from the elephant pens of the Animals' Hostel sets the eyes watering. The juice of steaks and the oily musk of smoked salmon drift from the flight catering kitchens. There is a clatter of machinery from the printing shed where embossed first-class menus in deep reds and blues, with epaulets and tassels of gold braid, are finalized with wild duck à l'orange for a flight to Chicago, poached turbot and prawns for West Africa.

Spinning blue strobe lights and the whoop-whoop of sirens move out of the fire centre. There is an emergency on average once every day at Heathrow. Alerts are graded from one to three, with a disaster category after an accident has happened. Any aircraft landing with an engine shut down or suspected undercarriage problems rates emergency treatment, hence the high turnout.

The fire service trucks link up at special rendezvous points with ambulances, which would first go to the nearby hospital at Hillingdon. They are guided over runways and taxiways by radio by the ground controller in the control tower. As the 'target' airliner comes in, traffic and aircraft are cleared from adjacent runways and taxiways. In a belly landing, a carpet of foam can be laid down the runway in under four minutes.

Aircraft in serious difficulties normally divert to a Royal Air Force base. The crash facilities are better, the teams (in view of the far higher accident rate in military flying) more experienced, and there are less people at risk, with no great concentration of passengers in terminals.

The drivers start as the aircraft crosses the threshold markers on the runway. That way they will be with the target for the longest time, they have calculated, so that they will not overshoot the crash spot and have to turn back, nor undershoot. Timing is vital, for a fuel fire is an uncontrollable and poisonous thing. Flooded with foam, a fire can be suppressed for a minute whilst the cutting teams get the passengers out.

The passengers in the aircraft are often unaware that there is an emergency. Everybody else knows. The news comes into the control tower from the pilot of the aircraft in trouble. It is then flashed to the police and to the fire and rescue services. The police alert local hospitals, giving the number of passengers aboard. If the emergency is serious, and the chances of a crash significant, hospitals go on standby. However, the special burns units would be too small to cope with a major crash of a Jumbo, DC10 or Tri-Star.

A special disaster room is kept free in the police station. Emergency mortuary areas have been designated and body bags for the dead are ready. Special equipment can link it to air traffic control or the national TV network. Banks of telephones await the next of kin, and cards to match, red for victims, white for inquirers.

Beyond the fire centre on the north side, not far from Runway 10 Left, is an old, blackened Argonaut. Its engines have been removed. The undercarriage has collapsed. But every month, it is set on fire with thousands of gallons of kerosene, the warm, sweet-smelling jet fuel that permeates the air of every airport. The airport fire brigade then practise putting the fire out, awkward in their heavy asbestos suits and breathing equipment.

Many experts feel that commercial airport fire facilities are inadequate compared with those of military airfields. With the military, special firefighting helicopters reach aircraft that crash a few miles from the airport in a minute or so. They carry fire-fighters, doctors, nurses, medical equipment and foam-throwers. No civil airport is equipped on this scale, even though the numbers involved in an airliner crash are normally far greater than in a military accident.

The public is a major menace at any crash. A fire engine got to a BA Trident that crashed after take-off within eight minutes, and an ambulance in eighteen minutes. Looters and sightseers beat them both. They caused such serious traffic jams and hampered rescue work to such an extent that the Home Secretary suggested television and radio should withhold news flashes on accidents until the emergency services were in control.

The three nearby hospitals at Hillingdon, Ashford and West Middlesex have mobile medical teams for crashes. The fire service have special hydraulic jacking tools and compressed-air cutting equipment, to minimize the risk of a spark starting a fuel explosion. Trained women will take calls from anxious relatives and hoaxers: they deal better with personal tragedy than men. There is even a recognized and expert firm of undertakers, J. H. Kenyon, which is retained by several international airlines to send teams to crashes. They deal with the identification of victims. This is often difficult, due to the high incidence of fire and the fact that many passengers travel under assumed names. Dental and medical records are often used. Once identification is complete, the firm deals with embalming, and repatriating the body or burying it locally.

Almost every trade and profession is represented at a great airport. Some are not on any official payroll, but certainly earn their livelihood from airports. In the spring come the international pickpockets, following the great society migration. In the high summer months, as the airport fills with its maximum flow of tourists, the people smugglers – the illegal immigrant runners – put in their greatest effort. Their clients would be too obvious in the winter: it is then that they try the Channel ports or the motorboats from Ostend across the Channel.

The summer also sees the cheque and credit card con-men at their height. Teams operate in fours. One man steals a wallet or handbag, looking more for cheque books and credit cards than cash. He immediately passes the booty on to another man. If he is challenged, he will be 'clean'. The second man takes the valuables and dumps the rest in a waste bin or toilet. The cheques and credit cards are passed to the 'cashers', the man and girl who use them to get cash from banks or easily saleable items like jewellery and watches. Some items like cashmeres and tweeds are ordered by a fence at their home base before the teams leave for abroad.

They travel on airline tickets bought with credit cards stolen in their last port of call. Airports give them mobility, victims, plenty of shopping and banking opportunities, plus a jet-speeded exit.

One gang arrived in London from France at 8.30 a.m. They never left the airport. By midday, they had accumulated ten cheque books and thirty-eight credit cards, and departed for Sweden. Their haul was £700 in cash from the airport banks, £500 in travellers' cheques, and £9,000 worth of perfume, fabrics, cameras and watches from the duty-free shops. They were caught eight airports later.

Prostitutes, 'call-button girls' as they call themselves, roam from airport to airport, operating from the airport hotels.* Most claim to be airline stewardesses. This is both a cover for the hotel, and a come-on to the customers, since stewardesses are international sex-symbols. There is a well-known bar on the Ginza in Tokyo where all the girls are dressed in the uniforms of the great international airlines. The allure of flying is great enough to ensure the bar's success.

Smugglers are locked in endless battle with the Customs. For the professionals, it is a battle of skill, with invoice forms and cargo manifests the keys. A minor change in description can alter the duty rate from 50 per cent to zero. For the amateur, it is often the grin in front of the hidden spyholes on the far, 'safe' side of Customs that gives away the man with the odd camera or extra bottle of Scotch. Glances picked up through the two-way mirrors in Immigration provide other clues.

With large amounts of cargo and passengers' valuables disappearing every year, some of the staff are also there for more than their salaries. Some staff at the car parks, the busiest in Europe, at one time bought their jobs from their predecessors. And small wonder, since it was found that some employees were pocketing half of the take in a sophisticated operation involving major criminals. Parking tickets were obtained by pushing loaded trolleys over the pressure pads at the entrance, and substituted for genuine long-term tickets after the customer had paid them.

* Protesters at the new Dallas/Fort Worth made it clear what they thought of airports. They took out advertisements in the local paper: 'Is this what we want? Cheap taverns? Honky tonks? Go-go dancers? Gay bars? Crime? Dope? It can happen here.' They failed to stop the airport.

Some simply steal cars, although, like much airport crime, this has become more difficult since intensive security against bombers and hijackers began. A more enterprising group started a flourishing car-hire firm. They worked in the off-airport car park, and knew how long each car would be left from the date of return given by the customers. The cars were hired to unwitting passengers at rates well below Hertz and Avis. They were caught only after a series of accidents brought in the police. All off-airport car parks now ask owners to record their mileage to prevent such rackets.

Few workers do their relaxing at the airport. The aircrew go to the hotels that mushroom along the Bath Road on the north side of the airport. Most have small 'key clubs' frequented by pilots. Aircrew are forbidden to drink eight hours before a flight. They avoid pubs when in uniform because the public cannot tell whether they are coming back from a flight or going out on one. Clubs avoid this sort of problem.

Airports spawn pretty girls: the biggest concentration of beauty in any country will be found at its major airport. They work in the big hotels, or the aircraft, or the check-in desks, in the duty-free shops, the departure bars and restaurants, for the car-hire firms and travel companies and banks. There are girl pilots, with Aeroflot and British Caledonian. DanAir, a British charter airline, has a lady captain.

Their public consists very largely of temporarily liberated men, away from home, footloose and fancy free. The girls quickly get bored with this. 'After a day of every passenger trying to flirt with you, the last thing you want to do is see them in the evening,' says an air girl. Hence the key club and room parties with visiting crews and stewardesses in airport hotels, in an attempt to relax away from the customers.

An airport has to cope with illness. Aircraft are met by an ambulance with a crew specially trained in using fork lift equipment to get patients out of aircraft doors. The airport has a medical centre, with eight nurses. Three doctors are on permanent call. The most common illness is a heart attack. About thirty people a year die of coronaries at Heathrow, or are dead on arrival in planes that land at it.

Other emergencies are more bizarre. Two Russian freighters *en route* to Bristol to pick up light aircraft from an aerobatic competition got lost in the control zone. They were short of fuel, and the pilots did not speak English. All incoming aircraft were stacked for an hour as an emergency appeal was put out over the public address systems in all the terminals for anyone who spoke Russian. Eventually, an airport employee found himself talking the aircraft down. His knowledge of Russian almost certainly avoided a crash.

The long-distance Number Three Terminal has had to cease operations temporarily several times as hundreds of Muslim passengers have faced Mecca, and knelt to pray.

Flights have their own rhythm which dictates the pulse of the airport. Far East and transatlantic flights arrive in Number Three between six and nine in the morning. They pull the taxi drivers, touts, trolley men, Customs and Immigration to that terminal. The airport has only 1,500 trolleys for luggage, and a scant thirty porters per shift per terminal.

By 9.30 a.m., the pace of Continental arrivals and departures is increasing. The tugs get busy pulling the snakes of trolleys round to Terminal Two, the Continental terminal. The peak of Continental travel is between 9.30 and 11 a.m. After 11 a.m. domestic flights and the 'milk run' routes to Paris, Zurich and Frankfurt account for most of a light trade. The emphasis is on the domestic terminal, Number One.

European flights pick up again in the early evening, before they are again superseded by intercontinental departures from ten in the evening until midnight. Noise abatement cuts flights between midnight and 6 a.m. to emergencies only.

The night silence at European airports is paid for by countries further east. Delhi, Karachi, Tehran, Beirut and Cairo take the brutal roar of jets ranging up from Australasia, the Far East, the Gulf and Southern Africa to Europe in the small hours. The flights from North America are also arranged to arrive just after dawn.

The complex schedules are thrown into chaos by fog. The mill of fogbound passengers mounts into night-long confusion. The caterers dig deep into their frozen food stocks to meet demands that can go up eighteen times. Telex and phone lines get jammed as incoming aircraft are diverted to Manchester, Paris or Glasgow, and anxious passengers and relations try to find out what is happening.

If fog hits the Low Countries, and Brussels and Amsterdam go out at the same time as Heathrow and Gatwick, the log jam of diverted aircraft will spread back all over Europe. If Paris is out too, few European flights will be possible. The stack of cancelled flights begins stretching back from New York to Chicago and Los Angeles. Aircraft on the transatlantic run are recalled if not too far out. Shannon and Dublin start to take the strain of diverted passengers. The Low Countries, Britain and Paris have been simultaneously fogbound only four times in the past eight years, but when this did happen, the air over the Atlantic and Europe became eerily silent.

2 Into the Jungle

The travelling public is continuously, if surreptitiously, watched by the citizens of the airport – at times with a view to fleecing the passenger, at others to prevent the passenger fleecing them. This jungle is seldom neutral.

The whole process begins with the buying of the tickets. On some flights it is possible that no two passengers have paid the same amount. Fares have become so complicated that there are more than twenty-five different rates on the North Atlantic alone. The cost depends on how early you book, how old you are, at what time of year you want to fly, how many weeks you will be away for, whether you are travelling with a group of friends. The time of day and the day of the week also make a difference, as does where you buy the ticket.

Many passengers pay too much, which is not surprising. Who in his right mind would assume that the cheapest way of getting to Calcutta from London is to fly to Bangkok, 1,400 miles further on, and then to buy another ticket for the 2,800-mile round trip from Bangkok to Calcutta?

And many pay too little. Airlines, anxious to fill empty aircraft, sell their tickets at less than the internationally agreed rate.* On many routes in the Far and Middle East and South America, no local would ever dream of paying the correct fare. These cut-rate tickets are marked Non-Transferable in the bottom left-hand corner. There is also, as we shall see, a flourishing trade in stolen tickets.

Once the ticket has been acquired, preferably in a legal manner and at the minimum price, the passenger must get to the airport. This can be difficult for those travelling in their native country.

---

* They are regularly fined by the International Air Transport Association (IATA) for doing so. British Airways were fined £144,000 for making improper discounts to the travelling public. Other airlines fined in 1976 were Iberia, KLM, Air France, Sabena, Pan Am, and Egyptair. Passengers not offered improper discounts could justifiably feel unlucky. *Business Traveller*, winter 1976.

Many airport taxi drivers strongly object to driving their fellow-countrymen, motivated not by concern for the foreigner but by the prospect of picking up a 'punter', someone who can safely be overcharged.

The case springs to mind of George Leggett, the amazing New Yorker who saw London on £790 a day. Mr Leggett had the impression that pounds were worth much less than dollars. He spent £100 each way on taxis to and from the airport, remarking that 'the drivers looked very pleased'. He tipped a waiter £5 for a meal that cost £2.50, and ran out of money in thirty-six hours. Mr Leggett's final words were: 'I am going home now because I think people could have been more helpful.'

Airport cab drivers throughout the world are rightly mistrusted. Most passengers realize that they should only take a licensed cab with a working meter. There have been plenty of warnings about 'pirate' or 'gypsy' cabs, where a man with his private car turns up at an airport or downtown terminal on the chance of catching a punter.

But people do strange things in strange countries. They get embarrassed, they do not speak the language, they do not know the currency. All this is instantly summed up by the drivers. There have been so many cases of people being charged up to forty times the correct fare on the short trip from the West London terminal to Piccadilly Circus that British Airways started putting spiked wheel clamps on any pirate car that turned up at the terminal. Airline buses have warning signs about non-licensed 'taxis'.

The British Airports Authority obtained injunctions in 1980 to prevent car-hire drivers illegally touting for trade. The Authority said: 'We are determined to protect passengers, particularly foreign visitors, who are unaware of their rights, from harassment by unauthorized drivers. These touts are uncontrolled and their passengers have little protection from excessive fares, unroadworthy vehicles or lack of insurance cover.'*

The easiest victims are girls flying into a foreign country for abortions, say from Italy to London. The drivers wait for British

---

* *The Times*, 1 July 1980.

Airways flights from Europe in the morning, and for European flights in the afternoon: that is how the traffic flows.

The girls are very easy to spot. 'They are probably looking distressed, and clutching a piece of paper with a clinic's address on it,' says an airport policeman. 'But the real giveaway is that they have hardly any luggage – and they never have any duty free bag with them.

'So the drivers know just who to go for. They know, too, that the girl will be carrying a lot of cash for the operation, and that she won't be in an arguing mood. With any luck, they'll not only rob them for the fare, they'll take them to another clinic and pick up a commission. They can make £250 off one fare.'

Nationality is an important clue for drivers. 'The Japanese and the Americans are the easiest,' says one pirate. 'The Japanese normally stick together in big groups, but if you get one on his own it's easy. They are very polite. They don't like scenes, especially if there are a lot of people around – which there always are at an airport or hotel. If they hesitate, you make it quite clear that there will be a hell of a row on the spot if they don't pay up pronto. They always do.

'Now, you never do that with a Frenchman or German. They know roughly what a trip should cost, because if you know one European city you'll know how far you've come in another. There's no cultural shock to get over, so you estimate distance easily. And a European knows damn well that a row is the last thing you want, especially at an hotel or airport, with doormen and police all over the place.

'Americans above all want to be loved when they are abroad. They stick their hand out full of notes and tell you to take the fare. Half of them don't know the denominations.'

Luggage is also a guide to the punter. 'If the suitcases are all covered with labels, gaudy hotel ones from exotic places like Hawaii and Hong Kong and the Caribbean, then that's perfect. I picked up one couple – pink matching luggage, stuck all over with stickers from the Mandarin Hotel, Hong Kong, and Aloha, Honolulu. £70 into town. The legal rate is eight. Luggage like that is lots of cash, no taste and wide open to flattery. You have to be nice and servile, that's all,' says a driver, extorting nine times the normal fare.

'You notice people who keep airline labels on their briefcases, sometimes a great wad of them. Now, that doesn't make sense for someone who travels all the time – every time you close it, you get the labels mixed up in the locks. So that means the owner is vain, and you can always play on vanity.

'The one you steer absolutely clear of, that you run from, is an old leather case with nothing on it except the remnants of a shipping line marker. Those people know it all backwards and they won't hesitate to call the law.'

The ideal victim comes off a long-distance flight, preferably one who has crossed several time zones. He will be disorientated as well as tired. The pirate will help him change money at the terminal bank.

'You'd be surprised how many people arrive without local money. Once you help them change it, you've got a moral hold on them. They have to trust you. Not only that, but the denominations won't have been explained to them. If they were on their own, they would ask. Because you're there, they don't,' says a driver at Palermo airport. The tricks of the trade are as international as flying itself.

Women are less easily fleeced than men, because they can instantly query a fare with a policeman, doorman or even a passerby without losing face. This enters the fare equation the driver makes of nationality, sex, baggage and exhaustion.

The moral pendulum swings on arrival at the terminal. It is now the passenger who may be up to no good. The ticket may be stolen or falsified. The passenger may have bought the return half of someone else's ticket, thus getting the benefit of a return rate on a single journey. He may be trying to travel before he has been away long enough to qualify for an excursion fare. With some concessionary fares a quarter the normal rate, the incentives to 'bend' a ticket with a little date alteration are great.

A passenger is a potential hijacker as well as a thief. There are several traits that indicate trouble to the check-in staff. The ordinary citizen should be carrying the average amount of luggage for the journey. Hijackers, many of them acting on the spur of the moment, often turn up without any luggage at all. The clothes should tally with the destination. It is suspicious to ask too many questions about the flight and the aircraft.

Concealed weapons, oddly enough, are no guide since so many non-hijackers carry them. A one-month haul at Le Bourget airport, Paris, comprised 96 rifles, ten revolvers, 8,100 rounds of ammunition, 56 daggers, 480 sheath-knives, 28 screwdrivers, 19 forks, 75 medical syringes and 21 paper-knives.

A passport is a more accurate clue. Many political hijackers travel on Arab diplomatic passports. Embarrassments happen. One 'terrorist' was relieved of his Bond-style gun, a loaded and gold-plated Walther PPK valued at £3,000. He turned out to be Prince Kalifa bin Ali Al'tani, the brother of the powerful and oil-rich ruler of Qatar. His temper did not improve when the Special Branch officer who took his gun managed to fire it accidentally through the floor of the terminal.

Great care must be taken to ensure that Arabs do not get on flights which fly via Israel, and vice versa. British Airways once diverted a Bangkok-bound charter flight from a refuelling stop in Dubai when it was realized that an Israeli woman was aboard.

If a potential hijacker is spotted, it will be at the check-in desk. The procedure is well established. The check-in man quietly stamps QQ against the seat number on the visual display screen. QQ alerts the security men at the flight gates for thorough searching of the marked passengers.

An AL after a name suggests a drunk. The captain will take a long look at the passenger before deciding whether to let him board. The cabin crew are told to keep a special eye on him, as they would if he was a CM, a 'compassionate case' after bereavement, or an NE, a 'non-English speaker', or a UC, an 'unaccompanied child'.

Not all security arrangements work. Pan Am allowed a young bearded man on board a Puerto Rico flight. He was wearing a combat jacket and a beret with a Cuban badge on it. Not surprisingly, he wanted the plane to overshoot Puerto Rico for Havana. The next day Marlon Brando was removed from an aircraft, merely for wearing a combat jacket.

The rules for sick passengers are strict, at least in principle. Thus women who are more than seven months pregnant should not fly. The pressure changes could affect the baby. This is as difficult to enforce as the rule that passengers must be able to walk 150 yards unaided and without needing a rest. 'If a woman says she isn't seven months gone, what are you supposed to do about it?' a ground hostess points out. 'And can you imagine what would happen if I asked an old dear to walk 150 yards before she got a boarding card?'

So occasionally babies are born in mid-air. When a Russian woman gave birth in a Jumbo over the North Atlantic as she sped back to Moscow from Washington, Pan Am said there was no means of proving the length of the pregnancy.

Ground staff must turn back passengers with wired jaws or eye injuries. Broken jaws could choke someone who got airsick; damaged eyes are very sensitive to pressure.

The 'No Go' list also includes contagious disease, heart attacks of any strength in the preceding eight weeks, anaemia, chest complaints, pneumonia and incontinence. The major hazard is pressure change: a mild 'chest cold' can turn into serious altitude sickness on a long flight.

Incontinence seems a strange reason for grounding a mature passenger, since babies can travel freely. However, states KLM: 'Changes in atmospheric pressure produce unexpected activity in those conditions and the resulting odours may be aesthetically offensive to other passengers in the enclosed cabin.'

Death is also frowned upon. 'The death of a passenger in flight,' writes KLM's Kanelis Vaandiagen, 'may cause serious delays and in some cases has produced international complications.' Now you know.

In a place as curious as an airport, even baggage is of interest, partly to the airline, if there is too much of it. Hiding a pile of heavy hand luggage whilst weighing in a single suitcase is an old trick. If the flight is not too full, most airlines will ignore it. They should not. Their own regulations strictly limit the amount of hand luggage that can be taken aboard. This is because bags and shopping strewn over the cabin make it much more difficult to get out of the aircraft in an emergency. It has little to do with weight: modern jets are powerful enough to carry much more than the prescribed twenty kilos per passenger.

If excess baggage is charged, an airline will inform all other airlines flying that route. There is thus little point in a passenger storming off and trying another airline. Cooperation is not a hallmark of the airline industry, but it is applied in this area.

A more probing and less welcome interest in baggage is shown by thieves, some of them employed as baggage handlers to load the aircraft.

'Something happens to people when they get to airports,' says a security man. 'They wouldn't dream of letting a suitcase out of their hand, let alone sight, at a subway station. At an airport they'll leave it and go for a stroll or buy a paper. They seem to think that because flying is expensive, you only get nice people at airports. Alas, nothing could be further from the truth.'

Far from the problems coming to an end when the baggage is handed over to the airline, that is often when they begin. Consider the cautionary tale of Alwin Schockemoehle, champion German showjumper. Herr Schockemoehle was flying home from Heathrow after a most successful week of prizewinning in England.

His smart, black leather briefcase, with its two differently numbered combination locks, contained the evidence of his equestrian skill. There was a gold watch won in the Nations Cup, another watch as a present for his wife, £400 in small notes for travelling expenses, a spare shirt and most of his winnings from the international competitions at Hickstead and Wembley – £500 in tens and £2,500 in ones and fives.

The British Airways flight to Bremen, BE618, was delayed by an hour. Herr Schockemoehle became a little worried: 'There were crowds of people around and I thought there was a chance the case might have been stolen. I thought it was safer to give it to British Airways.'

All he got at Bremen was his case, with the locks ripped off, and his shirt. Herr Schockemoehle was not aware of a fundamental airport tenet: any unusual or lavish baggage is likely to be stolen.

His baggage fell into both these categories. Briefcases are seldom sent as cargo, normally being carried aboard as cabin luggage by the owner. Briefcases made of black leather with combination locks indicate a certain lavishness. The baggage handler who opened it may well have thought that the case was being sent as cargo because the owner was smuggling out money and did not wish to take it through Emigration himself.

Schockemoehle happened to be perfectly entitled to export money from Britain. But often such cases were destined for Zurich and Geneva, not Bremen, and were stuffed with illegal amounts of sterling, lire, pesos, dollars. This was the perfect theft since it was very unlikely to be reported. If the owner reported the theft, he faced prosecution for trying to export the cash illegally in the first place. British Customs seized £1,000,000 of currency in 1976. It seems probable that airport thieves made something close to this in totally unreported crimes before British restrictions were eased. They keep a sophisticated eye on exchange rates, bank rates, currency regulations and other factors that indicate a flight of money out of the country.

Currency also comes into the country. Whilst it is legal for it to arrive it has probably illegally left a country with strict export regulations. Indians, Argentines, Chileans, Ugandans, South Africans and others who can take only a very limited amount of cash with them, may all be travelling with a wad of notes in their suitcases.

Baggage, or the absence of it, is also used by check-in staff as the ultimate sanction against rude passengers. It is 'accidentally' dispatched to Nairobi or Nassau. According to airline legend, luggage mistakenly sent to either of these places has never been found. Neither has much sent there deliberately.

Some passengers are immune to such treatment, no matter how rude they are. They are members of the exclusive airline clubs. Magical things happen to people who wear a tie with light blue stripes on a dark blue background, and a briefcase motif to ensure it is not confused with the equally magical Old Etonian tie. This immediately identifies the wearer as a member of the British Airways Business Travellers Club.

He can check in at a first-class counter, even if he is travelling economy. Before take-off, he is entertained to free drinks, free TV and free charm in a British Airways 'Monarch' hospitality suite. Extra swift, personal service speeds him through the formalities. If the aircraft is delayed, free telex and telephone ease the annoyance. Once aboard, the stewardesses call him by his name.

The 'Club' is not restricted to flight privileges. There is automatic membership at twenty-five golf clubs from Gleneagles to Bermuda and Corfu, and automatic discounts from hotels like the George V in Paris, the Grosvenor in London, the Plaza in New York. Club members usually qualify for a 'Q' (high credit) rating on their Air Travel Cards. This enables them to obtain unlimited numbers of tickets to any destination in the world on any of 140 airlines with the piece of green plastic. The ATC 'Q' is perhaps the world's classiest credit card.

Most airlines have their clubs – Pan Am's Clipper Club with its Clipper Skippers, TWA's Ambassador Club. Election depends on how much is spent or how far is flown with the airline, with qualification normally being around £5,000 a year or 100,000 miles. Most airlines review membership annually. Pan Am, however, is good to those who meet bad luck in their career and travel less. Their members are for life.

Ordinary passengers may resent the way others sail through a queue on the strength of a tie or a special baggage tag, blue for British Airways, silver for Pan Am, marked 'Service Plus' for Air France. Consolation is available from a French businessman. Befriended and unaccustomedly jovial in a German nightclub, he thought that a good way to cement his friendship with his seven new friends would be to fly them all to Tahiti on his 'Q' card. By the time he had sobered up, all eight of the happy throng were airborne on first-class tickets. A grand gesture, costing some £6,000.

In these private worlds, there are still people whose courage may win them awards (a British Airways stewardess was posthumously given Britain's highest medal for bravery at London airport for saving passengers in a burning 707) or whose cupidity may land them behind bars (a more common occurrence).

3 The Black List

It is chilling to listen to pilots describing the many airports they do not like. 'High, bad lights, difficult approach – with a strong southerly blowing you can keep it, thanks,' is one pilot's view of Ankara. Another says of Gothenburg: 'Short runway, prone to bad weather, surrounded by hills, I'll never fly it with an inexperienced crew.'

'Tehran has the most dangerous conditions I came across,' says a long-haul pilot. 'A combination of physical danger and human inefficiency. You have to descend close to high mountains with strong winds. The VHF radio is the worst of any major airport. It is virtually unintelligible, although I suppose that could be a blessing in disguise since the controllers are so bad you are better off without them. You find the lights going out, the navigation aids going out.'

No pilot enjoys flying to Rhodes at night when there is a westerly wind. He has to approach over a high col between hills only a mile and a half apart, and gusts can blow him off course. The International Federation of Airline Pilots' Associations (IFALPA) sums up this very busy holiday airport in alarming style: 'Inquiries have indicated that it is not possible to improve this aerodrome and that a completely new one should be constructed. High minima should be considered necessary, especially in high winds and gusty conditions.'

Malaga and Alicante, gateways to the Spanish Mediterranean coast, both have high ground to the north. They are tricky when southerlies blow at night. Corfu has hills dangerously close and is badly affected by gusts. Gibraltar is dangerous for purely political reasons. The Spanish, who are reclaiming 'the Rock' from the British, forbid aircraft to descend in Spanish airspace and a tricky let-down over the sea results. Ibiza has neither radar nor ILS despite the tourist invasion and the consequent flow of night landings.

Naples has very short runways, with Vesuvius waiting at one end and an area where there is a 'cone of radio silence' that affects navigation instruments. Alitalia lost a Viscount with forty-five aboard on Vesuvius. At Palermo in Sicily, pilots complain that there are no proper approach aids, despite the high ground immediately to the south of the airport and the frequent thunderstorms in spring and autumn. An Alitalia DC8 hit Mount Lunga in the approach in bad weather and 115 died. Venice, Milan and Bari are other Italian airports where inadequate equipment or landing aids have been criticized by the International Civil Aviation Organization.

The same weather pattern affects the Greek holiday airport at Corfu – another spot where IFALPA wants an entirely new airport built. 'It is difficult to see how this aerodrome can be improved,' the Pilots' Federation reports. 'Unless and until a new aerodrome is built, pilots should only operate here to high weather limits.' Innsbruck, a major airport for skiers, is at the end of a valley. Radio aids bounce off the mountainside and lured a propjet with more than eighty skiers into a peak in bad weather. Nicosia has sudden weather changes. Mist shrouds the heights round Lima. The Athens runways 'begin in the sea, end in the sea and have mountains at the side', says an American pilot.

IFALPA publishes a black list of the world airports it strenuously dislikes. Nassau in the Bahamas looms large – severe runway irregularity, poor runway and taxiway markings, no sea rescue launches, lack of navigational aids and obstruction lights on Runway 14.

So does Kai Tak, gateway to Hong Kong, positioned in the heart of bustling Kowloon with flats and hotels only fifty feet under the flight path. IFALPA has noted a deterioration in air traffic control, inadequate runway length (several aircraft have landed up in the harbour after overshooting), and inadequate separation between runway and taxiway. Surrounded by soaring, steep-sided hills, subject to mist and low cloud as well as typhoons, and with overflying of the Chinese mainland prohibited, Hong Kong is already a difficult enough place to fly to. And it is one of Asia's busiest tourist and business airports.

Pilots are disturbed by ground controllers unwilling to take a responsibility, notably in the Caribbean. The controllers do not like guiding pilots in with an instrument approach where they could be blamed if something went wrong. They prefer pilots to fly visually, where the whole liability rests on the pilots. 'You could circle Jamaica and Trinidad until you run out of fuel, and they won't give you instrument approach,' a British pilot says phlegmatically. 'If you don't go visual, you don't get down.'

IFALPA marks airports which its members reckon to be 'critically deficient by international standards' with a black star. Other airports, considered unsafe but less dangerously so, are classified with red and then orange stars.

Some famous international airports qualify for black stars. Boston's Logan International is a busy centre, but the pilots say that new noise-control rules mean that planes can be forced to take off or land downwind at night and require departing and arriving planes to fly towards each other on the same runway. At Los Angeles, noise rules mean that aircraft must land and take off over the ocean, forcing some planes to fly downwind rather than into the wind. A TWA 707 crashed whilst attempting a downwind landing in poor visibility.

St Thomas, in the Virgin Islands, is given black star status because its runway is too short for jets. An American Airlines jet ran off the end of the runway while trying to abort its landing. Pago Pago in American Samoa is slated for heavy rain and sea spray on the runway. There is no approach lighting on one direction and the runway and taxiway lighting is inadequate. Navigational aids and weather information are held to be poor. An optical illusion by rain was held partly to blame for a Pan Am crash there.*

Colombia is peppered with black stars. Bogota, Barranquilla, Cali, Cartagena, Leticia, San Andres Island and Medellin all need more and better fire and safety equipment and all those except Cartagena need more navigational aids. Bogota is very high in a mountain bowl that is subject to sudden mists. 'It's called Bogota Eldorado airport,' says a long-haul pilot. 'It's very apt. You feel you've struck gold just by finding it.'

The normal flying standards in Australia are high. But flight charts warn pilots to beware of kangaroos and birds on the runway

---

* All survived the TWA crash, on 16 January 1974. The American Airlines crash, on 27 April 1976, was also survivable. The Pan Am crash, on 30 January 1974, was not.

at Learmouth, and Kalgoorlie and Meekatharra are considered inadequate alternates for international flights.

Medan airport in Indonesia is one to miss. The controllers' English is poor, the taxiways are narrow, the fire equipment and firemen are inadequate, flight control clearances are 'unrealistic', landing control is 'virtually nonexistent', there are often pedestrians on the runway and gliders operate without control. Ujung Pandan, not far away, is not much better – difficult to contact by radio at night, short of qualified flight controllers and with poor communications equipment.

In Italy, Alghero has inadequate approach lighting, firefighting equipment and air traffic control services. Rimini, which has very congested traffic, needs approach lighting, a visual glide slope and runway identification lights.

Osaka in Japan has taxiways that are too close to the runways and the runways themselves are slippery when wet and need their approach lights altered. The navigational aids are inadequate and the missed approach procedure could result in a collision.

Penang, the holiday island off Malaya, has a rough runway surface, inadequate runway markings, pedestrians along the runways, an 'unrealistic' approach procedure, deficient navigational aids and no radar or windspeed indicator. Fua'amotu on Tonga has navigational aids that are either 'unsatisfactory or missing'.

Mexico City, Bombay and Nassau are amongst the busy airports that get red stars. So does New York JFK, for poor snow removal, unsafe noise control necessitating a curving approach, and too many maintenance trucks about. Honolulu has no runway grooving to prevent aquaplaning and there are no approach lights for landing. Anchorage, halfway point on the Polar route from Europe to Japan, gets its red star for danger during crosswinds.

Standards on isolated islands should be particularly high. Aircraft carry additional 'island reserve' to give them extra circling time as they have no alternative. Some pilots 'top up for Mum and Dad,' putting on extra fuel to get them to an alternate, such as New York from Bermuda. Bermuda is very isolated in the Atlantic. Yet it is criticized for approach and landing lighting, and for shortage of navigational equipment. Both Bermuda and Darwin, another 'island airport' in Australia, have only one runway.

If the plane in front crashes on it those following would have nowhere to land. An 'island airport' is categorized in terms of isolation. Thus Darwin qualifies even though it is on the Australian mainland.

St Martin in the Virgin Islands had no precision approach equipment when an Overseas National Airways approached it in bad weather. The pilot bit deeply into his fuel reserves during three attempts to land in torrential rain. He ditched in the sea thirty miles off St Croix when he finally ran out of fuel, killing twenty-three.

Even lonelier is Easter Island, in the Pacific. Yet it has no weather forecasts or reliable navigational aids. There are no obstruction lights in the dangerously high terrain on both sides of the runway. The approach lighting is bad, and the runway length substandard. Communications with Santiago and Tahiti are poor. There is no crash or salvage equipment, no first aid and no search and rescue facilities.

To cap it all, reports IFALPA, 'there is not enough information from the French about radiation levels after nuclear experiments'.

Further into the Pacific, Suva-Nausoui on Fiji has a narrow runway and unreliable navigational aids. Pools of water collect on the runway after heavy rain and cattle are frequently reported wandering in the airport.

Addis Ababa has an unsatisfactory runway surface, poor communications between Addis and aircraft in the Sahara area, and a shortage of navigational aids. Khartoum, the only other airport in this wild area of mountain and desert, has poor approach and runway lighting, bad air traffic control and 'antiquated, poorly sited and maintained equipment'.

Manila is slated for everything from unswept, dirty runways to lack of firefighting equipment and poor electricity supplies. The radar is unreliable, is frequently out of order and should be used for training only. Met briefings are inadequate and there are frequent navigation and lighting failures. Manila's primary alternate, where the aircraft will go in the not unlikely case of something being wrong with Manila, is Mactan, also in the Philippines. At Mactan, 'the power supply is unreliable, subject to failures, affecting all aids including runway lights'.

A pilot diverting here from Manila would already have some

problems.* But he could easily find himself over Mactan with no runway lights, no airport lights and no town lights. When the airport fuses, so does the town. 'You could very easily not know that Mactan existed. It's better blacked out than anything in the war,' says one pilot.

In Germany IFALPA has awarded a red star for a shortage of safety equipment on one runway at Frankfurt, Europe's second busiest airport. Bremen, Stuttgart and Saarbrucken have also been starred.

The busy airport at Djakarta, capital of Indonesia, is savaged by the pilots. 'Air traffic control procedures are in need of vast improvement; the taxiway and runway surface conditions are deteriorating rapidly; runway extension is required. Navaids and radar required; search and rescue facilities have inadequate coverage.' At one stage Australian pilots refused to fly there.

The control towers of Turkey's two major airports at Istanbul and Ankara lost all contact with planes in flight for more than two hours on 18 October 1976. At that time there were twenty aircraft that were airborne and dependent on the towers. Contact with them was only re-established through the Turkish military.

All the aircraft got down safely on that occasion. But a Turkish Airlines captain was on the approach to Istanbul airport on a January night in 1975 when all the lights and beacons went out. Although emergency power was restored later, he crashed the F-28 into the Sea of Marmara and all four crew and thirty-eight passengers died.

The predictable troubles with airports are lack of navigational aids (navaids), runway length and closeness to mountains or high ground. All these can be dangerous.

Delhi, for example, has long been notorious for bad navaids. Four aircraft crashed on the approach to Delhi in two years. A Qantas pilot† said he and his 150 passengers were lucky to survive

---

* An alternate should expect different weather to the main airport. This is usual if it is on the other side of high ground, or inland instead of coastal. If it is on the other side of a city or industrial area, simultaneous fog and haze is less likely.

† Captain McManus, the Qantas captain, said that the control tower had given a cloud base of 700 feet when it was in fact less than 500 feet. Commenting on the incident, Reuters noted that four aircraft had crashed on the Delhi approach in the past two years.

after nearly being steered into the ground. He said the airport 'cannot be depended upon at any stage'. He only survived by ignoring ground instructions and landing visually.

Cairo is disliked by many crews. 'If the controllers have got one aircraft in the sky, that's enough. They can't cope with two,' says an American pilot. Cairo became so bad that the International Pilots' Association refused to make night landings there after two crashes, one of which, a Pakistan International 707, killed 119 people. The airport was said to have insufficient firefighting equipment, inadequate landing aids and high ground on the approach to the runway.

Japanese radio controllers are over-anxious and often difficult to understand. English is the international language for air traffic control, and the Japanese have particular difficulty in pronouncing numerals clearly. Pilots flying to Japan have special lessons in poor English, which ranges from 'flight' becoming 'fright', to the more serious inability to pronounce words like 'vector' and 'steer'.

Air traffic controllers in French-speaking Canada went on strike to force pilots to use both French and English, and Air Canada was ordered to translate flight operation manuals into French, as part of the language tension there. Air Canada pilots complained that the issue threatened safety.

Moscow has notoriously sloppy controllers with very poor English, though the standards improve markedly further east on the routes from Europe to Japan. Moscow has no civil airport to divert to, and Western pilots are not given any details of military airfields for emergency landing. 'It's get in or die at Moscow,' says a British pilot.

Caracas can be fatally misleading. 'You don't realize the mountains are so close at night. You have to point in towards them before turning left for the runway. Some people have kept going too long,' says a charter pilot. The combination of mountains and sea produces sudden mists. Rio de Janeiro also has an approach towards mountains that is dangerous in bad weather.

Building work at an airport can be dangerous. TWA's prestige Flight 800 from Rome suffered a reversed engine on its take-off run. The 707 slewed off the runway. It then hit a parked steam-roller and burst into flames, killing fifty-one. A DC8 crashed at JFK airport because a small stone being asphalted on a new taxiway was thrown up by the engine wake on to the tail as it taxied past. When the pilot pulled back the elevator on take-off, the stone jammed the tail. The aircraft stalled and crashed.

Strong crosswinds sweep across the runways at Bermuda, Prestwick and Hong Kong in winter.* The maximum crosswind allowed for most jets is a steady twenty-five knots. Any more would risk bursting tyres through the sideways pressure on them. But pilots often have to fly on the maximum to Bermuda and Hong Kong, as the diversionary fields are far away in New York and Bangkok. With gusting winds, pilots must add up to twenty-three mph to their approach speed to ensure maximum control during the gusts.

American pilots have criticized Kansas City, where pilots had to land on a 7,000-foot runway, short for a big jet, with a downward slope of 0.8 per cent. At the far end of the runway there was an artificial hill and a road and a dyke.

High buildings are as dangerous close to airports as high ground. But large hotels have been built close to airports and on flight paths in Majorca, Miami and Beirut.

The most embarrassing airports to pilots are those that are side by side. Sharjah and Dubai in the Gulf of Iran, Bombay and Juhu in India, and London Heathrow and London Northolt are the best examples. They have similar-looking and parallel runways. In one week, five jets landed at Sharjah thinking it was Dubai. Jets have landed accidentally at both Juhu and Northolt. These have short runways, and the planes have to be stripped of their seats before they can take off again for Bombay and Heathrow.

Perversely, although almost everything in the air is regulated by international law, there are no international standards at all for the most important ground installation of all – the airport runways. Local authorities design their runways as they see fit. Aircraft are limited by length of runway, and by the degree of up-and-down slope, but not by the general design.

Why such a vital part of safe flight should not be regulated passes comprehension. Research shows that runway design has a profound effect on pilots' visual judgement, particularly when

* There are three main types of winds created by local topography to avoid: valley winds, with Innsbruck an example; mountain gap winds as at Genoa; and headland winds, which affect Gibraltar.

approaching in bad weather with only a few seconds of decision time to set up a safe landing. Fat, short runways make a pilot feel he is lower than he actually is, so that he may put on full power and overshoot. A long, thin runway creates an even more dangerous optical illusion. The pilot thinks he is higher than he is, so that he reduces power and may crash short of the runway.

As for facilities, a long-haul pilot was taxiing his aircraft out for take-off at Bangkok. He noticed sharp metal debris in front of him and stopped his laden 747. 'That is potentially disastrous debris,' he says. 'It could slash your tyres and put you out of control on the take-off run. I radioed through for the emergency services to clear it. By normal standards, there would have been a fire crew there in ninety seconds.

'I radioed eight times over a period of twenty-five minutes. Nothing. In the end I got through on our company frequency and our station manager had to come out and clear it himself. Never, never crash at Bangkok. And if you do, pray you never catch fire.'

Binoculars have replaced radar at some airports. Things became so chaotic during the rebuilding of Cairo airport in 1979 that the radar was out of use most of the time. The air traffic controllers took to using binoculars to keep tabs on aircraft.

One binocular-guided Egyptair 737 pilot found himself taking off directly into another jet that was landing from the opposite end of the runway.

'I lifted my head in time to see an Arab 707 rushing toward me,' said Captain Safwat Ismail.* 'I was taking off and he was landing into me. We were both over Runway 23. I took a fast swerve left in time to get out of his way. He just kept on coming.'

The controllers, searching the sky through their binoculars, thought that the 707 was coming in to land in the same direction as the Egyptair was taking off. They could not pick it up in their binoculars. This was not surprising since it was in fact flying in the opposite direction, towards the 737.

Captain Ismail commented: 'Cairo airport radar seldom works and the radio system is weak. I think the 300 passengers and

---

* *Al Ahram*, Cairo, 18 July 1979. The incident took place in broad daylight on 17 July 1979.

myself can count ourselves rather lucky.' A truly Anglo-Saxon understatement.

Cairo airport admitted that there was some room for improvement in safety standards. 'It does appear,' said an airport spokesman, 'that binoculars are not a complete substitute for radar.'

Many pilots feel that Tokyo's new Narita airport should have qualified for a black star as soon as it was opened, at a cost of £2 billion, after years of protests and rioting by students and farmers, in 1978. The passions surrounding it, they say, make it insecure. It also lacks navigational aids; it has only one runway whose alignment is contested; and the approach is in a corridor between two military air zones.

Pilots criticize Nassau, a popular tourist airport in the Bahamas, for its severe runway irregularity, poor runway and taxiway markings, and for its lack of sea-rescue launches and obstruction lights on Runway 14.

Things are not always that bad, of course – which is borne out by the fact that flying by commercial jet in a developed area like the USA is now fifteen times safer than driving in a car. Insurance companies charge pilots no more for policies than bank clerks.

And there are airports that pilots positively enjoy. In Europe, they like Heathrow, Amsterdam Schiphol, Paris de Gaulle and Frankfurt. In the US, they go for Dallas/Fort Worth, Minneapolis/St Paul, Kansas City, Miami and Dulles International.

But for pure and perverse danger no airport can compare with Kerman airport in Iran. Captain Moini, flying over it in his Iran Air jet, could get no reply from the control tower. He radioed the police to find out what was wrong. On entering the tower, Police Inspector Dohwar found it deserted. A note was propped up on the main control panel: 'I am leaving. My time is definitely up.'*

4 Thiefrow

Her Majesty's Judge Edie sentenced an airport loader for stealing from passenger baggage at Middlesex Crown Court in January 1976. 'We have to deal at this court with airport loaders, handlers and other people who seem to steal all the time. I sometimes wonder if they do much else. The place has literally become a cesspool. Dishonesty at airports is an international scandal.'

These are boom times for airport villains round the world. Thefts at JFK have run in excess of $10 million a year. At Heathrow, platinum losses have totalled over £300,000 a year, with diamonds at £600,000. Newspapers have rechristened the airport 'Thiefrow'. In one case £44,000 worth of Bank of America travellers' cheques were cashed in London before they had even been reported missing. Thefts at Heathrow have been as high as £5 million a year.

At the Central Criminal Court on 12 February 1980, Judge Brian Gibbens said that 'the stealing of consignments at Heathrow is an absolute epidemic'. He was sentencing British Airways baggage loaders for the theft of a total of £341,000 worth of travellers' cheques. The judge added: 'I have tried other cases like this and I feel that the people who do not steal might stand out like a sore thumb. What a wonderful advertisement for the shop-window of this country.'

The scale of thefts was alarming. A policeman told the court: 'It would seem that it is very, very difficult for an honest man to have a job as a loader with British Airways, because if he is an honest man when he goes there, he is quickly corrupted. Otherwise he cannot work. Nobody will work with him.'

The defence counsel's plea was: 'There was so much dishonesty going on it was impossible to keep out of it without being ostracized.' Poor chaps. If they didn't steal, nobody would speak to them.

The latest figures available in 1980 showed that thefts at Heathrow were running at £680,591 from passenger baggage, £375,667 from cargo and £683,350 from mail. Since passenger baggage and cargo passing through Heathrow have a combined value of £15 billion a year, the percentage of loss is very small. An airport like Heathrow attracts crooks because the potential pickings are much larger than anywhere else in the country.

Nevertheless, the crime rate is of concern and may be higher than revealed in official figures. And, in the pervasive airport atmosphere, the police are not seagreen incorruptible either. The second most senior police officer at Heathrow, a Detective Superintendent, was sentenced to two and a half years in December 1979 for the attempted blackmail of a passenger. Det. Supt. John Colligan had attempted to obtain £6,000 from Soraya Khashoggi, former wife of the Saudi arms billionaire Adnan Khashoggi, after she had put in an insurance claim for jewellery stolen whilst she flew from Paris to London.

The airlines' attitude is to prefer to describe things as lost rather than stolen. This plays right into the hands of the villains, in a place where the police motto is 'if it's there sooner or later it'll go'.

The police complement in a smart, five-cell police station near the taxi pool on the north side is 300 men. That is more than twice the force of a similarly sized city like Carlisle, but the CID say it is 'hopeless'. Most of the force has to look after parking, the public and security.

The time left for dealing with criminals is limited. Loaders face the most temptation, handling cargo and passenger baggage. They get recruited quickly. A new loader finds £40 in an envelope inside his locker. If he hands it in to his supervisor, he will find himself working on heavy loads at bad hours. If he forgets to hand it in, he is reminded on his first job on a baggage gang. Once recruited, he remains in. As he progresses to lower management, foreman or baggage master, he will still draw his cut for tipping off the loaders and protecting them.

Freight is at its most vulnerable when it is being loaded into the cargo bay of a passenger aircraft by a team of three or four loaders. There is only room in the bay for one man, who cannot be seen from outside.

Heathrow has a notably long tradition of crime. Its predecessor, Croydon, was the scene of one of the largest pre-war bullion raids when £21,000 went in 1935. The world's first recorded theft of jewels in transit was at Heathrow in 1949. Since then, a major airport robbery is supposed to have financed the Great Train Robbery. Diamonds worth £194,000 went over a period of two months to one gang and another stole £200,000 worth of bullion in a week.

When industrial diamonds worth £106,250 disappeared in a four-day spell, so sensitive was Heathrow to the charge they had been stolen there that the insurance company was refused permission to post reward notices, although it posted them everywhere else the planes had touched down on their way from South Africa to Holland.

The airport attracts some of the keenest criminal minds. Scotland Yard has described the robbery of one bullion van on its way to Heathrow as 'the most perfect crime of the century'.

The van was on a regular run to Heathrow from a City vault. Its cargo was £109,000 worth of bullion and jewels destined for overseas flights. It was going along Pall Mall, the heart of London's clubland. Outside the austere Athenaeum, the van was blocked by two men arguing with each other, their cars stopped in the middle of the road.

They moved off, still shouting at each other through their car windows. The van went up St James's, past Overton's and Lock's, turned left at the Ritz Hotel and drove down Piccadilly. At Hyde Park Corner, the van dipped out of sight down the underpass that leads to Knightsbridge and on down the Cromwell Road to Heathrow.

The two cars stopped, blocking the van again. The drivers did not argue this time. They threatened the bullion van crew with guns.

On the surface, at the start of the underpass, another two cars stopped. The drivers leapt out and carried on a furious argument. This blocked off the underpass, and a massive traffic jam built up back along Piccadilly. Even if the police had received an emergency call from the van, they could not have got to the scene – and the van's radio was ineffective, since it was twenty feet below the ground.

In four minutes, the van was stripped of its cargo and the crew tied up. The loot disappeared along Knightsbridge in the cars.

The drivers causing the Piccadilly jam settled their dispute and drove off. Apart from the empty van and crew, there has been no trace of anything since.

Other crimes have been as breathtakingly simple. A hitch-hiker, dressed in an airline anorak, stopped a British Airways van on the airport in 1973. He said he wanted a lift to another part of the airport. Once in the van he pulled out a revolver and escaped with its cargo – diamonds from a Ghana Airways flight and platinum from South African Airways, just arrived from Johannesburg. His haul was worth £467,000.

An airline anorak also figured in the theft of £491,000 in March 1976. One man wearing a British Airways anorak and another in the uniform of a senior security officer went to the British Airways strongroom in Heathrow. It had been improved after a previous raid, and had electrically operated steel doors, bulletproofed windows and a conveyor belt to move packages without opening the doors.

The two men were let through a massive steel door on the strength of their uniforms. The door automatically closed behind them, trapping them between the steel door and a counter surmounted by an armoured glass screen with grilles. They asked for a package from the counter clerk. He said it was not there, and the 'senior security officer' asked if he could use the phone.

This was the catch. The phone was behind the counter, where the counter clerk had no protection. The clerk pushed a switch to let in the 'security officer' and at once found himself faced with a gun. The strongroom was opened. The haul was seventeen packets of US dollars, totalling £258,300, six packets of diamonds worth £60,000, three gold bars at £83,000, £15,000 in gold coin and £75,000 in travellers' cheques.

Union shop stewards have advised their members to treat plain-clothes policemen on aircraft as hijackers if they refuse to identify themselves. The bad relations between police and workers have been conducive to nothing but further crime. The arrest of three loaders in 1976 led to a strike by ninety others. There was a further strike in 1980. A police hotline was set up so that anything suspicious could be reported. The number is 01-897 4343. So far, it has only been instrumental in solving the theft of a passenger's box of cigars.

Crime can be exaggerated. A vast amount of small-size, high-value cargo passes through airports, an ideal target for criminals. More potential loot is centred on Heathrow than anywhere else in the world. Over £20 million of goods a day passes through; of this, about £1 million is in banknotes, travellers' cheques or precious stones and metals. Some theft is inevitable.

Nevertheless, a disgraceful amount is stolen. One loader admitted at the Old Bailey that he had stolen £215,000 in cash, travellers' cheques, diamonds, gold bars and gold dust over a period of a few months.

Reported baggage thefts in the year from October 1974 to October 1975 amounted to £434,353 stolen from 1,589 cases. The clear-up rate was so low as to encourage crime: only £11,324 was recovered from 31 cases. Cargo thefts ran at £473,391 with £145,461 recovered. The police only accepted 24 cases of mail theft, from 62 allegations, totalling £290,967. None was recovered. The 38 cases which Heathrow refused to admit responsibility for were not even investigated.

The simplest crime netted the thief £2 million. He was working for an American air courier firm. One summer day in 1976 he went round the firm's clients, picking up the packets of money and valuables due to be forwarded by them. He then got on a plane and flew to Switzerland with the £2 million. His previous criminal record had not prevented his employment as a courier of banknotes, although the flashy behaviour that had tipped off police on his earlier crimes soon alerted the Swiss police.

A Swiss insurance company has put a 100-per-cent loading on cargoes going to or transitting in Heathrow. Things have got so bad with diamonds and currency that the mining corporation and the big dealers now send couriers with the gems: the air fares are cheaper than the premiums.

The couriers fly first class, in sober business suits, with an occasional glimpse of metal chain between immaculate shirt cuff and briefcase.

The élite are the mail bag thieves, reckoned by one CID man to 'average £30,000 a year, if they're not greedy, with little chance of being picked up'. The system gives generous odds to people who are 'on the slit'.

Registered mail bags are green with identifying letters fifteen inches by eight. The thieves' modus operandi is first to get their hand through the sealed neck of the outer bag. This is generally loose enough for them to be able to wriggle a wrist through without damaging the wax. They can then extract the postal form, the 'AV7' form, which accompanies high value items.

The form does not say what it is in the packets, but it does say who they are addressed to, which amounts to the same thing. 'You don't have to be a genius,' says a CID officer in exasperation, 'to know that a heavy packet addressed to Johnson Mathey or Mocatta and Goldsmid, bullion dealers, is not full of scrap iron.' A slit is made in the inner bag, and the thief locates the parcels that the AV7 form has told him are addressed to bullion dealers. Thus the postal regulation that requires valuables to be in parcels with sealing wax and string in fact reduces security by drawing attention to the contents.

Once the hand is withdrawn, the slit in the inner bag is invisible. The villains thus benefit from the unwritten airport law: 'Say it didn't happen, or at least say it didn't happen here.' It is often impossible to tell at what airport, even in which continent, a theft took place.

If the bag is outward, it will be signed for on arrival by the local post office. 'Say it's going to Abu Dhabi,' says the CID man. 'Abu Dhabi sign for it before they've opened it, on the basis of an intact seal. By the time they discover the inner bag has been cut it's too late. The GPO say: "The Abu Dhabi signature is *proof* it didn't happen here." And Abu Dhabi know full well nothing was nicked their end. So like a whole lot of airport crime it drifts into a convenient limbo.'

And the GPO does not know *what* is missing. 'They get a team down at LOMO (London Overseas Mail Office) with no idea of what they are looking for – just a packet with seals on it. It can be months before they let us know what we're supposed to be looking for.

'And you know something? At this mighty airport – with ceaseless vigilance by 300 men, over 25 million passengers, many of them crooks, and 53,000 permanent workers, and Interpol flashing, and all that – we haven't even got a telex.

'If Interpol do flash a telex message, it trickles through to

Hayes, and then if the operator feels like it he gives us a ring on the electric telephone.'

Heathrow's notoriety is world-wide. A recent consignment of £39,000 worth of polished diamonds failed to reach Hong Kong. The aircraft had stopped at London, Frankfurt, Tehran, Delhi and Bangkok on its way. Every airport at once blamed London – which shrugged and said, since there was no proof of what had happened, no crime had been committed.

Some shippers send valuable consignments of diamonds and gold as ordinary freight to beat insurance and be unobtrusive. Again the odds favour the thief. The casualness of some airlines towards freight is vividly shown in the case of £1 million worth of raw opium, 177 lb 12 oz in weight, stored in ordinary warehouses without lock and key. It was to be used in medical preparations, but a large proportion of it was stolen and sold on the black market to drug addicts.

'To allow such immensely and devastatingly dangerous packages to be stored in the way these were passes our comprehension,' said Ewen Montagu QC, Chairman of Middlesex Quarter Sessions, after the drugs were stolen. Besides Middlesex, Heathrow keeps the courts at Uxbridge and Hayes busy, and contributes more than its fair share to the Old Bailey.

One report made by British Airways listed these security lapses in the cargo area at Heathrow:

Huge quantities of freight are left standing outside the warehouses. Telltale documents giving details and values of freight are left lying around open but empty offices. Radio messages about valuable cargo are relayed on an airport channel which anyone with a radio can listen in to. Passes for staff cars are seldom checked – so thieves can drive in. Administrative buildings can be entered by anyone.

Freight collection departments often do not know which drivers are airline employees and which come from outside firms. Dispatch bills can be simply unclipped from a board, and they are the only authorization necessary to remove the cargo. Vans carrying very high-value items have no special alarms or security fitments, apart from a cheap padlock. Export freight has been found in parked vans left with the doors open and the keys in the ignition. The cold stores are not padlocked. In the neighbouring towns, where airport workers live, it is a standing joke that no cargo or catering worker buys fruit, veg or chocolate.

The mail bag men have their Galaxies and Mustangs and foreign holidays and deep-carpeted houses. The police swear that even the outside lavatories are carpeted.

Below them in wealth and status are those on the 'lucky dip'. These are the loaders who open likely looking suitcases. Almost any suitcase can be opened by one of three keys or a piece of Perspex. The combination lock suitcase did not fool the loaders for long: it is dropped hard on its corner, and obligingly opens.

Favourite targets are the Japanese and passengers from countries with financial problems. The Japanese normally travel with their suitcases packed with valuable photographic and electronic gear, and entire package tour groups can be stripped. Businessmen smuggling money in their suitcases are, as we have seen, unlikely to report thefts.

Expensive destinations like Nice or Cannes are widely looted. The villains know all the events in the international calendar. Lewis R. Wasserman of Universal Pictures checked in for a British Airways flight to Venice. The film festival was on – which indicated booty, in this case £40,000 worth of jewellery. Five loaders were caught and sentenced for this.

Geneva-bound flights get special attention when currency is in the news. 'I'm not saying that they actually sit down and base it all on the *Financial Times*, but they certainly read it. They call it the Sporting Pink. There was a currency upset the other day, and sure enough they did the Genevas. Got £20,000 in brand new tenners from one man. And he told us about it. Most of them don't for obvious reasons,' says a policeman.

Just as often, though, theft is the result of a casual feeling rather than a precise idea. Baggage and destination are combined into an educated guess. Thus the Countess of Woolton checked an unlocked suitcase on to a flight from Heathrow to Bermuda, and lost £11,000 worth of jewels. The loot is easily smuggled out in the stream of freight trucks, crew buses and food vans.

Cash is the most attractive target. Bank notes are negotiable with a fence at 70 per cent of face value, whereas metals and precious stones fetch only 15–20 per cent. Stones may have to be recut. Metals have identifying numbers on the bar, but if they are melted down the stamp of purity will be lost. Furthermore, many countries have regulations against individuals holding bullion. Gold coins like kruger rands do not have these disadvantages and are thus popular.

Although banknotes, travellers' cheques and gold coin appeal in Europe and the US, they are difficult to dispose of in less sophisticated areas. Clothing is the stock-in-trade of loaders at airports in Africa and the Far East, with cameras and tape recorders as targets of opportunity.

The essence of catching loaders is speed, and the speed of air travel itself works against detection. Flights are turned round in forty minutes, roar off a thousand miles away, and what the police called the 'jet blur' sets in. By the time a theft is discovered and it filters back to Heathrow many hours will have passed. The passenger's baggage has most likely been through foreign Customs, through foreign loaders and airport taxis or buses, to a foreign porter in a distant hotel before the passenger is aware that anything has gone.

Who, then, can say it's a Heathrow loader, when it could be a Japanese bell-hop? It is inevitable that crime gets off-loaded, and there is a fashion in the rest of the world to off-load it all on Heathrow. It is not the only place to have some dishonest loaders.

Indeed not. The most famed of them all was the Airborne Loader of Orly, one Fernand Romain, who had himself loaded in a packing case on to Air France flights. This gave him uninterrupted time to 'faire le lucky dip' before climbing back into his packing case on landing. On his last trip he successfully stole £22,000 worth of gems on an Orly–Algiers flight before an underworld informant ended his career. An American girl who tried the same thing in May 1981 almost froze.

Passengers themselves can be highly dishonest, blaming loaders for stealing non-existent but highly insured valuables. Kamuel M. Solomon, an Egyptian citizen domiciled in Frankfurt, checked four cases weighing seventy-three kilos on to a Paris–London flight. He paid the excess baggage charges.

He arrived at Heathrow to find his baggage had 'disappeared'. The baggage tabs with the excess amounts were firmly stapled on his ticket. He claimed that handmade shoes, overcoats and suits befitting a gentleman had all gone. He produced receipts for his typewriter, Polaroid camera outfit and a woman's fur coat.

The coat receipt was found to be fraudulent. That alone ended the lucrative career of Mr Solomon and presumably of his anonymous accomplice, who simply took the same flight as Mr Solomon and 'stole' his luggage at the destination airport by walking out with the cases. Mr Solomon had previously made claims against Alitalia, Lufthansa, Libyan Arab Airlines, Air France, Sabena, KLM, and Swissair.

Sometimes passengers pick up the wrong suitcase quite inadvertently, with startling results. An Australian girl flew to Shannon on an Aer Lingus flight from Copenhagen. Also on the flight were $77,000 worth of diamonds intended for the South African owned Shannon Diamond Company. Her luggage was wrongly labelled by SAS in Denmark. Instead of her case with her clothes, she left the airport with the diamonds.

Airborne crime is not unknown. Professionals flew the airlanes between Entebbe and Heathrow during the Ugandan Asian crisis. Many Asians were smuggling out money. In a typical case, a professional confidence trickster, an Asian from Birmingham, chatted up a Ugandan refugee.

He found the man had £3,000 concealed underneath photographs in a family album and in the frames of large wedding pictures. 'Aha,' said the con-man, 'it's illegal to bring that sort of money into the UK, but I'm from Birmingham and I understand these things, I know how you have to fix those British Customs officers. I'll be delighted to take it through for you.' The Ugandan was convinced and handed over the valuable photo collection.

There are airborne pickpockets, taking advantage of the casual way people leave jackets heavy with wallets, traveller's cheques and passports when they go to the lavatory. People are seldom as loaded with valuables as when they fly, and seldom so off their guard.

What hope for the honest passenger? Common sense, say the police. It is absurd to travel with valuables in a suitcase. The suitcase can be lost by the airline just as easily as it could be rifled. Yet time and again women travel with jewellery, and men with cameras in their suitcases. If a passenger has to put valuables in his luggage, experience shows that the safest thing is a cheap suitcase with plenty of string round it. Loaders are not likely to start playing round with knots when there are fat Antler or Samsonite cases around.

The airlines are partly to blame for the public ignorance of the high crime rate at airports. Police have tried to get warnings printed on tickets and baggage tags without success. In the same way as many airlines refuse to admit that a crash is a possibility, most prefer to pretend that crime does not exist.

Some thieves specialize in 'sob snatches' – taking luggage whilst the owner is tearfully saying goodbye, or being joyously reunited with his family, without a thought for his possessions.

Thieves inhabit the oddest corners of airports. Heathrow has had lead and copper removed from its radar system and tyres stolen from aircraft. A bulldozer and a tractor disappeared from a building site. Most bizarre of all, the mercury has been stolen from the instruments of aircraft being overhauled. 'We haven't had an aircraft stolen yet,' says a policeman. 'But it's happened at Miami and I expect we'll get it here soon enough.'

Heathrow is not alone. Paris Orly, Frankfurt and Rome are all notoriously bad, and there are growing problems in the Far East in Tokyo, Hong Kong and above all Manila.

In New York, fur robberies at JFK became so bad that an air freight company refused to truck fur shipments to the airport. Thefts of registered mail from the airport have amounted to many millions of dollars. In a three-year period, from 1967 to 1970, it was estimated that $70 million in negotiable and non-negotiable securities had been stolen.

To stop the thefts, the US Postal Service has had to start a security system similar to the old Wells Fargo stagecoaches. It is called Con-Con, short for Concentrated Conveyance. Armed guards accompany every shipment of mail to and from the airport. Postal security officers, wearing .38 calibre revolvers, accompany the mail trucks out to the aircraft and check the shipments into the holds.

Registered mail sacks are held at JFK under guard, until the flight is ready. After take-off security men in destination cities are warned. They meet the flight and guard the sacks to the post offices. Night flights were eliminated to make thefts harder. All registered mail to JFK travels only in daylight.

This has been good for the US Postal Service, but bad for everyone else, since the gangster's greed is now concentrated on them. During a typical four-month period at JFK, a wide variety of air cargo was stolen – pharmaceuticals worth $136,000, industrial diamonds, Wyoming jade, raw furs and leather, Italian sunglasses, cigarette lighters, baby foods, tape decks, wigs and machine tools.

Two murders occurred at JFK within a month in 1970, at the height of an airport crime wave. A barman was shotgunned by thieves for not emptying his cash register quickly enough. A rich businessman was robbed and shot.

A Permanent Senate Subcommittee set up to investigate crime at JFK heard evidence from a master mail thief who admitted stealing more than $100 million between September 1960 and September 1970. Robert F. Cudak said that he had received $1 million for his share, but had wasted it all gambling. Most had been stolen at New York and Florida airports, but Cudak said he had also 'hit' airports in Las Vagas and Los Angeles.

He started stealing mail shortly after starting work as a ramp man for Northwest Airlines at JFK. He left Northwest, where he said he had been employed despite a prior criminal record, for a full-time career of theft. He was so successful that he employed 'chopmen' who drove to the airport to collect stolen goods.

No photographs of Cudak were allowed at the hearing, and it was said that he would have to be given a new identity and completely new life to avoid a revenge murder by organized crime at the airport. John B. Eaton, a witness in a conspiracy case involving $43 million stolen at JFK, was shot dead near Miami International airport.

Airport theft has become so sophisticated that almost anything that is stolen can be sold. In a typical case, an importer flew in a large shipment of doeskin gloves to JFK, where they vanished. To his fury, the importer discovered in a few weeks that the gloves were being sold on the West Coast.

The gloves had been flown from JFK to Tijuana, Mexico, and sold as legitimate merchandise, at a reduced price, to a West Coast jobber. The jobber had then sold them to one of the largest department stores in San Diego.

Mafia control at JFK was so great that the leading world airlines were forced to use Mafia trucking companies.* An independent trucker known as Direct Airport Service Inc. tried to break the Mafia stranglhelold by hauling freight to the airport. National and Northwest Airlines, anxious to break the racket combine, attempted to use Direct.

Direct discovered that thirty-eight tyres on trucks it had parked at JFK had been slashed and ruined. A Direct truck on the crowded Long Island Expressway went out of control when its rear wheels came off. Investigation showed that the lugs on the wheels had been loosened. When the same thing happened to another Direct truck a few days later it was obvious that even the largest airlines, whatever their wishes, could not use Direct.

'This airport,' according to Queens District Attorney John J. Santucci, 'is a playground for the underworld. Any crime is possible here.'

Santucci revealed that members of his staff had been able to buy a wide selection of radios, stereos and tape recorders, cameras and guitars for ten per cent of market value. They had even been offered bulletproof vests and telephone debugging gadgets.

This particular racket involved a corrupt airport policeman, a delivery service manager, an airport truck driver, a freight shed foreman and an airport dispatcher. Although it also involved the theft of stock certificates in a multimillion-dollar operation, Santucci found that neither the airport nor the airlines, nor even the FBI, wanted to know.

'The FBI is part of a group telling me that there's no crime at Kennedy airport,' he says. 'I don't know why. At every meeting we are told that Kennedy is a Garden of Eden. Nobody cooperates in those investigations. If I want to fandango, I go to a dance, not to meetings with those law enforcement officials.'

Other airports are as bad. Captain Robert L. Herzog of the Massachusetts State Police echoed the old complaint that airlines were not notifying thefts at Boston's Logan International airport. He sent some detectives, disguised as truck drivers, to the airport

* Light was thrown on the Mafia in a long article in the *New York Times Magazine*, 12 April 1970. 'The Jackals at JFK', by Fred J. Cook, created a scandal which forced the Mafia to reduce its activities. Cook, the author of *The Secret Rulers*, is an expert on Mafia organization. The situation at JFK is now improved.

and filmed them in action 'stealing cartons of freight, driving away a truck loaded with freight'. The film was shown to the airlines – who did nothing. Chicago and Montreal, where stock thefts have reached $2 million and $500,000 respectively, are also crime-ridden.

Theft, the police say bitterly, is 'as easy as JFK'.

The easiest field is tickets. Ticket frauds are becoming commonplace. A blank ticket is as good as a blank traveller's cheque – except that you can fill in your own amount on it. And the maximum, putting down London–Sydney return for the route, and first class for the fare basis, would be over £1,000.

The Mafia and organized crime have exploited the complexities of ticketing to make an estimated $50 million a year in the US alone. It takes, on average, six weeks for a ticket to be checked out by the International Air Transport Association's (IATA) ticketing headquarters in Montreal.

IATA is the centre of international airlines which regulates fares, routes and services. Every flight coupon is individually cleared. This is when the airlines adjust payments to each other to take account of passengers switching flights and airlines. It is most unlikely that any irregularity will be discovered until the ticket has passed through the IATA machinery.

The criminals must first obtain blank tickets. These may be stolen directly from the printers or the airlines. As commonly, criminals infiltrate a failing travel agent, promising the owner cash if he turns a blind eye to his ticket stocks. He is kept in business for a few weeks.

The crook makes out properly routed tickets and sells them at a discount to travellers, without paying the airline, relying on his six weeks' lead time. More simply he can make out expensive tickets and cash them in for refunds, as 'unused'.

This is not confined to the US. One of the largest frauds came to light at Heathrow, when an observant Pan Am check-in clerk noted an alteration and a fare anomaly on a British Airways ticket.

It had been issued in the name of P. de Tilly. This apparent aristocrat turned out to be a former Canadian ticketing clerk, Galvin Brian Humphrie.

De Tilly's career as the 'phantom freak' of the world airways had begun with a modest cash purchase of a ticket from Manchester to Europe. Humphrie's knowledge of ticketing enabled him to alter the route to one of higher value. He then told a clerk that he wanted it altered back to a less expensive destination. The difference was made up with MCOs, Miscellaneous Charges Orders – good for any air transport purchases, and if refunded, as good as cash.

With his MCO, Humphrie purchased another low value ticket, altered that to a longer route and extended the spiral. He swapped airlines with exotic ease, getting 'free' tickets from JAL, British Airways, Pan Am, Air France, TWA, Qantas, KLM, Eastern, Northwest Orient, United, Austrian, Sabena, Finnair, and Varig.

The destinations included Sydney, Bombay, Kabul, Athens and New Delhi. On one ticket alone a rebate of $2413.40 was paid when Mr de Tilly decided that he wasn't going to Bermuda after all. When he did travel, which occasionally he did for pleasure, he altered Y to F (Economy to First) on his ticket and stayed in some of the world's best hotels at airline expense.

British Airways alone was taken for £30,000. The total, in a few months of operation, was well in excess of £100,000. Humphrie and an accomplice, Gary Schiano, were sentenced to four and one years' imprisonment respectively at the Old Bailey.

Check-in clerks are trained to look for obvious forgeries. Paper, print, inking on tickets are scrutinized. But the airlines do not help matters by habitually flouting their own fare rules, particularly in outlying parts. No expatriate returning from Bangkok to Europe or the US at his own, rather than company, expense would dream of paying the full fare when almost without exception the local offices of IATA carriers will give a 25-per-cent discount.

A new variation is based on credit card counterfoils. Instead of the bother and risk of stealing the card, the crook simply gets the card number and the name of the user from a counterfoil obtained by an accomplice in a restaurant or shop. He then simply rings up the airline and orders a ticket through the post on that name and debited to that card number. Since no card has been stolen, the airline's check with the credit card company will reveal nothing odd and the ticket will thus be issued.

People within the industry get up to similar tricks. 'Interline' tickets give an employee of one airline a reduction of from fifty to ninety per cent when he is travelling on another line. He can simply write 'staff ninety per cent' on the ticket coding, and SUBLO on the status ('subject to load'; if the plane is full, you don't fly in preference to the other passengers who, in theory at least, should be paying full rate) and sell it at a good profit to a member of the public.

Travel agents get a reduction, the 'AD 75', or the seventy-five per cent off for an agent discount. They can get OK (firm booking) on the status. Every agent can get two seventy-five per cent discount tickets per airline. It is highly tempting to sell them to the public.

This does not prevent the public from trying out its own cut-rate schemes. The most common is taking advantage of ITX, the very cheap Inclusive Tour fares. To qualify for this, the passenger should be on a fixed package tour to a hotel. There is, however, no way of proving that a passenger is a businessman with no intention of going near a beach or package hotel. Flying as a package tourist saves a businessman up to £110 on a trip from London to Athens, and over £350 to Johannesburg.

Schemes for saving money are greatly helped by the chaotic state of IATA's price-fixing. Excursion times often vary between different towns in the same country, let alone from country to country. To qualify for an excursion to Paris, for example, a passenger must stay four days – but in Prague, twelve. A passenger commuting between cities may not stay long enough on any air trip to qualify for an excursion fare. But if he knows the dates, as he will, he can buy a series of excursion tickets in advance.

By alternating outward and return halves, it will appear that he has stayed longer each time than he in practice has – thus qualifying him for considerable discounts. The saving is commonly of the order of fifty per cent.

No scheme is foolproof. Once a new system is recognized, the airlines and IATA find a way to counter it. Nevertheless, there is so much confusion over airline fares that anyone who pays full fare is entitled to feel bitter. The ultimate in discounts, package tours, fly-drive, advanced bookings, winter breaks and other excursion fares has now been reached. Several airlines have recognized that the few passengers who are paying the 'normal' full rate should travel in a special 'executive cabin' of their own.

The basic ticket form is laid down to international standards.

It is a more complicated document than it looks. Airline liability for death or injury is archaic, still based on the quaintly named Convention for the Unification of Certain Rules relating to International Carriage by Air, signed at Warsaw in 1929. The subject is controversial and very confused. Damages vary greatly depending on the airline, the place of the accident and where the ticket was bought.

In general, as we shall see, tickets claim a limited liability of $75,000 where a flight goes to the US, and $16,580 for injury elsewhere. Settlements for dead American passengers are an average of 500 per cent higher than for others. This does not reflect higher American incomes, since European and Japanese travellers earn the same and Gulf Arabs much more. It reflects the disgraceful inability of other countries to depart from 1929 standards, and catch up with the more realistic American settlements.

The ticket contains a great deal of information for the check-in clerks. It is not transferable and the passenger must be the person whose name is on it. This is exceedingly important, since it would otherwise be easy to sell the return half of an excursion ticket. In fact, names are rarely checked, and many people take advantage of this, buying a return ticket on an excursion discount but only using it one way themselves.

The fare basis shows whether a passenger is F, first class, or Y, economy. It also shows if the ticket can be used on another airline. YR means it can only be used on the airline which issued it, YO that it can be used on any airline. This will also be written out in the special Restrictions and Endorsement section.

A 'status' section shows the strength of the reservation on a flight. OK means a confirmed booking: the passenger has a definite seat on the flight. SBY or WL means that the passenger is on standby or on the 'wait list'. This is when a flight is full of reserved seats but 'no shows' – people with reservations who do not turn up – are expected. Seats that have not been taken thirty minutes before take-off are allocated to people on the waiting list. Check-in clerks have to be on their guard against knowledgeable passengers who have altered their reservation status to OK. Airlines, however, often overbook their own flights. Gulf Air in the Gulf of Iran holds the record, having booked 390 passengers on a flight to Muscat. The aircraft capacity was 42.

A box shows the form of payment, by cheque, cash or credit card. This can be stamped Non-Ref, meaning that it can only be refunded after the issuing office has cleared it. Similarly, a series of numbers show that it is part of a package holiday, when it is again non-refundable. The letters CY next to the fare shows the currency in which it was paid, an important item with floating currency rates.

Probably the most imaginative user of an air ticket was an American, who flew his wife and two children round the world for eighteen months before being apprehended. He paid for them in travellers' cheques which were in every way genuine, except that he had invented the bank on which they were drawn, and designed and printed the cheques himself. Bank clerks being more attuned to forgeries than to non-existent banks, and with more and more small banks now issuing their own cheques, it took a long time for authority to rumble that it had been had.

Airborne crime continues to grow. In September 1982, a hand was seen to emerge from a packing crate in the hold of an Australian cargo aircraft. Further investigation uncovered a man squashed inside the crate surmounted by thousands of banknotes. He had originally been sealed in a crate containing telephone directories of the same weight as the money. He transferred the telephone directories into another crate, and moved the cash into his own crate. The man, who had stuck out his hand to make an air hole, was found at Rockhampton, Queensland. Other men, in a £300,000 plot, were then found in other air cargo crates in Townsville and Brisbane.

5 Security

International airports are faced with every modern crime from credit card abuse to hijacking. They are sensitive to the slightest suggestion. A British clairvoyant's dream has been enough to start a massive security check. A man told the police that he had 'seen' a Jumbo with the flight number 743 being hijacked with a machine gun over France. An immediate check revealed that a Pan Am Jumbo on a round the world trip was at Frankfurt in transit for New York, flight PA 743. The airline decided on specially strict security measures.

Three more airlines were affected. TWA's Los Angeles jet flight 743 had just changed its number to 811 at Boston before going transatlantic to London, but was still searched. So was Qantas's Sydney to London QF 743 and BA's Copenhagen to London BA 743. The British Airports Authority commented with dignity: 'Airlines operating flights with this number have been informed and countersteps have been taken. Security officials have been given details of the dream.'

All calls have to be taken seriously, as do bomb threats. These are almost always sparked off by a press or TV report. All the big airlines employ security staff, or hire private firms. A chart on the wall of the security office marks off the bomb threats. Threats to specific aircraft are marked in red: the caller mentions an actual flight number or route. Non-specific threats are marked in blue. Yellow on the same square indicates that the aircraft is on the ground, green means that it is in flight. Ground installations are marked in brown. Clearly a combination of red and green is the most worrying: a threat to a specific aircraft in flight.

Airlines do not like talking about bomb threats, with good reason. The incidents go in very distinct waves, and the crests are always when bombs are much in the news on TV or in the press.

Heathrow has a decompression chamber, in an isolated corner of the airport, where the pressure can be lowered to reproduce that of an aircraft in flight. Suspicious parcels are put into it to see whether they explode as 'height' is reached – the chamber is a heavily sandbagged bunker. Most aerial sabotage is done with altimeter bombs, set to explode when a certain height is reached.

The control towers at both Heathrow and JFK have been totally evacuated on occasion, although the hoaxers would be disappointed to know that landings are handled from an emergency trailer. Generally, says one security man, 'you just weigh it up. If you get a young male voice on the phone saying "there's a bomb on one of your planes", you put it down as non-specific. If you get a mature voice with a pronounced national accent and a particular flight in mind, then you're going to pay a lot more attention.

'Unfortunately, people with the hoax mentality exist. It's something we have all learnt to live with.'

Those old-fashioned travellers, stowaways, have survived into the jet age. One fourteen-year-old, Stephen Grimes, got on a BA Trident that took him to Dublin and back, and then on to Malta. Only on the return trip from Malta was he found hiding behind a seat. A three-year-old made it on to an intercontinental flight from Los Angeles to London. His father was aboard on his way to attend a family funeral. The boy was found playing happily in a lavatory an hour and a half out.

A classic example of the breed is the 'Wigan steward'. This sixteen-year-old hitched down to London from his native Lancashire. He chatted up British Airways stewards about their jobs, and soon knew enough to get a new uniform from stores. He obtained a British Airways crew identity card in much the same way. Then he was ready to start flying, with Nairobi his first stop. He merely walked on to a British Airways jet in uniform. It was assumed he was being positioned to Nairobi. When the flight was airborne a member of the cabin crew asked him to take off his jacket and wear a pullover to cover his uniform shirt. 'The passengers might not realize you're on a positioning flight,' he was told. He offered to help out but was told to relax and enjoy himself.

In Nairobi he checked into the British Airways crew hotel for a pleasant free stay that included trips to game parks. He got back to London, and out to the Far East before eventually being caught in Hong Kong because he had no passport.

Once back in Wigan he soon got bored. He returned to London

and flew to the Caribbean before being apprehended. He was returned to Wigan, and again went missing. This time security men at airports round the world had to look for something different. Stealing a case from outside a crew room, he went into a lavatory and emerged as a very young British Airways second officer. He had stolen a pilot's uniform. Finding himself short of cash but in possession of a cheque book, he cashed a cheque at an airport bank branch. With customary caution, the manager checked with the branch, and found that the young 'pilot' was overdrawn. He had a severe word with him but agreed to extend his overdraft by £20.

It is, however, more difficult for supernumerary pilots to sit around cabins than for stewards. He only made it as far as Frankfurt. The lesson of this Lancashire lad is that security on airlines is not easy to enforce against those with a certain amount of nerve and originality.

Airport anti-hijack networks have often been shown to have holes in them. A spokesman for the British pilots' union was able to clamber unhindered at night over aircraft at Heathrow despite his beard, spy-type epauletted raincoat and an international hijack scare that was on at the time. A dinner-jacketed figure was found asleep at the controls of a parked jet (escaping the breathalyser that would certainly have pursued him had he stuck to his car).

The situation is not helped by the splits in the responsibility for security at many airports. There is doubt as to who guards what, and argument over who pays for what. In theory the airport authorities are responsible for runways, tarmacs, parking areas and buildings.

The airlines have accepted responsibility for all passenger and baggage security. For example, the airlines themselves pay for and lay down the standards of passenger search. Thus El Al uses entirely different techniques, including written questionnaires, from most airlines. The airport authorities have nothing to do with direct passenger security and so airport security is as weak as the weakest airline.

Airport police concede that American standards are higher than elsewhere in the world, and that Zurich is probably the only really well looked after airport in Europe. Heathrow is typical of the major airports outside North America. Geography is against it, since it is surrounded by public roads. The northern perimeter road is a big hazard: 'Anyone with a .22 could puncture the jets from the road,' said an experienced sergeant. Opposite the shabby prefabs and unglamorous potholed roads of the north side, a man could hit six or seven jets as they wait to take off west. Indeed, it is possible for people to picnic at the east end of the main runways, and since people seem to believe that airports belong to the public, they often do.

The public can get down roads that will take them within a hundred yards of crowded holding points at the west end as well, simply by driving off public roads and ignoring small 'private' signs. A spinney at the southwest corner is full of cars at lunchtime. 'Of course it's secretaries necking with bosses, but it could be a gunman,' says a police officer.

The only way to make an airport really secure is to put a barbed wire fence round it and call in the army. The quick-reaction Army Unit, specially trained in airport security, is based twenty minutes away in Windsor and many police at Heathrow feel that there are not enough men to keep it even relatively secure.

It is chilling to remember that two students, for a dare during a rag week, were able to penetrate the huge maintenance area. They took four lifejackets, three ashtrays, and a pair of goggles from a 747. They could just as easily have planted a bomb.

Some airlines carry armed men for protection.* Tarom, the Romanian airline, carries up to three revolvers on every flight. They are sometimes carried by stewardesses. On arrival they are locked in a box which is riveted to the floor of the flight deck. Aeroflot carries guns on all flights, domestic and international. Up to five Russian-made automatic pistols are carried, and they have been used in one aerial shoot-out in which both pilots were killed and the plane crashed. The guns are distributed throughout the plane in flight, and pilots and navigators are always armed.

El Al carries three guards on every plane. They are Israeli Government employees, and are armed with Belgian automatics. Two sub-machine guns are carried in specially adapted briefcases which look like ordinary businessmen's cases. On the Arab side,

---

* *The Carriage of Arms for the Protection of Aircraft*, HM Government, London.

Royal Jordanian Airlines carry six armed guards on their jets, all revolver-carrying serving members of the Royal Jordanian Army.

The Iraqis pack plenty of punch: three guards with pistols, and, as a back-up, two machine guns in briefcases. Ghana Airways carry two armed men, as do Ethiopian Airways. Armed skymarshals fly on many American flights, but no Western European airlines have yet resorted to weapons.

6 Anything to Declare?

Once a month a sad ritual is performed at the Queen's Warehouse at Heathrow. Four Customs men open hundreds of bottles of impounded liquor, and invert them into crude wooden bottle racks. The spirit pours directly into a main drain, called the Queen's Sewer, thus foiling anyone who might want to catch and rebottle the evil, eye-watering mixture of wines and strange spirits.

The cloying scene of alcohol is sharpened by tobacco fumes as cartons of cigarettes and cigars are burned in an incinerator known as the Queen's Pipe.

The warehouse is a large basement in the main Customs House on the north side of the airport, conveniently close to the police station. It is stuffed with goods seized by Customs in the Queen's name. The shelves are crammed with bottles, each tagged with the airline flight number and the name of the passenger it was taken from.

Some is sold off at regular auctions. But there are no buyers for the exotic, or for bottles that have export labels or airline stickers on them. It is not worth the expense of relabelling and rebottling for the home market.

So every month the doomed bottles are picked out, Yugoslav slivovitz, Polish blackcurrant vodka, Thai Mekong whisky, sake and tequila. Occasionally a man will pause from his work before starting a jeroboam of Moet Chandon or a two-gallon bottle of Black Label Scotch on its ignominious trip to the sewage works.

The warehouse reflects the trends in amateur smuggling by passengers, since professionals nowadays often 'smuggle' goods by altering the import tax on invoices. The 'traditional' goods, as the Customs men call them, still stand out in pure volume. In a typical year, 1976, passengers arriving in Britain were relieved of 2,824 proof gallons of spirits, and 1,879 watches. More than 11,000 of them had 20,716 lb of tobacco confiscated. Most of this will pass through the warehouse, together with the expected haul of cameras and photographic equipment.

Although these traditional goods are smuggled at a constant

rate, with Customs men reckoning that a full 10 per cent of passengers are dishonest, there is an alarming rise in the two big new areas. These are drugs and pornography. The 1976 total of 4,147 kilos of drugs was exceeded in the first seven months of 1977, with cocaine, opium and heroin all showing a particularly marked rate of increase. Pornography seizures run into tons of publications. These also pass through the Queen's Warehouse.

A special cold store is crammed with minks and other furs – as well as a consignment of pig semen, a reminder that import laws are a lot more complicated than they used to be. Jewellery goes into a high value area.

The only slump in old-style smuggling has come with perfume. Concessions are now so high that the profit has gone. But newer items have taken its place. There are special shelves for musical equipment which fill fast with amplifiers, drum sets, electric guitars and the other accoutrements of pop groups. One group alone, the Tremeloes, were discovered with four uncustomed guitars, one set of drums and four amplifiers and speakers. They had sold their old equipment in Buenos Aires and stocked up again at considerable profit in New York.

A specially wired-off section contains the cannabis of drug smugglers who never made it – 'enough to keep a town the size of Saffron Walden high for a year'. A mass of drug containers goes up to the roof, mainly suitcases and bongo drums and camel saddles. Aqualung tanks have also become fashionable hiding places.

Businessmen have smuggling as much in their blood as hippies. Enough pocket calculators, desk-top computers, tape systems and electric typewriters to supply a thirty-storey office block are discovered every year.

The amateurs give the Customs men their biggest challenge, for least reward. The professionals, smuggling cannabis by the hundredweight and cameras by the £100,000 worth, are often caught after tip-offs. The small-time returning holidaymaker has to be detected, and all the knowledge acquired at the Customs Training School in Southend is needed.

A good nose, or what the victim might consider sixth sense, is vital. The Customs people call it 'smuggler's eye'. It is indefinable, of course, but it is the quality that makes a really good Customs man as he screens hundreds of passengers pouring past him on a six-hour shift. One man who had it was Liam Sumption, a legendary Irishman who pulled passengers out of the Green Channel at Heathrow for bets with his fellow officers, and is rumoured never to have challenged an innocent traveller.

Every guilty passenger has tell-tale traits. The normally timid become over-boisterous, the placid bite their lips, the domineering are ingratiating, bossy women turn sweet. The 'eye' is mainly a question of feeling who is acting out of type.

'A lot of people look nervous when they walk through the Green,' says a Customs man. 'The art is spotting types who do not seem to be naturally nervous.' The process starts much earlier than most passengers realize – at the moment when they pick their luggage off the conveyor belt. It is there that the Customs men weigh up attitudes. Most people who are stopped in the Green Channel have been earmarked for inspection from the moment they first picked up their case.

Smugglers like to go through Customs in the middle of the queue. If their bag comes up first, they will often let it go round on the conveyor belt and only pick it up after other passengers from the flight have started off through the channels. Likewise, they get agitated if the bag is late and they have to go through at the end.

They also visibly relax when they pass through the Customs hall without being challenged, not knowing that plainclothes men mingle with the crowds in the terminals. An international drug smuggling gang was caught after a courier, an attractive and well-educated girl, ordered a double brandy in a terminal bar after clearing Customs. Young girls do not normally travel alone or take stiff drinks. Drugs were discovered in special compartments in her brassiere and wig. She was being paid £1,000 a trip to smuggle. Upper-class girls, who would have passed unchallenged almost automatically ten years ago, are now commonly used as drug couriers.

Baggage tags indicating the airline and origin of the flight are important. Duty-free prices in the Arabian Gulf, particularly Bahrein, are rock bottom. Amsterdam's Schiphol airport has a huge duty-free shopping complex. Many people make a point of flying via Amsterdam to take advantage of it. At Addis Ababa, a passenger can buy everything from duty-free washing machines to automatic gearboxes for a Mercedes.

'We get people off a Hong Kong flight. They'll hang around and come through with a flight from Zurich and they're actually surprised we pick them up,' says a Customs man. 'Yet their original flight number and airline tags are on every bit of their luggage.

'It's the same with hippies and drugs. They know we keep an eye on flights from North Africa or the East, so they come back via Frankfurt or Paris. It doesn't cost them any more for the ticket, and they think they can "launder" their image. But you don't pick up a deep suntan and dusty suitcases hanging round Germany or the Louvre.'

Terminal Three, the long-haul terminal, has the highest proportion of successful challenges by Customs officials.

Some attempts are almost as old as smuggling itself. Passengers are caught with a two-gallon bottle of Scotch, and say innocently that they thought they were allowed a single bottle duty free, irrespective of its size. They put old straps on new watches and new cameras in old cases. Fur coats are picked out because they have no labels, or because the shop label that 'proves' the coat was not brought abroad has been sewn in by hand instead of machine and is clearly older than the coat.

'I had one lady who challenged me to look at the Harrods label in her mink. It was Harrods all right – Harrods Man's Shop,' says a Customs man.

Other smugglers show a touching belief that priests, doctors and other respectable men are not searched. A house painter arrived at Heathrow with 300 watches hidden in a woman's girdle round his waist. He was dressed as a Roman Catholic priest with a passport to match. He was fined for the watches, and imprisoned for smuggling when disguised in Holy Orders. Few amateurs have heard of section 73 of the Customs and Excise Act. It provides that anyone either armed with an offensive weapon or in disguise whilst attempting to avoid Customs duty is liable to imprisonment.

Customs men the world over know what to expect on particular flights. People returning from England will be laden with woollens and cashmeres, silver tableware and fine china. From Hong Kong and Singapore come cameras, tape recorders, and hi-fi equipment.

From South America, there will be emeralds and alligator hand-bags, and from South Africa diamonds and animal skins. From Mexico there is onyx, and from the US new electronic gadgets which will later be copied and come in from the East.

And from the Far and Middle East, North Africa and South America come drugs. The big syndicates rarely use passengers as carriers. Freight is safer. But semi-professionals still use suitcases. If they get a few pounds through, the profits will keep them going in Europe for a year or more in some style.

False bottoms are not in great demand now. The entire suitcase is now built round the cannabis, lining it top, bottom and sides. A distinctive suitcase, respectable-looking and easy to copy, is the Samsonite. Genuine handles and the maker's name-plate are taken and imitations built round them, normally in Turkey. These are exported to Afghanistan, Morocco, the Lebanon and India – where they cost three times as much as a genuine Samsonite case.

Up to twenty kilos of hashish can be used to form the frame of the suitcase. This puts the case close to the airline weight limit. Filling them with light clothes, mainly shirts and underclothes, is the normal answer. But Customs men are quick to suspect a case that has no heavier shoes, suits or books. The Queen's Ware-house is full of these fake 'Samsonites', hanging in groups of two or three. A man who will risk one is normally greedy enough to try more. One Jordanian was arrested because he had seven ident-ical 'Samsonites'.

Crews smuggle too. One incentive is that they only get half the normal duty-free allowances on many trips, offset by the threat of losing a career. After leaving the aircraft, the crew go through their own Clearway Customs system. Sometimes a 'rummage squad' of élite Customs men boards the aircraft before the crew leave it, and takes both plane and crew luggage to pieces.

Crew members who do smuggle often choose another airline to do it on. Thus stewardesses working for the Far Eastern airline Cathay Pacific smuggled suitcases full of Japanese cameras into Heathrow, but flew off-duty on British Airways flights from Hong Kong to London.

Large quantities of gems, drugs or watches have been found by rummage squads. Couriers dump their corset load of contraband in a special compartment on the aircraft before landing. It is picked up later by another member of the gang who has access to the plane when it is not surrounded by Customs men, a maintenance engineer, a cleaner, a loader or a mechanic.

This is how, for example, 988 watches and 3,000 watch movements were found in the toilet of a jet that flew in from Zurich to London. The rummage squad found them before the man – or woman – on the ground could get to them.

Gold smuggling grew up with aviation, and bars of gold dumped by frightened couriers have been found on many planes. It will flourish as long as countries restrict gold hoarding. During the halcyon days of the 'golden stewards', cabin crew and passengers smuggled gold by the waistcoat-full into India and Pakistan.

The demand for gold in those countries is insatiable. It alone represents security and status, and smuggling became a major industry with profits of over 200 per cent. One 'courier' could make £20,000 a trip. Aircraft flew into India with parts of their tailplanes made of gold; typewriters with gold space bars were brought in as hand luggage. Gold pellets replaced the stones in dates carried by pilgrims from Mecca to Karachi.

Couriers were recruited by vaguely worded advertisements in leading European papers promising quick money in return for travel. They were then flown to Zurich, where they were trained by a woman in a broken-down house near the Hauptbahnhof.

The first priority was to get the reluctant adventurers fit. An early courier was arrested in India because he sat down whilst waiting to go through Customs. Tired and weighed down with 80 lb of gold above his belt, he was unable to stand up again. His successors could be seen jogging round the early morning streets of Zurich, practising the knees-bend-with-straight-back that was vital to their trade.

Even so the weight on the long flights to the East could be crushing. One man dropped two bars of gold down the lavatory of a 707 whilst adjusting his load an hour out from Delhi. The lavatory jammed, and the $8,000 mistake was discovered.

Couriers were instructed to dress 'English', with collar and tie, and to avoid casual clothes. They were told to be polite and relaxed with officials – but never humble. A nine-page advice list gave them such advice as: 'Immediately before arrival, it is a good idea to *have a wash and shave* so that you may look as fresh and as lively as possible.'*

To stop people bumping into their golden torsos, they were told to carry hand baggage or a camera. Rule 6 in the list pointed out that 'this is to give you distance from any person touching you while queueing or when in the gangway of the plane'. Further advice encouraged them to 'sleep with your head towards the aisle so that the steward will not nudge your chest to wake you up for food or a transit stop'.

Rule 13 was more comforting: 'In certain transit stops such as Karachi a gentleman in uniform may come on to the plane and stay there while the native cleaners are on board. This gentleman, no matter how ominous he looks, is there to make sure the cleaners do not pinch anything. Completely ignore him and go to sleep.'

Once trained, the courier is fitted with a special canvas waistcoat that will accommodate over $150,000 worth of gold. It has forty small pockets and a one-kilo bar will fit in each. The gold is bought quite legally in Europe. From Switzerland, it will be stamped with the name of a bank; in London with the name of bullion dealers, such as Johnson Mathey. In both cases, the bar has the magic number 999 engraved on it – proof that it is 99.9-per-cent pure gold.

A few couriers made golden nest eggs and retired. Others still languish in prisons in the Indian subcontinent. The big operators made fortunes. Some had a working capital of over £1 million, and could afford to write off seizures of £100,000 as acceptable business losses. But the change in gold prices, and the difficulties of getting couriers through routine anti-hijack searches, have affected the business.

There are one thousand Customs men at a big international airport. The bulk of them are not concerned with Red and Green Channels. These were introduced so that more men could be spared to fight the professional smuggler.

The modern smuggler's stock-in-trade is playing dull but highly

* A former gold smuggler, who was imprisoned in India, told his detailed story to *Town* magazine.

lucrative games with paperwork. A false certificate of origin showing that Japanese goods apparently come from New Zealand can mean a 25-per-cent preferential reduction in duty. Over a year's trading, this is worth thousands of pounds.

Evading restrictions on prohibited imports and exports is again largely a paper exercise. Large profits are made by altering the description of some electronic equipment, embargoed for security reasons, so that it can get into a Communist country.

Pornography is imported as 'comics'. In Britain alone 41,000 such 'comics' are seized every year. So are 1,000 films which are certainly not 'educational' in the normal sense.

Ocelot is listed as jaguar to get round animal protection laws. £80,000 worth of Japanese ivory carvings were carefully dated as early nineteenth century since antiques more than a century old bear no import duty. It was discovered that they had been chemically aged.

£18 million computers and hundreds of thousands of forms help fight the modern smuggler. A busy airport like Heathrow handles 1,500,000 consignments coming in, and two million going out every year. Each is fed into the computer system, to be retrieved at over 200 visual display terminals. More than ninety per cent of smuggled goods come in like this, anonymously as freight.

Drugs are a constant worry, increasing at over twenty per cent a year. There are some clues for Customs. Large consignments of low value items are natural targets: airfreight is expensive, normally only for high value cargo. Half a ton of meat tenderizer revealed 200 lb of drugs.

Exotic foods are now flown into Europe and the US for immigrants and for Asian restaurants. Chilli pickle from Bombay, pickled mustard plants from Hong Kong, black mangoes from Jamaica, egg jam from Singapore, coriander leaves from Cyprus – they have all included drugs.

'Sometimes the smugglers almost dare you,' says a drugs expert. 'We thought there was some heroin in some priceless carvings from Hong Kong. The ivory was flawless and very valuable. We took the risk and broke one open. The powder had been injected.'

Most seizures like this are based on tip-offs. Consignments are followed step by step from the poppy fields of Turkey and the Lebanon, or the 'Golden Triangle' on the borders of Thailand and

Burma where private armies still hold sway, to the departure airports at Beirut or Bangkok. The 'informers' are usually business rivals.

'Foolproof' schemes are discovered through jealousy. One was to send tatty suitcases, supposedly containing immigrants' personal effects, to await collection at airports in Europe. The suitcases would lie in bond, unexamined, until they were claimed by the 'immigrant' on his arrival.

In fact, they were stuffed with drugs, but whilst in bond they were safe from detection. They were not claimed for some time, and gradually were pushed to the side of the freight sheds. They were then replaced with identical suitcases, the original labels switched, and driven out of the bonded area.

The substitute suitcases were full of precisely chosen effects, cheap Indian clothes, tatty shoes, cooking vessels. When they were claimed by the 'newly arrived immigrant', the Customs check revealed nothing.

It was too good a scheme not to upset other drug dealers.

One method has been used many times. The smuggler puts identical suitcases on to the aircraft – one with the merchandise, the other quite 'clean' with clothes and so forth. On arrival he picks up the suitcase with the smuggled goods. If challenged when going through the Green Channel, the smuggler says he has picked up the wrong case. On returning to the luggage pick-up point, he will, of course, find 'his' identical suitcase filled with innocent items.

This system can fail, as Henry Patrick Solomon discovered. A former Nigerian police officer from Lagos, he was ambitious enough to try to get £40,000 worth of cannabis through Heathrow.

Things went wrong. The case with the cannabis was accidentally misrouted at Madrid on to a KLM flight. When Solomon arrived at Heathrow, there was no sign of it on the conveyor. He panicked and left without even the 'clean' bag. He later returned for the 'clean' bag, but Customs were suspicious, since they knew by now that one bag on the flight had accidentally been sent to Amsterdam. Solomon was arrested on its arrival. It was opened, and he got three and a half years, all because of a baggage handler's inefficiency in far-off Madrid.

Another old favourite is the secret compartment in an animal cage. Whenever Customs are suspicious they call in an expert to look after the animal whilst they search the cage. The haul has included heroin in a tank of coral snakes, and hashish in an oversize dog basket.

The Customs consider that currently the most stupid place to hide contraband is in the soles of platform shoes. Nevertheless, people still try it.

But in spite of all this there is no doubt that the smuggler has come fully to terms with aircraft and airports. American Customs reckon on picking up only one smuggler in ten at airports, and the British admit to about one in eight; the scale of smuggling is increasing.

Drug smuggling is the big business in the USA, growing every day. 'I remember the old marijuana days, eleven years ago,' says JFK Customs agent Pat Solan. 'People would pour off the Avianca flights with big vests full of the stuff, wearing ponchos to hide it. You had to see them to believe it. I made eight seizures one night with twenty-five pounds of the stuff. All from people wearing ponchos.'

The big amounts come in as cargo, by ship or by special aircraft. Individual passengers carry 5 to 6 lb unless they are in the diplomatic racket, when their bag can be full of 40 lb or more. Diplomatic passports, normally Latin American but including some European and Middle Eastern countries, and United Nations passports are being widely used. They are particularly used in getting Customs preclearance for the US in Canada and Bermuda.

Some smuggle for their own use, but most are 'mules', paid $1,500 or so a trip. They are frequently paid in counterfeit money. 'They come in all shapes, sizes and colours,' says a JFK Customs man, one of 300 at the airport. 'Most are from the twenty to forty-five age group, but we've had grandmothers, and mothers who have hidden stuff on infants.' Mules have included a former Los Angeles probation officer, a priest and several doctors.

Cocaine can be dissolved in liquor or perfume, and is easily recovered after passing through Customs. Water containing dissolved cocaine can be soaked into cotton clothes and the cocaine retrieved days later with a loss of only ten per cent.

The profit can be very great. Anyone flying in from Bogota can make $10,000 tax free selling a pound of cocaine, no bigger than a paperback book. Or he can get three years to life.

The most used flight into the US for cocaine is Braniff 922 from Bogota to Los Angeles. A favourite ploy is for the passengers to hide the powder on the plane, clear Customs in LA, get back aboard for the connection to San Francisco, and collect the hidden drugs there. Eight pounds of unclaimed cocaine were found in the nose cone of one DC8. Panel bolts on others are worn from smugglers' screwdrivers. Los Angeles-bound smugglers also use Avianca 080.

There is a clear pattern to drug-smuggling routes from Colombia. On direct routes, JFK Customs agents take a hard look at the Avianca 727 on Flight 204, and Braniff's 908. At Dallas/Fort Worth an eye is kept on Eastern's 990, which connects with drug flights from Miami. In Chicago, Eastern's 78 is checked out.

Even closer to the source of supply, some smugglers fly out of Cartagena on Avianca 068 to Miami. They can connect on to Houston with National 53. Or they fly from Medellin to Miami on Condor 144.

But direct routes are losing their appeal. 'We still get numbskulls who haven't figured out that we take a keen interest in anybody who flies in from Colombia,' says Pat Solan. 'But some of them have got the message. We had three recently who came into JFK on Pan Am 800 from Tokyo.

'Pan Am is an interesting airline for us. You get a mixture of everything and everybody. The unexpected is always happening. Unlike, say, TWA or British Airways, which are more straightforward. But you wouldn't expect much on Pan Am from Tokyo. And the first guy was a returning military man, normally very clean.

'But he didn't fit the profile. The profile says two bags. He had eight. The profile says sets of clothes. He only seemed to have shirts. Sure enough, he had heroin. That's the new thing – the smugglers position themselves to fly in from a really innocent-seeming city.'

Besides Tokyo, there have been cases of smugglers flying from Bogota to Madrid and Brussels, and then going on to the US. More commonly, and less expensively, a number will come in via the Caribbean. Pan Am 436 from Santo Domingo to Miami has aroused interest, as well as American 658 to New York. Haiti is equally suspect.

A near foolproof scheme to bring cocaine into the US was found in Port-au-Prince and Santo Domingo. Four women would book a one-week Caribbean cruise out of Miami or Caracas. The liner would make a stop at Santo Domingo or Port-au-Prince, where the women would return to the cruise ship carrying twelve kilos or more of cocaine in wicker baskets or shoulder bags.

When the cruise ship stopped at Puerto Rico, the cocaine would be taken to the distributor who had arranged the deal. The women couriers would return to the ship and continue the cruise. The cocaine was then put into suitcases and flown to JFK on normal commercial flights. There are no Customs examinations of flights from Puerto Rico, so the smuggling carried almost no risk.

One gang is thought to have made more than $4 million in two years with this scheme. The women couriers operated on Commodore Cruise Lines' *Boheme*, Chandris Lines' *Amerikanis* and the Yugoslav liner *Istra*.

Even safer has been the use of diplomatic passports. In one case, involving high Panamanian officials, 175 lb of heroin valued at $20 million was found by Customs agents on a passenger arriving at JFK on a Braniff flight. Rafael Richard, the son of the Panamanian Ambassador to Taiwan, claimed immunity by way of his diplomatic passport. That would normally have put an end to it, but agents found that he did not have full immunity and was subject to arrest.

'Normally, there's not a damn thing you can do to a "diplomat". And remember, the whole goddamn Embassy gets immunity – drivers, switchboard clerks, cooks, cleaners, the lot,' says a Customs agent. 'They get very cheeky. They know you can take the stuff off them, but you can't touch them. I had one who had cocaine in 35-mm cameras. I asked him what it was for. "For my nose," he said, as cool as you please.'

The agents sniff out smugglers with the help of the 'profile' of the normal traveller. One agent says:

Simply put, the average traveller is very average. He has two cases, and the things in those cases accurately reflect his position in life and his journey. Let's say he's a businessman back from Europe. He may have had a rather complex journey, been to a few capitals over there. His cases will have a fair bit of paper work in them. He'll have a couple of pairs of shoes, good shoes, and a Brooks Brothers suit or whatever, three or four silk ties, and a good selection of shirts and socks, all neatly laundered by a hotel. There will be a little stack of laundered handkerchiefs and a couple of hardcover books.

Now, if he's an oilman, even a fairly senior one, he'll be very different. If his travels have taken him to the North Sea, he'll have bought a couple of tartan rugs – for certain, they all do. He's going to have slacks, maybe a plaid jacket, and sports shirts, and a pair of boots. He may have a paperback and a shooting or hunting magazine, and almost certainly a couple of bottles of straight malt whisky. Don't ask me why oilmen have dirty laundry – maybe Scottish hotels won't do it. But they have it, as certainly as really starched shirts tell you the man in front of you is, depending on the maker, a US merchant marine officer or a British military type.

People think I'm boasting when I say I can tell a Midwesterner, a New Englander or a New Yorker purely from his luggage, but I can. I've spent my working life looking at people and their luggage. A New Yorker will have English shirts from Harrods or Mr Fish. A New Englander will have one from New York, and a Midwesterner from Sears. New York women pack everything carefully so the label shows: you don't get New Yorkers creasing labels, not if they are good labels. Whereas California and Texas women just chuck clothes in. They are much less finicky than Easterners.

When we get somebody whose luggage doesn't match his appearance, or his story, or his route, then we get curious. Like with Pan Am 800. Why should people carrying light clothes, slacks and short-sleeved shirts be coming from Tokyo in February? Why should they have suntan oil in their toilet kits? Because they started out from Colombia.

They may claim to be students. What is a student doing in Tokyo in February? He's surely not on vacation. So where is he studying? Or a businessman. So how come he's not carrying lots of papers, commercial samples, sales aids?

Smugglers never accumulate all the rubbish in their cases that an ordinary traveller does – phrase books, torn street-maps, half-filled-in post-cards, used rolls of film, hotel receipts, book matches, curios, presents for the children. And they can make real fools of themselves. They'll say, 'Colombia, where's that?' And then you point out that their shirt wrappers – back to shirts again – are labelled Bogota Hotel, or that their toothpaste or shaving cream is Colombian.

You get some who are so stupid that they don't even fill their suitcases. They seem to think that we won't find it odd that they are travelling with an empty case. Those who fill them often get the mix wrong. There will be masses of clothes, but not heavier shoes or books. The clothes themselves are often suspicious: shirts of different sizes, trousers that don't seem they would fit the passenger, labels with little giveaways – Ind. Col., Colombian made. Or all the other clothes will obviously be new. Or they don't suit the personality of the owner. We had one, a macho type, and he had all dull gabardine trousers and chunky sweaters. Totally out of character, though the cocaine we found wasn't. It takes a lot of skill to fool a man who's been looking at suitcases for fifteen years.

7 Illegal Entry

Not only things are smuggled. People are too, in what has become one of the most lucrative and fast-growing commodities of all, the illegal immigrant. Perhaps the most fanciful of all intending illegal immigrants to visit Heathrow was Asraf Mohammed Ali, a Pakistani. He arrived from Karachi one late summer day, just in time for the opening of the football season.

He explained to the Immigration officers that he had come for a trial with Woolwich Queen's Park Athletic. His best position was centre forward and this was where he expected to play for his new club. He gave his age as twenty-three.

There was a Woolwich Arsenal in 1900. There still exists a Queens Park Rangers, known as QPR, and a Charlton Athletic. There never has been a WQPA. Asraf produced a letter of invitation from the 'club', but the spelling was wrong. He finally admitted that he was forty-one, and that he had written the letter himself. He was flown home.

Another manoeuvre in the immigration war was the four-day 'see the England of the Bard' tours from Scandinavia to Stratford. A remarkably high proportion of Pakistanis were turning up on these tours. And, although a number of Pakistanis do work in Sweden, most of them were using the package tours as an excuse to get into England and disappear.

Heathrow is the main battleground for illegal entry into Britain, and the problem is growing. Where 8,945 were refused entry in 1974, 17,014 were turned back in 1980. The number of Commonwealth citizens turned back was up from 3,255 to 5,386. India, Nigeria and Ghana again headed the list, with 1,238, 1,176 and 695. Cyprus, another traditional source of illegal immigrants, registered a slight drop to 274. The West Indies rate much lower than is generally supposed, with Trinidad and Tobago at 17 and Jamaica at 82.

There was a sharp increase in foreign nationals who were denied permission to enter the country. The figures were up from 5,690 to 11,628. Many of these resulted from the Ayatollah Khomeini.

Iranians scarcely figured in the lists in 1974, but in 1980 topped all countries with 2,294. Algerians and Pakistanis also topped the 1,000 mark. Spain and Turkey, who provide illegal workers in the restaurant trade, were high at 578 and 798.

Many of these fall into the penniless student category rather than potential illegal immigrants. But the problem, and the controversy of virginity tests applied to check marital or fiancée status, show no signs of going away.

The cost of illegal entry into Britain is now running at about £2,000. Punjabis and Sikhs are highest on the list, and the schools for would-be immigrants are getting so sophisticated that the Immigration Service has established its own Intelligence Unit to get knowledge on racketeering, particularly checking Karachi, Delhi, Bombay, Dacca and Sylhet.

The plastic seal over the photograph on new passports has made things more difficult, but not impossible.

An awkward page on a legitimate passport, one that, for example, restricts the holder to a stay of three months, can be 'reconstituted' in the same way. 'Completely forged passports are rare,' says a senior IO. 'It is too easy to steal a genuine one, although it has to be used fairly quickly before it gets on the stolen list.'

Suitable doctoring of a returning Indian resident's family passport can enable them to bring in an extra child. Children under sixteen are entitled to admission if they are accompanied by a parent, and greatly overaged sons, nephews and cousins still try to come in. X-rays of the wrist bones are used to verify real age. Pregnant women frequently slip in as tourists for short visits – and leave after their children are born in Britain and thus entitled to British passports.

The emphasis is now switching from Terminal Three to Terminals One and Two, the short-haul routes from Europe. This gives the would-be immigrant a few more bites at the cherry. If he fails the first time, he is not shuttled back to India or Pakistan but just back across the Channel where he can obscure the vertical cross of the Commonwealth refused entry (foreigners get diagonal crosses) and try again.

Airports of origin for the short-haulers are Frankfurt, Paris and Amsterdam. Any Asian with a ticket booked directly onwards from the subcontinent to Heathrow via any of these European airports is almost automatically suspect.

Visitors' restrictions can be 'laundered'. One worried London travel agent checked with IATA after he had issued several hundred tickets to Asians, which had been returned for full refunds. IATA confirmed that the tickets had not been used fraudulently. Why should individuals buy so many tickets and then not use them? Because with a ticket to a European country they could approach foreign Embassies and obtain visas. Once they had filled up their passports with visas, fresh passports could legitimately be obtained from their London High Commissions and Embassies. And the fresh passports would *not* show the original three month restriction on stay in Britain.

The latest scheme, particularly with Indians – and the Immigration authorities rely a great deal on nationalities consistently using the same method – is a ticket through to Canada, with a 'holiday stopover' in Britain to visit relatives whilst *en route* for a new life. This gives the illegal immigrant the chance of trying Britain – and if that fails, going on to Canada for another attempt.

Pakistanis favour the 'returning resident' approach. They are rehearsed with street maps, National Insurance documents, and details of their jobs at a travel agent's 'school'.

Turks are known to have a flourishing business with forged work permits. 'It is good work, fresh printed, not altered. Like a lot of papers that give people away, they're too good. You don't expect an Indian birth certificate to be perfect. Much less do you expect the typing and spelling on a Turkish permit to be exact to the nearest comma,' says an IO.

Moroccans, and to a lesser extent Italians, have genuine work permits, almost invariably in catering. They obtain them by faking their catering experience and references on their application forms. For a waiter to get a work permit in Britain would normally mean at least three years' higher grade work abroad.

With Cypriots, the short visit for a 'cousin's wedding' is often used. As with any successful approach, it could well be genuine. 'That is why we get so many complaints about questioning legitimate passengers,' says an IO. 'The racketeers don't feed their customers cover stories or documents that aren't being used truthfully by others.'

Detection is partly instinct. 'When you've been through a plane load and there's one passport or ticket that's somehow different to the others, then the suspicion just flicks into your mind.' Partly it is because certain flights or tickets are known to be suspect: 'KLM run two flights a week that correspond with PIA flights from Karachi. Clearly you're going to be interested in anyone who's changed at Schiphol instead of flying direct. Nicosia flights in Terminal One are also musts,' says an IO.

All non-British passengers are held at a gate before being told which IO's desk to go to. This enables behaviour to be seen. 'There's normally the stool pigeon IO, the one who looks an easy touch, just as there used to be with Customs before the channel system. If you see anyone hanging back, being over nervous, then you start checking.'

Theoretically, every IO should look up every immigrant in the 'look-out book', which has details of 18,000 prohibited or suspect aliens under twenty different codes (political, expelled for work permit, morals, and so on). This weeds out some, although not everyone in the 'look-out book' is barred from entry. The IO will ring the Home Office for confirmation before refusing entry. Diplomats, of course, have to be allowed in even if they are suspected of spying. If a diplomat on the look-out list appears, the IO will immediately telephone a special Diplomatic Passport Section in London, which will keep the diplomat under surveillance.

Experience is as helpful as the 'look-out book'. 'The illegal immigrant can be word perfect on the difficult stuff, particularly the "returning resident" who has never even been here before and thinks Bradford is as big as Calcutta,' an IO explains. 'But you ask them, "What do British policemen look like?" and they say, "Well, they carry guns." Or you take a ten pence piece out of your pocket and the chap, although he'll know exactly what he should be earning in his fictitious job, will say it's a penny. Or you ask them what tram they go to work on. The suits are a dead giveaway – obviously bazaar not Burtons, although there's a trade in Burtons and St Michael labels.'

Luggage is often a considerable clue, though it must be opened by Customs. The IO has no such powers of search. 'If you find someone has his school reports, or job references or exam results in his suitcase you can be fairly certain he's not just on holiday.

People get upset when we read diaries and letters – but there are a lot of clues you can pick up.'

Suspect waiters are asked to show their tickets. As they pull them out, the IO looks for blisters, short nails or other signs of manual work. If they are there, he can and probably will get the terminal restaurant staff to bring a table and cutlery into the room and ask the passenger to lay the table.

A German girl at Terminal Two was recently suspected of being a prostitute. A search of her luggage revealed a whip, riding hat, boots and spurs and a letter confirming accommodation in a £100-a-week King's Road flat. 'But of course she just said she liked riding, and she got in.'

Customs only reckon to catch about fifteen per cent of total traffic. It is probable that more illegals are getting through. The pick-ups are often too chancy. 'We had a lot of Indian dependants coming in, between twelve and eighteen, all just coming up to working age. They were being met by people who obviously weren't their fathers. But there was instant recognition between "son" and "father" on every flight.

'Then we realized the children were all wearing ties, which was unusual. So we altered the ties on one flight, and all the "fathers" went for the wrong "sons". But it is difficult not to be one play behind the game,' says a former IO.

Forging passport stamps is not easy. Each IO has his own individually numbered stamp. Exact duplicates of all stamps in the country are on hand at every port. Each stamp has its own peculiarity – the three sides of the triangle are not of equal thickness, spacing between letters varies, and some words are deliberately off-centre. It is as peculiar to its owner as his signature, and more difficult to forge. 'You get so you can read them. And it isn't easy to cut fake ones. The effects are got through varying the thickness of rubber, so that no two stamps squash on to the paper in the same way. You could make a perfect facsimile of a stamp – but it wouldn't work the same when you hit the paper.'

Special Branch men stand beside the Immigration officers. If they want an IO to stop a passenger they simply put their foot on his high stool. Their interests are different to the IO: they look for nationals rather than foreigners, and for people leaving rather than entering the country.

The main job for the IO with outward-bound passengers is to see whether the passport has been stolen, or whether the bearer is a Ward of Court. Many children are made Wards of Court specifically to stop one parent from snatching them abroad. It is the IO's responsibility to stop these 'tug-of-love' cases.

The Special Branch man beside him is interested in a lot more – the person's moral record, his destination, his spying proclivities, or whether he is on the criminal wanted list, although contrary to romance wanted criminals are hardly ever picked up at airports.

He checks everyone booked on to the Communist airlines – Aeroflot, Hungary's Malev, Czechoslovakia's CSA, Poland's LOT. If an IO makes pleasantries to a passenger without asking any specific questions, it is probably because the sour-looking Special Branch man standing next to him is interested.

Oddly, an IO cannot prevent nationals from leaving or entering even if the passport is out of date. Although they can cause a lot of trouble, they have little legal power over their own nationals.

But their powers over foreigners are very considerable. Without giving any reason, they can refuse them entry; detain them for five days maximum in the Queen's Building, which has eighteen beds; or put them in Harmondsworth detention centre (capacity fifty-three, with an overflow to Pentonville) without time limit. Much of the guarding is not done by the police or Immigration Service but by private security men.

Language can be difficult. There are 190 IOs who speak French and 68 German, but they are down to three with Hindi and Punjabi and one with Arabic and Chinese. IOs also have to watch out for airport workers. Several Pakistani men dressed in baggy trousers and pink smocks, with jewelled noses, have emerged from the lavatories of Paris flights. They hoped to pass off as airport cleaners, most of whom are Asian women.

There are 416 men at the airport with Terminal Three still leading with 193, Two with 128 and One with 95. Almost half the British Immigration Service is at Heathrow.

Part Two
Skypeople and Others

8 Pilots

The typical captain is forty-three, married with two children, a dog and two cars. He lives in a detached house with a large garden within thirty miles of his home airport. His only real interests outside flying are golf, fishing and gardening. He will be politically and socially conservative. For recognition he has four gold bars on his sleeve. First officers have three.

It is a very reassuring profile. Unfortunately, as Dr Herbert Haynes of the important American Federal Aviation Authority points out: 'We have no effective screening methods to make sure pilots are sane.' Pilots are rigorously, although not always successfully, checked to make sure they are in the pink of physical condition. They are examined for heart conditions, bad teeth, cancer and syphilis; their physical health must be excellent but nobody challenges their sanity.

On 9 February 1982 a Japan Air Lines DC8 with 174 passengers aboard was approaching Tokyo's Haneda airport after a flight from Fukuoka. It was at 200 feet and 126 mph when it nosedived. An automatic warning sounded in the cockpit, a tape recording saying 'Glide slope, glide slope' as the aircraft lost height. The co-pilot shouted, 'Captain, please stop it.' The aircraft crashed into Tokyo Bay just short of the runway, killing twenty-four people.

The captain, Seiji Katagiri, had put one engine into reverse thrust and had pushed the control column forward causing the crash. The flight engineer, Yoshimi Ozaki, had fought with him and the co-pilot Yoshijumi Ishigawa had tried but failed to lift the nose.

Katagiri told investigators that 'immediately after I switched from auto to manual operation on the landing approach I felt a sense of terror and completely lost consciousness. I heard an inner voice telling me to "Go! Go!" ' The day before the accident Katagiri banked his aircraft dangerously, but crew members did not report his erratic flying.

He had been diagnosed as a psychosomatic case in November

1980 after refusing to fly an aircraft from Moscow to Tokyo because he felt 'too tired'. JAL grounded him for a month and demoted him to co-pilot. Katagiri was advised to seek psychiatric help in March 1981 and in August 1981 was found to be suffering from 'autonomic imbalance'. But he returned to full duties as a captain in November 1981.

Remarkably, the Japanese labour ministry discovered that Japan Air Lines employed doctors only on a part-time basis. Medical checks after the crash revealed that twelve JAL cockpit crews and trainees had records of psychosomatic ailments or neurosis.* Fortunately eccentricity is more common than tragedy.

The captain of a United Airlines scheduled flight from San Diego to Seattle was told by the stewardess that the last hot dinner aboard had been served to a passenger. Furious, the captain announced that he would make an unscheduled stop in San Francisco for 'resupply'. He put the big jet down in San Francisco, had a restaurant dinner, and then rejoined the plane to take it to Seattle.

An instructor pilot, who was examining another airline pilot on a Boeing 707, suddenly wrenched the plane into a steep climbing turn and yelled: 'Damn Japs down there are putting up a lot of flak. Guadalcanal will always be a tough target.' He was over Oklahoma City at the time. The crew had to knock him out.

A Boston-based pilot counts the black passengers who board his aircraft, and delays the flight by ten minutes for each one. A French pilot who had a radio argument with a flight dispatcher lost his temper and hitchhiked 370 miles home, abandoning his passengers on the aircraft.

The captain of an Alitalia DC10 stormed off the plane, which was waiting to take off on a flight from Rome to Bangkok, when the airline refused to let his daughter take the flight on a ten-per-cent discount ticket. It was August 1976, and Alitalia do not allow staff discounts in the peak season. Another captain had to be found for the pilotless plane.

An expert British doctor, L. T. C. Hayward of Graylingwell Hospital in Chichester, has written an 'Assessment of Stress Tol-

* *Guardian*, 25 February 1982.

erances in Commercial Pilots'.* He reported: 'There is some reason to believe that many pilots, at the peak of their physical health and outwardly calm and composed, are inwardly suppressing a seething sea of emotional turbulence born of domestic worries, administrative frustration, technical hazards, and operational fatigue.' Another British doctor, Anthony Hall of the Hospital for Tropical Diseases in London, revealed in 1981 that he had examined seventeen pilots over the preceding five years.† He had diagnosed alcoholism in nine, hypertension in six and partial blindness in one.

'My clinical experience,' said Dr Hall, 'and my collection of books and press cuttings indicate that a high proportion of pilots are physically, and/or mentally, unfit to fly.'

The pressures on the older pilot are clear. His contemporaries are often beginning to achieve recognition and power in their late forties. His career is virtually finished at fifty. Above that age, it would be too expensive to retrain him on new aircraft.

He may worry about crashing, perhaps to the point of obsession. The danger periods to a pilot are said to be three hours after the first solo, and with 300, 3,000, 13,000 and 23,000 hours. Few pilots get in enough hours to qualify for the last, which represents over two and a half years in the air. But many worry badly about the other danger points. Pilots who have made it to retirement warn the younger generation: 'There are old pilots and bold pilots, but there are no old bold pilots.' They are all supposedly dead at one of the danger points.

A pilot is put through tests four times a year. Failure in any one can end his career immediately. Two are flying proficiency tests. The others are rigorous medical checks. The strain is enormous: career and family well-being depend entirely on him passing. Pilots are not the totally self-confident figures, serene and godlike in the cockpit, that they seem to passengers.

Very occasionally a substandard pilot can get by and still fly. A United Airlines captain, Gale C. Kehmeire, received a poor report when he was being trained to fly DC8s: 'A review of Captain Kehmeire's record still indicates unsatisfactory performance in the

* *Flight Safety* 1 12–18, 1967.
† *Daily Telegraph*, 22 January 1981.

areas of command, judgement, Standard Operating Procedure, landing techniques and smoothness and coordination. On the basis of the above I recommend Captain Kehmeire's DC8 transition to be terminated.' This unsatisfactory showing in almost every aspect crucial to flying notwithstanding, Captain Kehmeire was later in command of a United Boeing 727 when it crashed at Salt Lake City.*

The insecurity of employment means that many take up second jobs which can be tiring. Pan American pilot Jim Zockoll says: 'No matter how fit I feel, I always get the collywobbles every six months when I go for my medical. And that goes for nearly every pilot. There's this terrible inbuilt insecurity.' So Zockoll started a company that unblocked drains, Dyno-Rod, which now has branches in Germany, Belgium and Britain.

British pilots have a peculiar penchant for chicken farming. Others go into property, travel agencies and yacht building.

A British Airways VC10 pilot, Captain David Ferguson, started a chicken farm. 'He was pushed into his second string with chickens eighteen years ago when he was thirty-four and did lose his licence,' said his wife Betty.† 'He needed an operation for a stomach ulcer and his licence went for six months. There was no guarantee at all that he would ever get it back, and this is the fear that haunts pilots. They all dread that day when some doctor is going to turn round and say: "Sorry, old chap, it's not on, not any more." '

The tension is international. The divorce rate for pilots is high, especially those on the long-distance routes. They are away from home much of the time. When they come back, they have to spend days reacclimatizing to the new time clock.

A wife gets the compensation of duty-free gifts, a high salary, the latest gadgets and foreign holidays at very little cost. But many of them tire of being left alone to struggle with the children, house repairs, medical emergencies. Some are former stewardesses, which does not quieten the nagging fear of their husband's infidelity on a trip.

Pilots can also seem very authoritarian. They are notoriously

* Aircraft Accident Report. United Air Lines Boeing 727, Salt Lake City, Utah, 11 November 1965.
† *Daily Mail*, 28 September 1973.

sticky about status. A former chairman of British Airways called them 'spoiled children'. They complain about trivialities: stewards getting gold rings on their sleeves in case the passengers thought that diminished their own importance; other pilots calling air traffic controllers 'sir'; being checked out by younger men for flying skill; being checked by Customs at all. One captain insisted on having his tea served on a silver tray; another allowed his engineer to smoke two cigarettes an hour – on the hour and the half-hour.

A long-haul captain, at forty-three, will probably have spent the last twenty years of his life on endless journeys. But he cannot seek help too obviously if he begins to get jaded. He could easily be grounded as mentally unfit.

A pilot who has suffered a recognized psychiatric condition has great difficulty in obtaining reinstatement to flying duties, however successful his treatment appears to have been. Dr Hayward writes in *Flight Safety*: 'Pilots with self-perceived problems of a patently psychiatric nature are therefore reluctant to disclose them to the flight surgeon, until the seriousness of the developing situation forces his hand.' So tired and sleepless men are advised to relax by 'drink, drugs or sleeping with the stewardess', as airline doctors put it.

The chief medical officer to the Department of Trade and Industry, Dr Geoffrey Bennett, claims that two per cent of all pilots are alcoholics, shielded by their fellows. He says that they fight a 'continual battle against adversity', with unhappy wives, strained marriages and short job prospects. One British Airways captain died of acute alcoholic poisoning less than a month after being in charge of an airliner between Hong Kong and London.

The Russian airline Aeroflot breathalyses all crew members before commercial flights. If anyone is positive for alcohol, the entire crew is changed.

A Japan Air Lines DC8 was preparing to take off on a scheduled flight from Anchorage, Alaska. It first attempted to take off, in heavy fog, from halfway down the wrong runway. The tower warned of its improper position, and the aircraft finally positioned itself at the start of the correct runway. It lifted off, climbed 150 feet, veered and crashed beyond the runway. The five aboard were killed.

Tests on the captain showed that he had a blood alcohol of 298 milligrams. This is well over three times the level at which car drivers are convicted.

A taxi driver who had driven the flight crew to the airport had reported the captain's condition to his dispatcher, but JAL operations staff were not notified. The National Transportation Safety Board commented: 'It is extremely difficult for crew members to challenge a captain, even when the captain offers a threat to the safety of the flight.'

Pilots are subject to the same stresses as everyone else. They can and sometimes do develop severe fear of flying. There have been many cases of blacking out. Vertigo is common. Fourteen per cent of all the fatal crashes in the American Air Force are attributed to vertigo. Vertigo accidents are likely when the pilot is under stress and without experience to hold his nerve, typically whilst flying a new type of aircraft, or in weather conditions he has not met before. Momentary disorientation going into and out of cloud, from flying off instruments to looking out of the window, is normal. It takes forty-five seconds for the senses to change completely from visual flying to instruments, a more difficult transition than the other way round.

A Pensacola Naval Study revealed surprisingly large errors in judging degree of bank – the amount the aircraft is 'banking' or tilting. Some pilots identified sixty degrees of bank as straight and level.

The US Navy logged fourteen epileptic attacks to airborne flight crew members. Dr Hayward records that EEGs give some indication of psychiatric abnormality. One suggestion was continuously to monitor the EEGs in flight, so that if one crew member showed signs of abnormality the machine would warn the others to take over.

It has been established that the human brain cannot judge some apparently simple situations. Boeing were worried after four of their 727s had crashed in quick succession. All had landed short of the runway.

An engineering psychologist and chief scientist for the Personnel Subsystem of Boeing's Commercial Aircraft Division began to investigate the landing-short phenomenon using a night-landing simulator. A model of a lighted city was linked to the cockpit controls of the simulator. The pilots flew a visual approach, looking at the city lights, with all the cockpit instruments working except the altimeter.

Boeing used twelve of their most experienced captains who had averaged over 10,000 hours of flight time each. They thought the exercise would be easy. The model city was projected either on a flat plane with the runway or on a slight three degree upwards slope.

Eleven out of twelve crashed short of the runway. The twelfth man was a former Navy carrier pilot with a special knowledge of landing on a moving deck at sea.

The pilots were shocked. But it was clear that the problem exceeded human visual ability. The brain cannot work out the right angle of descent on to flat ground at night. The experiment proved vividly that it is indeed possible to fly straight into the ground unless the altimeter is checked constantly.*

The short-haul pilots, on European scheduled or holiday routes, are tired by heavy concentration on radio messages and frequency settings, and the many take-offs and landings. The greater speed and the smaller crews mean they cannot get back into the cabin. Most holiday aircraft like the 1–11 or the DC9 and Boeing 737 have only two pilots, without the flight engineer and navigator of ten years ago.

Thus the pilots spend the whole flight with the aircraft 'strapped to their backside', as they put it, without even momentary relaxation. Backache is the most common occupational disease. The pilots also claim that the absence of contact with the passengers is turning them into bus drivers.

The long-haul pilots have fatigue problems, with upset appetites, sleep patterns and biological rhythms.

The tiredness is obvious. Some flights begin in temperatures of −20°F and end in the hot nineties. Aeroflot pilots on the Moscow to Havana routes in winter, or Air Canada pilots flying down to Jamaica from Montreal and Toronto must endure these extremes

---

* *British Airways Air Safety Review.* A high initial accident rate was common with the early jets. Thus the 707 had eighteen accidents in its first million hours, dropping to thirteen for the second and eight for the fifth million hours. But the introduction of the new big jets, the 747, DC10, Tri-Stars and Airbus, has been notably safer than before.

of cold and Caribbean heat as a matter of course. Pilots often work for fourteen hours non-stop, try to shut their eyes in a strange hotel room when their body clock thinks it is afternoon, and then put in another long flight.

A Japan Air Lines survey of pilots and engineers shows how many factors affect crew fatigue. In ascending order the percentage thinking themselves 'seriously affected' was 34 per cent by lack of exercise due to continuous seating, 71 per cent by time zone differences, in-flight humidity and sunlight, 74 per cent by after-midnight flying, and 80 per cent by weather.

What do they do on the flight deck on those long stretches across the Atlantic and Pacific? The passengers know they cannot be very busy, and they are not. The tempo on a long trans-oceanic flight is slow. But they do not have secret drinking parties, or orgies with the stewardesses, or wild card games, as a passenger staring at the flight deck door might think.

All too often, they simply fall asleep. All of them. A British Airways VC10 captain on a night flight in the Far East found himself nodding off.* He shook himself awake. He found his co-pilot sleeping peacefully next to him. The flight engineer had slumped on his instrument console, and was snoring. The crew had black coffee all round, and flew on.

Pilots can, and occasionally do, drop dead at the controls of airliners. Flying is taxing on the heart. Heart rates go up to 140 on take-off, and a wearing 150 on landing. The norm is the steady 80 of the cruise. An official report on the hearts of two pilots on an actual transatlantic crossing also noted that the rate increased to 100 when the stewardess leant over with their meal trays. Sitting on a chair in cramped conditions, with it virtually impossible to move or take exercise, is not good for avoiding coronaries. Heart conditions are the most common cause for loss of licence.

The odds of death in flight are small. But seventeen captains died in American airliners in a six-year period: all the deaths were caused by heart attacks, but only one fatal crash resulted. Although pilots are trained to cope with this emergency in the next seat, there were five accidents and five near misses. A heart

* *Flight Fatigue*, Report of the Special Committee BALPA, London 1973.

attack to a British Airways Trident captain was a factor in the worst crash in Britain, when 117 died after the plane stalled shortly after taking off from Heathrow.*

More typical is a DC8 of KLM on Flight 863 to Tokyo. The aircraft was less than thirty seconds from touchdown at a scant 150 feet when Captain de Gloot died of a massive coronary. He had been fully in charge of the flight at its most crucial phase, when transition to the co-pilot would never normally be attempted.

With only twelve seconds of decision time left to him, the co-pilot, Cornelius de Jager, took over the controls. Putting on full power, he was able to go round again. He moved the dead pilot from his seat with the help of the steward and dragged him into first class as the aircraft flew on automatic pilot. The worst danger is of controls jammed by the body leading to a crash, rather than just the sudden death of one pilot, since a co-pilot should be able to fly the plane adequately on his own. The co-pilot returned to the cockpit and made a perfect landing.†

However four months before the Tokyo incident, on 22 April 1966, an Electra on a military charter flight crashed in Oklahoma after the captain died of a heart attack on the landing approach. Only 15 of the 98 aboard survived.‡ The dead pilot was Captain Reed W. Pigman. All seven crew died, together with 77 of the 92 passengers. Captain Pigman, who was the founder of the airline, American Flyers, had a very serious heart condition of long standing and also suffered from diabetes. He had falsified his medical record to keep his licence.

The Federal Aviation Agency estimates on statistical evidence that about three US pilots will die in flight each year.

Food poisoning has ceased to be an acute danger since flight crews were forbidden to eat identical meals in the 1950s.

But crews have been poisoned by things other than food. The crew of a Pan Am freighter died after nitric acid reacted with sawdust in a packing case to produce choking smoke, and they crashed at Boston.§ Intoxicated by carbon monoxide fumes from

* CAA Report 4173. The crash was on 18 June 1972.
† CAA *World Airline Accident Summary* 22/66.
‡ CAA *World Airline Accident Summary* 14/66.
§ CAA *World Airline Accident Summary* 31/73.

a faulty cockpit heater, the crew of a holiday flight from Manchester to Perpignan flew into a mountain killing all eighty-nine aboard.*

This is the sort of schedule that a pilot can expect in a typical eight-day period. First he 'deadheads' (flies as a passenger) from Paris to Singapore. He pilots the aircraft from Singapore to Sydney, and again from Sydney to Darwin. He deadheads home to Europe.

The actual flying hours involved are small, with only thirty hours on duty. But there are tiring time changes and the disorientation of sleeping through six hotels. Flying conditions vary from the lush warmth of Singapore to the vicious gales of the Tasman Sea. As a pilot says: 'You're always just on that edge of tiredness where it only needs a whine from the air conditioning to keep you awake all night; where an egg that's overboiled will put you off your food for the day; and one flip remark from a floor service waiter has you snapping your head off in the cockpit eight hours later.'

A pilot on a 'bus stop' or holiday charter route will be saturated with radio transmissions and complex landings. Aircraft on these routes often get 'stacked', kept circling in the air waiting their turn to land in an aerial traffic jam.

A pilot has to retune his radios fourteen times on a 55-minute trip from London to Frankfurt. The most familiar noise in the cockpit of a short-haul jet is not the whine of the engines and the rush of air playing round the windscreens in the breathless way of the long-haul jets. It is the clatter as the radio channels trip from one frequency to another.

The holiday airfields in the Mediterranean get very cluttered in July, August and September, December and January. Pilots must queue to land and take off, weaving intricate patterns in the sky to the orders of traffic controllers who are often not skilled, above airports that are seldom fully radar-equipped.

Punctuality is almost more important on holiday flights than on scheduled services. 'The big airlines can always roll out another aircraft if one goes u/s (unserviceable),' says a charter pilot. 'We don't have spare equipment. And if we start getting behind, it

* HMSO CAP 312.

snowballs. Miss one flight, and the holiday bookings for a whole season start snowballing into each other. The hotels can't cope. You have to keep to times to avoid a nightmare. It erodes safety standards.'

Training for pilots usually starts at eighteen. Commercial pilots are much younger than most passengers realize. British Airways has some nineteen-year-olds on its Tridents, and twenty-year-olds are not exceptional.

Captains and senior first officers are usually former military pilots. In countries that still produce plenty of young ex-Air Force pilots, like the United States and France, virtually all pilots have military experience.

But in Britain and Germany, the big airlines run their own training schools. They take their pilots direct from school. At thirty-two, they consider the ex-military pilot too old to justify the expense of commercial retraining. The young captains and the new first officers are not tough, moustachioed men who learned their flying on bombers in sheepskin flying jackets. They were taught at a trim little airfield at Hamble, near Southampton Water, or in Arizona, and they wear short hair and neat blazers with badges.

Modern selection is designed to get the stable, level-headed personality rather than the individualist. Lufthansa has a week of non-stop screening of personality to select the one in eight of serious applicants who will get pilot training.

During the week, the would-be pilots play several games of basketball. The good team player is preferred to the original or creative player: a showy attitude might lead to friction in the cockpit at a later stage.

The highly individualistic 'up and at 'em' pilot is the product of fiction. In fact, airlines try to avoid them. A recent US Navy study by Dr Robert A. Alkov states that in crashes caused by pilot error, the pilot involved frequently had a 'John Wayne' attitude about their lives and flying. Dr Alkov said that a composite profile of such pilots 'reveals an individual who is an egocentric perfectionist with a high opinion of himself'.

Such a pilot is 'resentful of authority which he feels puts unfair restrictions on his superior performance. He portrays himself as a sociable extrovert, the life of the party, and a ladies' man. He has a low tolerance for tension and is less in harmony with his environment and drinks too much. He feels he is above ordinary mortals and lives by his own rules.'

Individual flair and skill, however, can still play a vital part in commercial flying. This is particularly true if an aircraft gets into what pilots call 'EA', or an extreme attitude.

An Air India 747 had taken off from Bombay at night. At 1,400 feet the captain started a gentle climbing right-hand turn. His attitude indicator then failed, although he was unaware of this. With his instrument showing a gentle bank to the right, the captain started applying left bank to get level.

He did not sense that the aircraft was responding. Believing the instrument, he kept applying left bank. The aircraft rolled so far to the left that the wings went eighteen degrees past the vertical. The captain continued the left bank until the aircraft hit the sea, with a nose-down attitude of thirty-five degrees and its wings well beyond the vertical.

By contrast, a Trans World Airways captain was flying at 39,000 feet in April 1979 when a leading edge-flap on the starboard wing broke loose. It was dark and there was no horizon. The aircraft rolled beyond the vertical to the right, began to yaw and went into a spiral dive. Out of control, the speed increased to near the speed of sound and the aircraft was losing 16,000 feet a minute.

The captain and co-pilot did not know what had caused the EA. Nevertheless, they controlled the speed by lowering the undercarriage, and eased the aircraft out of the spiral dive. They eventually levelled out at 6,000 feet and landed safely thirty minutes after the initial loss of control.

The pilot, Captain Harvey Gibson, explained that he was able to cope with a situation many airline pilots might have been unable to handle because he was a current aerobatic pilot. He was thus accustomed to maintaining his reference while flying aircraft through unusual and extreme attitudes. This type of individual aerobatic skill is not sought by most airlines in pilot selection.

A system is used to measure personality, aptitude and intelligence.

It is a sort of super eleven-plus, with psychological tests thrown in.

'Pilots rate their skills very highly. They point out that few of their fellow countrymen can take a hundred tons of metal and fuel 3,000 miles through the night, and land it like a feather in another continent. But the war showed that a very large percentage of young males are perfectly capable of flying aircraft, even though they may not wish to spend their lives doing it,' says a veteran medical officer.

'Basically, if you can pass the eleven-plus or a similar intelligence test, can see and hear all right, and are good at something that requires coordination and judging distances – clay pigeon shooting would be a perfect example, but football or driving a car would do almost as well – there is good reason to suppose that you would make a competent pilot. People think a pilot should be fit, dashing, tall, handsome. None of those qualities is necessary. In fact, they are rather thrown away by leading a life strapped to a chair.'

The student pilot spends twenty-one months flying on single- and twin-engined light planes. By the end of training school, he will have 250 hours flying time, and a grasp of the basics of navigation and engineering. When he joins the airline, at nineteen or twenty, his first job is a month learning the nuts and bolts of the jet airliner he will be flying.

His first approach to the plane is to a 'cardboard bomber', a mock-up of all the dials and instruments in the cockpit. Every switch, every button is mocked up exactly as it is on the plane. But nothing works or moves. The pilot sits in the 'bomber' on an ordinary chair checking the panels until he knows instinctively and in the dark where each instrument and control is. It is called 'cockpit familiarization', the first step in teaching the pilot to fly a jet without the expense and risk of actually putting him up in one.

The next simulator is slightly more sophisticated. The systems instruments 'work', the dials move for the hydraulics, fuel systems, engine temperature gauges and so forth. The flight instruments and controls are dummies.

Then the pilot moves on to the big simulator, a machine that is as close to the real thing as several million pounds can make it.

Everything works. Indeed, the pitch, roll and yaw movements of an aircraft are reproduced by motors. Pull back on the stick, and the nose comes up just as it would in flight. Push the throttle forward, and the airspeed indicator and fuel gauges and other instruments will react. Even the noise of the engines, and the thump of the undercarriage, is reproduced.

Accurate models of airports and countryside are mounted on moving belts. Television cameras roam over these, picking up the commands of precise height and angle sent to it from the pilot at the controls. It feels the same, it behaves the same, it sounds the same, and it looks the same, as the colour television transmits pictures of the ground through the windscreen.

This is where the pilot learns to fly a jet. Indeed, at the end of the course he acquires an Instrument Rating on the airliner he is to fly – without necessarily having seen one, let alone flown in one.

Anything can be thrown at him: multiple engine failure, hydraulic breakdowns and loss of instruments, stalls. The simulator can 'crash', signifying this by acute juddering and banging.

Each simulator represents one particular aircraft type, having that plane's exact performance and criteria built into it. Airlines used to lose many expensive jets, and expensive crews, on training accidents. On 8 March 1971 the training captain of a 707 shut down an engine on take-off in Scotland.* The aircraft took off normally but immediately afterwards started to roll to the right and continued to do so despite full left rudder and left aileron. The captain got a measure of control back by opening up the 'failed' engine. On the landing run the aircraft again veered to the right before landing successfully. The strain of the training 'emergency engine failure' had fractured the lugs on the rudder power control unit.

On 31 March 1971 a 707 of Western Airlines in California† had a similar simulated engine failure on landing. The training captain advised the pilot to overshoot. The aircraft climbed to 500 feet, rolled to the right and crashed vertically into the ground. The lugs on the rudder unit had fractured.

* HMSO CAP 361.
† National Transportation Safety Board NTSB *AAR* 72–18.

Thus aircraft and crews are destroyed on training flights that could be carried out safely on simulators. Aircraft which normally carry passengers are subjected to dangerous manoeuvres which may weaken them. In this case, three weeks passed without vital information getting from Scotland to California.

To help with air traffic control, simulator training normally builds in garbled messages, broken pidgin English, very bad radio reception and static. It would be entirely possible for a crew who had never seen a real aircraft to emerge from a simulator, walk on to a flight deck and fly round the world.

Indeed, some British pilots have forty hours on a simulator followed by only twenty hours of base training on actual jets. They then go 'on the line' for their first scheduled flight, with twenty hours flying a jet transport in their logbooks. The young co-pilot of a British Airways Trident had just seventy-nine hours and five minutes flying experience of jets when the immensely experienced captain collapsed in the seat next to him. He would have been expected to fly the aircraft back to safety himself, had it not already been in a fatal stall.

The inexperience was held to be partly responsible for the crash. Only two days before the Trident crash, a Japan Air Lines DC8 crashed on the outskirts of Delhi, on the banks of the River Yamuna. Crew inexperience was again held to be a cause.

JAL was replacing its senior American pilots with Japanese, and the crew of the Bangkok–Delhi sector of JAL's Flight 471 from Tokyo to London was relatively inexperienced. Approaching Delhi on a very hot sultry day – the temperature was 47°C, 116°F, and the wind twenty knots on 14 June 1972 – with the sky obscured by a dust haze, the aircraft ploughed into the ground, killing eighty-six.

The various factors which combined to cause the accident* were so shattering that JAL was obliged to restrict its routes whilst pilots were trained. An investigation found that a comparatively inexperienced captain and co-pilot were flying the jet, although they filled the legal requirements. Neither of the pilots was very familiar with the route, and they had misconceptions about the facilities available at Delhi.

* CAA *World Airline Accident Summary* 18/72–19/72.

They did not follow the laid-down procedures in calling out Landing and Approach checks, 'which shows indiscipline and slackness'. In conditions where an Instrument Flight Rules approach was preferable though not necessary, flight instruments were ignored after incorrect runway lights sighting was first made.

The aircraft was only cleared down to 3,500 feet. Having come down to 2,100 feet instead of levelling off at 3,500 feet, the pilot continued to descend on sighting lights and landmarks near the crash site. Poor orientation led the crew to believe they had reached the outskirts of Delhi airport, instead of a village several miles away.

Further, the co-pilot was allowed to make the approach, in spite of being inexperienced, by a pilot who himself could not be regarded as very experienced. The total instrument flight time of the co-pilot in DC8s was 'most inadequate to make an approach to an airport on a route on which he had no flight checks'.

The captain did not perform the functions of a co-pilot after putting the co-pilot at the controls. The pilots ignored the altimeters. The aircraft was down to a critical height before it was realized that the runway was not actually in sight. The 'overshoot' command at this stage was late, and the engine did not develop full thrust in the six-second time lapse between the command and crash.

The accident report summed up: 'The immediate cause of the accident, therefore, appears to be the total disregard of laid-down procedures, abandoning all instrument indications without properly ensuring sighting of the runway by the flight crew. The "cause behind the cause" was pilot inexperience and pilot error. It was particularly worrying that both JAL and the Japanese Government sought to blame a false glide slope signal being transmitted from the ground. The investigator said this contention is not accepted.' It is disgraceful that a national airline and government should have made it.

For the first year of line service in Britain, a thin brown line is marked under the pilot's name on the roster. The pilot can only fly with an experienced training captain for his first two and a half months: the Brown Line stands between the public and total inexperience on three-crew Tridents and 707s.

The pilot is then cleared to fly as co-pilot, and becomes a second officer with one stripe. After two years, he automatically becomes an acting first officer. After two and a half years, with around 1,400 hours of flying time, he takes a difficult examination for a senior pilots' licence – the Senior Commercial or Airline Transport Pilots' Licence. After passing it, he gets two stripes in this stripe-conscious world, but is still only an acting first officer.

Four years after entering the airline, the pilot becomes a first officer. He is not promoted again for six years. He then becomes a senior first officer with three stripes, or, if he is lucky, he gets his first command with four stripes on a small airliner or a freighter, like a BAC1–11 or Vanguard.

The only individual input in this automaton-like progress comes after two years. At that stage, pilots are placed on a promotion ladder by being given a nominal day of entry to the airline. From then on, promotion is totally automatic, depending on the position on the ladder. The only way in which exceptional skill can be rewarded is when the day of entry is allocated. If BA hires five pilots on, say, 1 January, after two years the best will remain on 1 January and the other four be demoted from 2 to 5 January. But an immensely experienced former military pilot joining at thirty-four will have exactly the same seniority as a youth joining the same week from a training school.

There is thus a great orderliness about a pilot's profession, in which promotion and increased salary comes through the unwinding of the calendar, and not through particular skill.

And pilots are extremely well paid. The big Continental airlines like Air France and Lufthansa start their pilots off at £12,000 a year – at twenty-two, this makes them amongst the highest paid young men in Europe. By the time they get their first commands at thirty-four, they will be on £24,000 a year. The pilots joke that the Jumbo has a great bulbous nose under the cockpit so that the pilot can sit on his wallet: 747 captains get £42,000 a year. In badly off Britain, top captains get under half that. Pilots, as a rule, are amongst the top-paid one per cent of the population they come from. They normally retire at fifty-five.

This does not stop them from being fractious and strike-happy. Their international union, IFALPA, first drew attention to the serious deterioration in the relationship between management and pilots back in 1968. The situation has improved little.

'They've got managers everywhere,' says a young British Airways pilot. 'A little chap rushes up and says you're leaving at such and such a time, here's your lunch, here's your Met report, here's your passenger list, now get going. You *are* just a bus driver.'

The bitterness spills over into the cockpit. Pilots scrawl anti-management slogans on the flight deck. The crashed BA Trident had a wide range of graffiti: 'No to Keyline management' (a reference to the dead pilot, Captain Key), 'Grim Jim for the chop', 'Charles . . . is a . . .'

Increased speed, and increased passenger capacity, has cut the pilots off from the public. Chatting with passengers was always thought great therapy. 'You walked back from the cockpit,' says a French pilot, 'and you knew at least some people thought you were still God. It was very good for the morale. You felt your link with the great sea captains, with the captain's table.'

Some pilots made a great art of passenger relations. None more so in Europe than the legendary Captain Thompson, a Scot with British Airways. The first edict asking captains to provide 'in-flight entertainment' for passengers came in 1951. Most captains took it as meaning a chat with passengers, preferably adoring girls. Captain Thompson emerged from his cockpit in a kilt, strumming a ukulele and singing 'When I'm cleaning windows' (a well-known dirty song).

Captain Thompson would always arrive after the passengers had boarded on night flights. He would then tap his way up the aisle, with a white stick and dark glasses. The cockpit door slammed, the engines started. Then the passengers would see him open the door, and grope round pinning up a message. As the door closed, and the passengers could read the notice, he started the take-off run. It read: 'Blind Flying Tonight.'

Towards the end of his career, he flew an old biplane on the routes in the Scottish islands, where there was no separate passenger compartment. The pilot merely sat in the very front seat.

Thompson would board with the other passengers, taking a seat at the back, wearing plus fours, a tweed jacket and carrying a deerstalker. He and his fellow passengers would get increasingly irritated at the non-arrival of the pilot. Thompson declared that he had read a book about flying, and thought he could manage to get the thing up and probably down. Indeed, if the damn pilot didn't turn up in three minutes he'd try it.

Time up, he then strode to the pilot's seat. He took off, flying in a deliberately eccentric manner whilst musing aloud about which chapter had said what about landing.

Nowadays, on Jumbos, fewer and fewer pilots even bother to point out anything to the passengers over the public address system. All information is left to prerecorded cassettes. Thompson himself has enjoyed a well-earned retirement in Scotland.

The modern pilot is a rather remote figure, far from legend. He is basically a systems engineer, operating and checking very complex electronic equipment, and only a small part artist. Even his emergency training will have been done, coldly and clinically, in a simulator.

Indeed, some pilots think that it is easier to fly a real aircraft than a simulator. 'In a simulator it's tense, with examiners and instructors breathing down your neck. On the actual aircraft you can get navigational assistance from the ground, use the autopilot, all the aids. It's less sweat,' says one pilot.

There are criticisms of the artificiality of much training. Young Lufthansa pilots, for example, are taught to fly in the cloudless skies above the Arizona desert. Only ground training is done in Bremen. So clear and uncrowded is the Arizona weather that each training aircraft can fly 1,700 hours in visual weather conditions against an average of 600 hours in Germany.

But, although cloud can be simulated in the air – by making a pilot wear a visor, so that he can see nothing but the instrument panel – there is still something lacking in the desert air. German Luftwaffe pilots also train in Arizona, something that has been put forward as a partial reason for an appalling accident rate for German Air Force Starfighters.

'You simply cannot simulate a filthy day over the Ruhr. You can almost smell the factory fumes at 30,000 feet, there is a yellowish grease about the clouds. It's a crossroads for civilian and military flights. There is no way you could reproduce it in Arizona,' says a senior captain.

Most of the conversion training to a new aircraft type is now done on simulators. Propeller pilots converting to new jets like the 707 in the 1960s averaged twenty-two hours of actual flying, and eighteen hours on a simulator. But a modern 707 pilot converting to a 747 or DC10 averages fourteen hours on a simulator and only six actually in the air.

One fatal crash at Heathrow was caused by too much simulator training.* The pilot had only practised overshooting in bad weather on a simulator.

Instruments on the simulator responded immediately and accurately to actual changes in attitude. But on the aircraft they took time to register and change. The pilot pulled up in the fog to go round. Nine seconds before the crash, his instruments showed that his speed had not built up although his rate of climb was good. He relaxed his pull on the elevators. With six seconds to go, his speed was still not very fast, although the rate-of-climb indicator showed that he was climbing at 850 feet a minute. He put the nose further down.

The accident report reveals: 'At four seconds before impact the vertical speed indicator was probably showing a substantial rate of climb, and the altimeter a gain in height, though the aircraft was in fact losing height.' The pilot put the nose further down, and the aircraft ploughed into the airport, killing all aboard. If the pilot had trained on a real aircraft, this might not have happened. He would have known the lag of his instruments.

The pilot is expected to do more than simply fly the aircraft nowadays. The modern twin-jets, like the DC9 and Boeing 737, only have two-man crews. The captain, in the left-hand seat, flies the aircraft. The co-pilot has to work the fuel systems, navigate, operate control levers at the captain's command, and continually monitor radio channels. On larger three-man aircraft like the three-engined Trident and Boeing 727, the third pilot is mainly responsible for checking engine performance and the actions of the others. Most big jets only carry three crew – Boeing 707s, the Airbus, the Tristar and the 747 all operate with three. There are two pilots, with a third pilot acting as navigator and radio operator.

Very few aircraft now carry navigators. Getting lost in the air is almost a thing of the past. An aircraft flies from beacon to beacon along airways. Doppler sets work out ground speed, pos-

* CAA 27/65.

ition, and course to steer. With a computer it also gives the distance flown and the distance to go. Distance-measuring equipment gives the distance to go to ground beacons. Some navigation equipment records the position of an aircraft automatically on a chart in the cockpit.

With inertial guidance systems, a pilot has a precise map display of his position. This is based on gyros. The pilot dials in his position at the start of the flight. So accurate are these systems that he can dial in the exact latitude and longitude of the particular pier he is at. The piers have their geographical position marked on them for this reason.

Thus even a high-speed run on a holiday charter flight, to an under-equipped holiday airfield in the southern Mediterranean or a Greek island, a plane with 150 holidaymakers is considered quite safe with just two pilots. One will fly the aircraft. The other will navigate, largely a business of punching buttons on radio consoles. He will also monitor the engine instruments carefully.

Teamwork is equally mechanical. Most airlines do not keep crews together, as air forces do. The pilots on a flight may very well be complete strangers, who are introduced to each other at the beginning of the day. Thus there is no room for personal quirks, or for making up others' weaknesses.

The flight deck is a completely professional place, where the cockpit drills are so thorough that a group of strangers can work together safely. That is the theory. But one incident was caused by an engineer closing the throttle when the pilot, whom he had not worked with before, yelled 'take-off power'. The pilot meant him to open the throttle to the power setting for take-off. The engineer literally took off the power, and 'crashed' the plane.

Fortunately these strangers met on a simulator.

9 Airline Girls

A passenger's life is held in a pilot's hands. However, his more immediate welfare rests with the stewardess. She has considerable power over him, and is backed by well-tested methods of dealing with him should he be rude or difficult or if she is having an off-day.

The check-in staff, or 'checkers', take the most abuse from the public. They have to relay the bad news that an aircraft is late, that fog has closed the destination airport, that baggage is over-weight. They are not responsible for these things, but they take the blame for them.

By nature they may not be vindictive. But years of harassment have built in safety mechanisms designed to get their own back on those who annoy them. Their prime power is over seat allocations.

In principle, this is on a 'first come, first served' basis, with an aircraft layout displayed on the check-in counter for the passenger to choose a seat from those remaining. In fact, the clerks have found that displaying it leads to trouble. Passengers resent their favourite places being taken. Arguments follow.

So many checkers keep the layout concealed on a shelf on their side of the counter. The passenger cannot choose: he takes what he is given. And this lets the checkers punish those who meet with their disfavour. Businessmen are seated with families with children, or next to talkative old ladies. Smokers are put in seats in non-smoking zones. Those who inquire over-strenuously about the movie will wind up in window seats two rows back from the screen, the worst place in the plane for film-watching.

Experienced travellers will always avoid seats close to the toilets on long night flights, knowing that they will be woken up frequently. The check-in staff are also well aware of this, allocating these seats to those who irritate them. They know, too, that for safety reasons mothers with infants should have the wide leg-room found at the ends of cabins near the bulkheads. That is also a very tempting place to seat the unsuspecting passenger, who thinks he will get room and the privacy of not staring at a head in the row in front. In practice, he will get a howling infant.

'It is amazing how stupid passengers can be, especially those who pride themselves on being well travelled,' says a Paris-based checker girl. 'Those are normally the ones we have trouble with, who get arrogant. They fall for the cabin front seat every time. The great thing is that if they do start complaining about the baby in the next seat they are not going to get any sympathy.

'People can be stuck next to each other for fifteen hours on some flights. They know all about window seats, and where the noise is worst. But they simply don't realize that it is the person they are sitting next to, or the people they are sitting between, who make the real difference to their flight.

'Of course, normally we just let them sort it out themselves. But I had one businessman who was unbelievably patronizing. Knew it all. Off to Los Angeles. He still won't know that it wasn't just chance that had him stuck between a smelly hippie and a merchant seaman for eleven hours. You get people you like, of course, and you put attractive people together. I often wonder how many love affairs I've started by simple seat allocations.'

Weight on modern jets only plays a critical part when a full fuel load coincides with a very hot day at a high altitude airport – both height and heat make the air thinner and reduce power on take-off. On internal American flights, the size and not the weight of baggage is the governing factor. But a difficult passenger can expect his baggage to be minutely weighed and excess charged if applicable. His hand luggage is restricted to the legal maximum of one overnight bag, one camera or pair of binoculars, and one umbrella. His boarding card is marked QQ or AL so that he is rigorously searched as a potential hijacker or drunk.

Once on the aircraft, the cabin crew take over with their torments. Somebody who makes an immediate bad impression is likely to be greeted with a flannel that has been greatly overheated in the microwave oven. Later, his meal is overcooked. The trolley bumps persistently against him as he tries to sleep. He is left until last on the duty free trolley, and is then told that Customs now demand that the duty free be sealed.

In cases where the cabin crew are out of sorts, or all the passengers annoy them, they can inflict subtle misery by turning the lights from dim to full brilliance at breakfast time, blinding people awake, or by altering the cabin heat from full, warm to cool and back.

A stewardess's rage can follow the wretched passenger off the plane. She can tell the ramp controller on arrival that he is a suspected smuggler. This is then radioed through to Customs, and his baggage will be searched.

There are warnings on what makes passengers qualify for this inhuman treatment. 'I hate the ones who say "Hey, miss!", the ones that click their fingers, the ones that poke you, the ones who are always asking what the time is in Timbuctu or where are we,' says a stewardess. 'Then there are the ones who ask several of us for the same things. I'd like to give all passengers a book of rules. The first one would be: Don't ask more than one stewardess for a glass of water. The second rule would say: Occupied means there's someone in the lav.'

It is not jaundiced opinion, that stewardesses are getting older.* It is a fact. During the swinging sixties, the average girl worked in the sky for just eighteen months before leaving to get married. In the late 70s, it crept up to five years for women, and ten years for stewards.

The main reason is that unions have been successful in lifting the ban on married stewardesses. Further, more stewardesses now marry stewards who want them to keep at the job. In the sixties, a higher proportion married passengers, who were anxious for them to give up flying.

The most wizened cabin crew are undoubtedly the stewards on British Airways long-haul routes. Many of them came off the transatlantic liners in the days when BA had a commerical link with Cunard. They average twenty years' service, against the girls' three and a half. The long-distance French line UTA averages fifteen years. Air India has perhaps the youngest stewardesses, keeping them an average of just eighteen months. Others with noticeably young girls include Air California, Braniff, Gulf Air, Japan Air Lines and South African Airways.

* Stewardesses were first used by Air France in 1931. They were thought of as nurses to deal with airsickness and other problems. Glamour crept in, ironically, in the Second World War, when nurses were unavailable.

This does not please the airlines. One airline journal noted sourly: 'Airlines are forced to keep married stewardesses far beyond the period where they are an asset to the airlines' promotional efforts.' It embarrasses them when they are older than the girls in the seductive 'Fly Me' ads.

The airlines do their best to keep them looking fashionable by changing uniform styles completely every three years on average. Since this means buying 200,000 new uniforms, on a world airline basis, it is a highly expensive bit of promotion.

If their age has noticeably increased, from an average of twenty-two in 1968 in the US to thirty in 1981, so has their ill-temper. Mary Ellen King, head of the stewardesses' union at Pan Am, says: 'The glamour image isn't there any more. We have a non-stop from San Francisco to Hong Kong which serves three meals and shows two movies. There's nothing glamorous about working that hard for anyone.'

An anonymous TWA girl revealed to the *New York Times* an attitude passengers will, alas, have little difficulty in recognizing: 'The big difference is that ten years ago you had a "customer is always right" attitude. Today if someone gives me a hard time, I don't stand for it.'

All too often, asking for a cup of coffee or a bottle of duty free is taken as giving a hard time. Today, the passenger is only right if he is asleep or mute. 'If flight safety had deteriorated as much as cabin service has in the past ten years,' says a businessman, 'there wouldn't be many airliners getting through. Cabin staff have become arrogant to a totally unacceptable level.'

The airlines adopt a superior indifference to the flagrant ill manners of their cabin staff. But they have become a very real problem. A survey by the Airline Passengers' Association* is a deep indictment of how rude cabin staff have become. Passengers were given a list of suggestions to improve airlines. Just after the old pleas for more leg-room and wider seats, and way ahead of items like better scheduling, more safety and fewer delays, came 'more courteous and competent employees'.

Eighty per cent of the association's members who voted Eastern

---

* Airline Passengers' Association, 800 Airport West Freeway, Irving, Texas 75062.

as America's most avoided domestic airline* did so because of poor service and lack of courtesy.

Passengers who feel themselves ill-treated should complain to the captain on arrival. This is most simply done by using the forward exit on disembarking: the flight deck is just in front, and the door is often ajar and usually unlocked after landing. Knock, enter and give the captain details of the cabin staff's names and behaviour. A captain is responsible for the whole aircraft, and must take a dim view of sloppy stewards and stewardesses. A complaint forwarded by a captain will have far more weight with the airline than a beef that comes directly from a passenger.

The old standards are unrecognizable today. The Association of Flight Attendants' handbook of 1930† laid service on the line:

Remember at all times when on duty to maintain the respectful reserve of a well-trained servant. A ready smile is essential but never permit yourself the intimate attitude of a travelling companion . . . Keep the cabin windowsills dusted and use a small broom on the floor before every flight. Swat flies in the cabin before take-off . . . Carry a railway timetable in case the plane is grounded . . . Warn passengers against throwing lighted

---

* Pan Am, in my view, is singularly lucky that the APA restricted itself to domestic airlines. It is said that 10,000 girls a year apply to Pan Am. Given that wide choice, Pan Am's ability to select the pettiest and meanest-minded girls this side of Aeroflot is stunning. With other airlines, some routes are worse than others – like American Airlines' La Guardia–Dallas/Fort Worth ('Relax, will yah – that will dry-clean out, no sweat'), British Airways' notorious London–Glasgow shuttle ('Coffee, sir? Sir must be joking'), Air France's Paris–West Africa ('We 'ave ze right to sleep too, m'sieur'). Pan Am's system-wide lack of courtesy is unique. Only Gulf Air, Kuwait Airways and Air Malawi in the non-Communist world would run as close seconds.

As far as ground courtesy is concerned, despite short tempers and long lines at Miami's International and Chicago's O'Hare in particular, London's Heathrow is in a no-contest situation. The British Airports Authority is in a global league of its own when it comes to slovenliness and hostile incompetence. Despite being the proprietor of the world's largest international airport, the BAA was unable to deal with a snowfall of less than three inches in early 1979 and Heathrow was closed down. Incredible but true. Connoisseurs of airline irony may have noted that Pan Am considered withholding landing fees from the BAA to recoup revenue lost during this bizarre closure. The prospect of the world's rudest airline fighting the world's trashiest airport authority would warm the cockles of many a passenger's heart.

† Quoted in *BA ASR*, 10 October 1977.

cigar butts out of the windows, particularly over populated areas . . .
Assist the passenger to remove his shoes, if he so desires, and clean them
thoroughly before returning them to him.

Against this, modern flying is incomparably more comfortable
than it was. Cabin service in the old days had to be good because
so much else could go wrong. A westbound transatlantic flight
today is a seven-and-a-half-hour outing once the passenger is clear
of the airport and airborne. Before the jet arrived at the beginning
of the sixties, one prop pilot never flew London–New York direct
in more than seven years, although this was the advertised flight
for his Stratocruiser, the Boeing 377.

The schedule was seventeen hours but twenty-four hours was
more common, with stops at Prestwick, Iceland and Nova Scotia
and frequent diversions to Boston and Montreal. Aircraft would
lag halfway and more across the Atlantic – because the prevalent
westerlies were blowing the aircraft back towards Europe, the
halfway time in a trip happened well after the actual halfway
distance – and then 'do a 180° degrees and turn back to Ireland'.

The aircraft often bumped the whole way across in cloud or
heavy icing conditions as the navigators coped with the captain's
point of no return (insufficient fuel to turn around and head back
home) and the PLE, the prudent limit of endurance.

Passengers needed coddling.

Nowadays the job itself is straightforward. The girls check in
eighty minutes before take-off. The first-class girls are given lists
of their passengers and a quick briefing on the likes and dislikes
of any VIPs. Economy girls are given just the number of their
passengers, together with any special categories, compassionates,
unaccompanied children, non-English speakers.

They collect a bar float. Once aboard, they have to take care of
paperwork as well as serving passengers. This includes checking
for forged currency. The airline business is plagued with forgeries.
Descriptions of counterfeit numbers are telexed round the world,
and issued to stewardesses on their Exchange Rate lists on international flights. The most notorious notes are Italian 10,000 lire
notes numbered L171–4117, US $20 bills B06063685 and
B06073685C, Australian $10 notes with a weak metallic thread,
and Argentinian 5,000-peso notes from 457001A to 4583000A.

Stewardesses are not medically trained. The emphasis in the

short training period is on personal appearance, and on serving food in a cabin mock-up. On many airlines, the girls have only a rudimentary knowledge of first aid and evacuating the aircraft. Cabin staff panic has been a feature of several crashes.

'What happens if someone dies? Oh, we're trained to cover him up with a blanket so he looks as if he's asleep. We get a half-hour lecture on how to deliver babies, but I've never needed it, thank heavens,' says one girl. So it is standard practice to ask if there is a doctor on board if someone is taken ill.

A typical training schedule gives one week on safety equipment, two days on medicine, one day each on fire, deportment, grooming and hairstyling, and three weeks on cabin service.

The stewardesses have two medical boxes. A turquoise box holds the A2 medical kit – aspirin, airsickness tablets, Dettol, bandages, eye drops, scissors. The black A10 box is sealed and locked and the girls can only open it with the captain's permission. It has the heart stimulant Nikethamide, the heavy sedative Amatol, and morphine.*

The cabin crew routine is hard. A typical seventeen-day trip starts with Frankfurt to Tehran via Beirut, a thirteen-hour haul. Twenty-four hours off in Tehran (not a favourite with its insistent youths and men) is followed by a six-hour flight 'deadheading' to Delhi as a passenger. From Delhi, the girl works on the five-hour trip to Bahrein before getting her next 24-hour rest.

From Bahrein, she goes on to Hong Kong via Bangkok, a thirteen-hour working day, followed by another twenty-four hours off at Hong Kong. From there, the girl jets to Sydney and a

---

* In a real emergency, it can be important to have a doctor amongst one's fellow passengers. A friend of mine was taken violently ill on a flight from London to Boston in August 1980. His temperature rose quickly to 104°F and he lapsed into semi-consciousness. The cabin staff laid him out in the first-class section and gave him oxygen. The chief steward brought him good news: 'Hang in there, sir. I just checked the manifest and we have a doctor on board. I'll go get him.'

The chief steward returned a few minutes later. 'Don't panic, sir. He's not in his seat right now, but I'll find him.' 'What's his name?' asked my friend. 'Dr Mobbs,' said the chief steward. 'Oh, God,' said my friend. 'I'm Dr Mobbs.'

I am pleased to report that he survived.

three-day stopover before working her way back along the route to London.

There are compensations. The girls only pay ten per cent of regular airfares when they go on holiday. Big hotel chains, like Intercontinental, Holiday Inns and Hilton give a fifty-per-cent discount.

Some hotels in the Gulf will pay stewardesses to stay there, since they drum up bar and night club custom from well-heeled locals merely by being there.

Weekends in New York go for £15 all inclusive: a week in Rio from Europe can be had for under £40. Small wonder, then, that the girls look like walking travel posters. Their ten-destination baggage tags are marked CREW in red capitals. The hotel stickers on the faded tote bags (new girls leave them out in the sun to fade, much as the pilots do with the gold stripes on their uniforms), read Antigua, Trinidad Hilton, President Bangkok, Bermuda, Casa Mia Jo'burg, Swinging Seychelles. These status symbols, too, are carefully dirtied and torn, as if they were only there because some irritating hotel baggage boy put them there. Stewardesses are just as big travel snobs as their passengers.

Stewardess parties are a blend of the same self-conscious internationalism. The cigarettes come in all sizes and brands, the liquor out of old, often refilled bottles, the talk and the suntans from many countries.

There is a flight crew camaraderie that encircles the world, with the same vaguely dull jokes and catch names for airlines. It's 'Dangling the Dunlops' where the layman might lower the undercarriage, 'dropping the rubber jungle' when the oxygen masks come down in the passenger cabin.

The airlines are Pandemonium Scareways, Air Chance, Try Walking Airlines, Queer and Nice Types of Stewards.* There is Can't Promise Anything, Sweet and Sexy, Hysteria Airlines of Spain, Stay At Home Stay Alive of Honduras, even Good Airline Run under Dutch Administration for GARUDA of Indonesia (which the Dutch abandoned many years ago). Better on a Camel

* Qantas stands for Queensland and Northern Territories Aerial Services, one of the world's oldest airlines.

(or, at the height of the Profumo scandal, Bend over again Christine) and Back Every Afternoon have now been merged into the boring and as yet unnicknamed BA. (For clarity, British Airways is referred to throughout this book, rather than to the old BOAC and BEA).

Even the practical jokes are international. New girls are asked for a sick bag by the co-pilot. A can of vegetable soup is poured into the bag. When the girl goes back to collect it, the captain tastes it with a finger – 'Ummm, not bad.' Or she is asked to put all the air vents at full blow and pointing backwards to get additional speed. She will get her revenge on a new pilot with a Junior Jet badge and a baby's bottle.

There are RT, radio transmission, jokes for every country. The Frankfurt RT joke shows the standard. Ground: 'Vy haf you stopped taxiing?' Captain: 'We've just ingested one of your seagulls into an engine.' Ground: 'Vich one?' Captain: 'Dunno. You've seen one seagull, you've seen them all.'

And airline jokes. The legendary South African Airways pilot Captain van der Merwe is asked for his height and position. Quick as a flash, he radios back: 'Six foot two and in the cockpit.'

The wit shown by one girl fired by BA has, alas, long passed. 'What is the servant situation like in England?' she was asked by a domineering woman in first. 'Madam,' she replied, 'I am sure you will have no difficulty in finding a position.'

Stewardesses talk the new language of the air: 'no shows', passengers who do not turn up to join the flight they are booked on; 'slipstops', points where an aircraft changes or 'slips' its crew; 'shooting a letdown', for an approach and landing; 'interliners', passengers transferring from one airline to another at a transit stop.

They learn some pilots' jargon as well. 'Alternates' are the airports listed on the flight plan to fly to if the aircraft is diverted from its destination. 'Holding' is the pattern flown by an aircraft waiting to land, a 'stack' is made up of all the aircraft flying holding patterns. 'Notams' are the notices to airmen used for route information.

Airports themselves are abbreviated by international three-letter codes, although the stewardess will know by now that an airport should always be called a 'station'. They must be memorized, and they are not logical or easy. ORD is Chicago's O'Hare Field,* GIG turns out to be Rio's Galaeo airport, and an aircraft going to YEG is *en route* to Edmonton International.

The abbreviations are important, as they are used on tickets, baggage tags and itineraries. A mistake can mean a passenger or baggage going to the wrong destination. The reason for the confusion is that most airports, unlike sea ports, have different names to the parent city, and some cities have three or more airports. Thus Detroit has DET, DTW and YIP, for the City, Wayne County and Willow Run airports. Paris comes on flight schedules as ORY, LBG, CDG and ISS for Orly, Le Bourget, Charles de Gaulle and Issy-Les Moulineaux airports.

Flight numbers help passengers make sure they are catching the right aircraft. It is notoriously easy to get on the wrong aircraft, as Mrs Shirley McVay will testify. She and her two-year-old son boarded a plane at Los Angeles after going to her father's funeral. She thought it was going to Chicago, although she was puzzled by the time it took and the large expanse of water it crossed. After eleven-and a half hours, she arrived in London.

At least in theory, all flights travelling either north or east have flight numbers which are even, and those flying south or west have flight numbers which are odd. Thus a flight from Baltimore to Dallas would have an odd number since it goes westward, where Madrid to Munich would be even for eastward.

Cabin staff have a developed sense of fringe benefits. An efficient cabin crew can strip a 707 in twenty minutes. They often do so, commonly when the lights are dimmed after dinner and before breakfast on a long-haul flight. Some crews prefer the final approach, when passengers are strapped in and the curtains round the galleys are pulled shut. The restless or observant passenger may notice that the cabin crew are moving softly with large bags to the rear of the aircraft and hovering around the galley area.

Methodically, the stewards first 'rumble' the dry stores. 'Rumbling' is the professional word for looting. Tins of chicken supreme, minced beef, Dundee cake, bottles of Bovril and instant coffee, tea bags and Ryvita crisp bread slide into 'coat bags'.

* Years ago, it was called Orchard Place airport, hence ORD.

The coat bag is the greedy steward's best friend, and the reason why he can always outloot stewardesses. It is a large bag into which he puts his starched uniform jackets. There is plenty of room for more than clothes.

The steward cooks his looted meals in his hotel room by using a 'dipstick' or a 'hotcup'. The first is an electrical filament that can be slipped into any liquid to heat it, the latter a cup-shaped heating pot that will scramble eggs.

By using the dry stores and milk and fruit juice from the galley, a steward can get through a three-day stopover abroad without spending anything. His $40-a-day meal allowance goes straight into his pocket.

He can be more ambitious at home and can stock up for the whole household. The Stilton jar from first, the unused, still-frozen steaks, the vegetables, the fruit disappear into the coat bag. As the galley is thoroughly done over, liquor from the first-class bar is decanted into plastic squash bottles. The drinks are free in first, and consequently the airline has no idea how much has actually been consumed by passengers and how much has gone as perks. Plastic bottles are used because the original glass ones have the name of the airline printed on them, and would be incriminating evidence at home.

Even the mixers go. 'Some stewards think the war's still on and there's rationing,' says a British Airways stewardess. 'You get back to the galley before touchdown just wanting a couple of oranges, and the men have had the lot. I mean, even the yoghurt and the cornflakes. They come along with Tupperware all ready for the prawn cocktails.'

After the food and the complimentary cigarettes and liquor have gone, there is a mad rush for the lavatories. Here at least the girls are permitted by tradition to have first claim on the baby powder, skin tonic, the milky cleanser, moisture and hand lotion, eau de cologne and Tampax. The perfumes and lotions are decanted into plastic containers.

The stewards then clean out the after- and pre-shave lotions, the talc and the Kleenex. The toothpaste is requisitioned. The first-aid kit is denuded of Dettol, aspirin, elastoplast, scissors and eye drops.

Rumbling is relatively safe away from home base. As long as

the liquor and cigarettes stolen are within local duty-free limits, they are of as little interest to Customs officials as the tins of chicken and candy bars. At home base, Customs have no authority either except on dutiable items, but they are far more likely to pass on the names of the rumblers to the airline.

The Customs swarm on to an aircraft immediately the last passenger is off. First they check the bar seals, which are put on by the crew before landing, and take the removable stores list. They put their own seals on the bars and check the crew list for declarations. The moment of truth for the crew comes when they go down the steps to the crew bus.

Company security men may be on it, and they can dismiss cabin staff for a stolen can of tonic. The Customs 'Rummage Squad' could be there, too. It will take a crew and their luggage, and if need be their aircraft, to pieces. 'They're sitting waiting for you in the bus, smiling at you just a little. Then it's straight off in the bus to the Customs sheds, and they go through the lot. And when they rummage they do all of it – squeeze the toothpaste, sniff all your ciggies for hash. Even if there's nothing there they practise on you. Cabin crew are the sort of tame thing for experimenting on. The public wouldn't stand for it,' says an American girl.

Perks extend beyond stripping an aircraft. Some cabin crew are basically self-employed businessmen. They have wives or boyfriends running shops and boutiques at home which are stocked with curios they fly back wholesale. An Air France man flies to Nairobi with piles of old clothes bought in the Flea Market. He trades these in for wooden carvings which his girlfriend sells on the Left Bank.

Each route has its favoured goods. Onyx chess sets from Mexico, camel saddles and leather bags from Beirut, cameras and hi-fi from Hong Kong, crocodile handbags and watchstraps from Rio and Buenos Aires, avocados from Nairobi – all can be bought, shipped home free and sold at a guaranteed profit, after full duty has been paid.

Free shipping can be overdone. A British airline captain was discovered to be running a flourishing fruit importing business purely on the ability to freight in fresh fruit jet-quick, and completely free, in the forward freight compartment of his 707. A group of American pilots maintained a chain of highly successful seafood restaurants on the East Coast because they were flying in cheap West Coast seafood at a cost only to their unwitting company.

Both these businesses were uncovered because of the scale of the operation. The 707 skipper was flying an aircraft that was so fuel-thirsty on its return flights from East Africa that a young lad being trained by the airline thought he would take this aircraft and crew as a theoretical problem in fuel management.

There seemed no reason for the excess consumption. Why should a captain be 'heavy' on the throttles and burn up the fuel only when returning from Africa – not when going out, and not when returning from anywhere else? The aircraft engines were well within maintenance times, and were not normally expensive on fuel. Headwinds were not affecting other pilots.

The aircraft settled out of a leaden winter sky from Africa and was surrounded by security men. The boy's final theory proved correct, in the form of a ton of avocados, oranges, passion fruit and paw paws that were not on the cargo manifest.

The seafood pilots were as unlucky. They abandoned a take-off and the heavy braking resulted in the electrical circuits being flooded. It was a strange experience for the company to find an aircraft full of water. An investigation showed up the lobster tanks, which had spilled over during the emergency stop.

'Freefreighting',* as it is called, is quite widespread. Employees, including ground staff, are often given 100 kilos freight concession a year for 'personal goods'. Arabs and Asians working for French and British airlines have used this concession to start highly successful freight and import-export businesses.

A new trend is for check-in staff to insist on being paid for excess baggage in cash. There is, of course, no reason why the passenger should not pay by credit card. But the check-in staff will say that the airline does not accept cards for excess baggage because of the charge made by the credit companies. They then

---

* It is most common in the military. A sergeant in the Delta area of Vietnam put Milo Minderbinder, the freefreighting star of *Catch 22*, to shame. This ingenious American, nominally a machine gunner, hired most of a transport squadron from the pilots. He used it to ferry in neon signs, juke boxes and bar equipment for the red-light district he was developing.

simply pocket the cash. Beware those 'friendly' types who, having calculated excess baggage at, say, £28.47, enthuse: 'Why don't we call it a straight £25 in notes?'

It is tempting to settle for £25. Even if it goes to the employee and not the airline, that is hardly the passenger's affair, and a saving of £3.47 is not to be sniffed at. It is, however, often possible to circumvent the charge entirely. A passenger should be given an excess baggage ticket: this prevents the employee from gypping the airline since it is traceable.

The instant reaction to a request for a receipt is normally: 'In that case, we'll have to charge the full amount.' At this stage the passenger is strongly recommended to call the airline supervisor and to reveal the bargaining that has been going on. The charge is likely to be dropped entirely.

Few passengers do this in practice. That is why ground staff, notably in Rio, Rome and Madrid, have turned excess baggage into a profitable fringe benefit.

Some cabin crew have airborne businesses, with the travelling public as the customers. Even relatively crude ideas work. Stewards sell wrapped cutlery sets as souvenir packs for a few dollars, and leave saucers in the toilets for tips. A Royal Air Laos crew rechristened their loos Cloakrooms, with well-tipped attendants. Inexperienced holiday travellers often fall for these simple ploys.

In-flight entertainment has given wide and well-grasped opportunities to the crew. Thus earphones are rented out for £1 or $2 for watching movies or listening to stereo music by the airlines. Many girls are skilled at resealing the packs. The apparently brand new issue, neatly and freshly wrapped, will in fact have been resealed several times. The money goes straight to the crew.

Some girls 'own' their own earphones, accumulated slowly over flights from 'breakages' and those 'taken off by passengers'. They dole them out on a fifty-fifty basis with the airline's headsets. On movie flights (popular anyway with cabin crews because they keep the passengers quiet), a girl can make twenty-five or more rentings of her own equipment, or £25 of pure profit a flight.

A cursory examination of a steward's effects as he boards an aircraft might reveal the odd fact that he is taking empty miniatures and quarter wine bottles aboard, together with a funnel and a child's bendy drinking straw.

He needs the empties to start business. During take-off, with people still strapped in but the complimentary liquor for first-class passengers already flowing and the tourist bar about to open, the steward busily funnels liquor from the first-class bottles into miniatures. This is called 'dipping'. Without taking on his own empties, he would have to wait until passengers drank a first 'genuine' round before entering business on his own account.

The miniature market is vast. Pan Am sells over 10 million a year, BA 6 million, United 15 million, Lufthansa 1 million. World-wide over 177 million are sold, some of them purely for the profit of the crew.

An indication can be a solicitous steward who insists on opening the miniature. Breaking the seal can indeed be awkward, though the steward will often 'open' it for the very good reason that the seal was broken several flights before, and the bottle is full of first-class gin or whisky.

The money paid goes straight into the steward's or stewardess's pocket. With a full first-class compartment on a 707 of 16 (cabin layouts and numbers differ) the equivalent of 32 miniatures of spirits, and 16 splits of champagne or wine can be siphoned off with little chance of discovery. These are sold to tourist-class passengers for some £30.*

Enterprising cabin crew also find that they can undercut their employers by selling duty-free cigarettes and liquor. Cigarettes sell duty free for 50p a carton in Bahrein. Yet most airlines charge £1.50 for them off the duty-free trolley. That profit margin has proved irresistible to many stewards on the great Europe–Far East routes which transit Bahrein. They buy their own duty-free cartons and sell them to passengers at the airline price – a 200-per-cent profit for them. Scarves, ties, gold lighters are also traded in similar fashion. Cartier tank watches sold for £600 in flights from the Middle East are bought by the cabin crew for £250 in Kuwait.

In reverse, liquor and cigarettes are smuggled into places where they cost more than on the aircraft. The crew buy up the duty free from the trolley, noting it on the liquor and cigarette sheets as having been bought by passengers. The airline will not query

* The rewards on the wide-body jets, with their hundreds of passengers, are correspondingly higher. Thus BA cabin staff call their Tri-Stars the 'Big Dippers'.

a pleasant upsurge in sales: indeed, it will usually pay the crew a commission on the goods they have in fact bought for themselves.

The actual smuggling is normally left to ground staff and cleaners. A steward might try making £5 a bottle on Scotch in Tehran or £8 in Delhi with four or five in his coat bag. But if he's a serious operator, who has just bought up the aircraft's total supplies of perhaps ten dozen bottles, he will leave a ground operator to get them past Customs and settles for fifty per cent of the profit.

Few cabin crew deny what goes on. Flight deck crew are seldom involved. 'It's partly because, with their money and skill, it's not worth the risk,' says a steward. 'But also it's because we wouldn't let them. Those are our perks. They get enough in salary.'

Visits to their flats show there would be little point in denials. The fridges bulge with quarts of milk and orange juice from the US which cannot be bought in London. The whisky bottles are always the same, the label getting more faded as they are constantly refilled from the plastic squash bottles. The bathrooms are full of colognes and creams, awash with Kleenex and small tubes of toothpaste.

The cigarettes are a wild assortment of brands, tastes and countries of origin. The sugar comes in tiny plastic bags. The pepper and salt comes in individual airline packs. The food will be pleasantly out of season, the fruit exotic.

The top British rumbler lives in a snug south coast flat. He has perfected his perks to the point of fetishism. The cutlery, linen, china, glasses, all come from aircraft cabins, still with incriminating airline motifs stamped on them.

The meal is served from an aircraft first-class trolley, which the host proudly explains he was able to 'rumble' despite its size.

The wines and liqueurs are poured from bottles bearing the airline's names. The menu is written out neatly. For a small dinner party, smoked Scotch salmon, sirloin steak in white wine sauce, mushrooms and tomato, buttered asparagus spears with pommes parisienne, palm heart salad, assorted cheese, fruit basket, friandises, all of it rumbled from a plane that day.

In May 1981, British Airways estimated that they were losing £2.5 million a year to staff 'perks'.

It might be thought that such goings-on are restricted to the employees of decadent capitalist airlines. Not so. The Soviet journal *Vozdushny Transport* reported that three cabin staff of the Russian airline Aeroflot were caught after stealing from passengers' baggage during a flight from Siberia to Moscow.

The three, the stewardess in charge and two stewards, were on an Il-18 airliner. The passengers' baggage was stored in an unsealed compartment in the cabin. They stole bottles of liquor, jewellery and a leather coat. The coat was their undoing. The owner noticed that his suitcase seemed to have lost weight on the journey, investigated and reported the theft.

The captain was hauled over the coals for commending the three for their excellent service on the flight, and for not noticing that they had arrived at Vnukovo airport drunk from the liquor they had rumbled during the flight.

As for the three, they were sentenced to a term of imprisonment in the place they had just flown from – Siberia.

10 Passengers

People behave strangely on aircraft. Take this telex message from H. Rodrigues, a shift supervisor for British Airways in Honolulu. It is filed as supervisor report flight BA591/459:

Prior to arrival Captain Thompson radioed operations advising that he wanted a British Airways senior official to meet his aircraft on arrival at Honolulu. He stated he had two passengers on board the aircraft who were creating problems. What the actual problem was, was unknown at this time. Ops advised Station Manager Mr Benson who came out to meet the aircraft.

On arrival Mr Benson and myself contacted Captain Thompson to see what the problem was. We were advised that a man in seat 25A and a married woman seated 19A got together during flight and were using profane language and molesting one another. They were both in the last row of seats, row 25. Two other passengers seated directly in front of them complained to the chief steward. The CS approached them to control their actions as they were causing an inconvenience to other passengers.

The lady became quite irate and requested to see the captain. This was arranged and the captain advised her that he could not permit these sort of actions on board the aircraft. She told the captain that she was going to kill him on arrival in Honolulu. Captain Thompson advised her to take her seat or he would turn her over to the police on arrival. She returned to her seat but only to carry on where she had left off with Mr—.

Per Captain Thompson and the chief steward both passengers had sexual intercourse right in the plain sight of all other passengers. Captain Thompson stated once this was completed they both settled down and went to sleep and were of no bother from that point on. As a result Captain Thompson did not feel they should be offloaded. As far as he was concerned they just needed to get it off and would not be of any more inconvenience to other passengers. Outgoing captain and chief steward were contacted and advised of the situation and both agreed to leave well alone. Both of these passengers were travelling JFK/SYD.

The incident was on a British Airways VC10 flight from JFK to Sydney.

Such sexual escapades are by no means rare. They usually involve passengers who have never seen each other before. 'Love at first flight' is how the airlines put it. In the majority of cases, they do not even share the same destination. This is a major attraction: the affair is totally fancy-free, with no chance of complicating follow-ups.

Modern aircraft are less suitable for lovemaking than the gracious giants of the past. The Imperial flying boats had smoking rooms where a couple could be alone. The post-war Stratocruisers, double-deckers that serviced the North Atlantic, had curtained-off luxurious bunks.

Connoisseurs claim that the last great Five Mile High Machine (the Five Mile High Club being an institution for those who claim to have made love in the air) was the turboprop Lockheed Electra. In the first-class cabin back in the tail was a long daybed which was easily locked off from the rest of the aircraft. The Electra itself suffered from a tendency to shed its wings in flight at one point, but this merely added a wholesome sense of urgency to proceedings on the bed.

Passengers with an eye for the stewardesses should, however, remember the cautionary tale of Aubrey Bumguard. A Texan oilworker on leave from the North Sea, Bumguard took a National Airlines flight from London to Miami on 20 January 1977. He slapped two stewardesses, Patti Dewbody and Jane Otto, on their bottoms. Contrary to National's 'Fly Me' image, he was reported and charged under the Federal Air Piracy Act in Miami. This makes it a felony 'whilst on an aircraft to assault, intimidate or threaten a crew member or flight attendant so as to interfere with their duties'. The maximum penalty is twenty years and a £4,000 fine.

Mr Bumguard's case was referred to a grand jury, and he got six months' probation and a £293 fine.

First-class travel today appears exotic in the brief moments when the curtain is pulled aside and it can be glimpsed from the economy cabin. The first-class passenger has already checked in at a special counter, waited in a special lounge, been driven out to the aircraft in a special coach and walked up special steps.

The free bar, together with free cigarettes and cigars, starts before take-off with champagne cocktails. The seats are more like armchairs, deep, with wide arms. On 747s there is an upstairs bar, behind the cockpit and reached by a circular staircase from the normal cabin level. It has casual sofas and coffee tables, and its own barman.

The food is superb, served by the cream of the airline's stewardesses.* IATA regulations allow five courses at dinner and lunch, where only three are permitted in economy. Personal attention is excellent. Buttons are sewn back on, letters and postcards are taken to be posted on arrival, coats and jackets are hung up in wardrobes; and passengers are addressed by their names.

There are free presents, to a maximum of $3, such as cologne, slippers and sleeping masks, kimonos and golf caps.

But, this is not a great deal extra for paying half as much again as the economy passenger. It mainly appeals to businessmen on expense accounts, who now make up eighty-five per cent of first class. This is sad, since it makes first on the business routes a more boring and predictable cabin than economy.

This is not to rule out every first-class passenger as a dullard. Lady Beaverbrook, refused permission to take her dog into first class (dogs should travel in the hold), promptly chartered the whole plane, an Air Canada DC8, to take her from London to Canada. It cost her £8,400. Aspiring actresses book themselves first on flights to Venice and Nice (for Cannes) to be near directors, turning the jets at film festival times into casting couches. It is revealing to see how many arrive first at Las Vegas, and leave economy. For sheer beauty and wealth, however, first class on the 747s and Concorde from Paris to Rio in February, for the Carnival, is perhaps unequalled.

Drunkenness is common to both classes on all but Muslim airlines, more and more of which are strictly dry. People drink too much through fear or tension, and the effects are multiplied by the rarefied air of the cabin. This is the equivalent of being on top of a 6,000-foot mountain, with half the moisture of the air in the middle of the Sahara desert. This combination makes a drink in the air worth at least two on the ground. The effect is even greater on a flight at very high altitude, above 37,000 feet, where cabin air is thinner still.

Particular types get drunk and worry cabin crews the world

* Most American and European airlines have had to bow to pressure from militant feminists and first-class stewardesses are appointed by seniority, and not looks. As a result, the high payers at the front wind up with some of the more mature girls. The level of service, however, is vastly better than in tourist.

over. 'You recognize the danger signs even if you're dealing with a race of people you know nothing about,' says a stewardess. It's people who are not used to drinking. You can tell very simply. They will always ask for whisky. It's the only drink that means alcohol to them. And they won't have the first idea of what to put in it: offer ice or water or ginger ale and they'll say "Yes, please" to all three.'

A captain can arrest any passenger whose behaviour is prejudicial to safety, and the passenger can then be sentenced by a court on arrival at the destination. In practice, however, airlines do not prosecute their passengers.

Many people who, for the strictest religious or social reasons, would never normally drink change in the air. Among those most affected are Chinese and Muslims. 'Charter flights back from Hong Kong with Chinese kitchen workers can be real hell,' says a pilot. 'They get very drunk very quickly. They all play Mah Jong, which doesn't help because it's the perfect fuel for rows and fights.

'I've been back plenty of times. It's like a Conrad ship – you get them trying to open the doors, fighting, shouting. But the uniform calms them pretty quickly.'

Crews are agreed that the ultimate horror is sportsmen, particularly in teams. The same pilot says he would rather fly a hundred Chinese charters than one sector he did back from Mexico City after the Olympics. 'They are all either super-angry, because they haven't won a medal after years of training, or super-elated. They are also super-fit. That means they get super-drunk super-fast. It also means you can't push them around. The uniform doesn't do much to that lot,' he said.

The most common affliction to passengers is fear. It affects at least twenty per cent of those who fly: an Air Canada survey of passengers puts it at twenty-seven per cent. It can hit anywhere at any time. A former flying doctor suddenly had phobias: 'My personal fear is particularly embarrassing as first, being a doctor, I feel I should be able to overcome the phobia, and second because for nearly three years I ran a "flying doctor" type service over the jungles of Malaya and Borneo for the Marines with whom I was a medical officer in the early 1960s.

'Not only did I enjoy every minute of this rather dangerous

flying but frequently piloted the helicopters and Beavers myself, including trips to situations under fire from the other side.

'I am sure my phobia originates in a near fatal incident in a British Eagle Trooping Britannia at Bombay airport. Since then I have looked upon flying as a passenger in abject terror although I have, in the past, deliberately flown from London to Scotland to test my reactions. I arrive at the destination in such a state of stress that I feel that it is no longer worth trying.'

This fear is held in common by Mohammed Ali, Doris Day, stuntman Evel Knievel, rock superstar David Bowie, golfer Neil Coles, comedian Eric Morecambe, columnist Marjorie Proops, Hermione Gingold: the list is long.

Mohammed Ali, asked on television what he was most frightened of, replied: 'Flying. That's the only thing that terrifies me. I'm flying all the time and I feel it's time for one to crash. I don't control the airplane. Some pilot does.

'Say we're between America and England. And the engines stop. Now even if it gets down there without the engines, how am I gonna find my life-raft? And even if I do, how are they gonna see me in the dark? And what happens if a shark comes along and rubs against it . . . ?'

Few airlines bother to give special training to cabin crew on flying phobia. This is despite the fact that pilots are every bit as prone to the fear as anyone else. The Airline Pilots' Associations admit to having their own 'white knuckle brigade'.

Doctors think there are three main causes: claustrophobia (most passengers are happier in partly empty aircraft), vertigo, and a phobia that the lump of metal cannot stay in the sky. Treatment is difficult, although Air Canada claims a ninety-per-cent success rate on its course. There are societies for sufferers. The British one is called SCOFF – the Society for the Conquest of Flying Fear.

There are seminars, often held in hangars since many people find it difficult just to visit an airport. Pilots give talks explaining how an aircraft works. This often develops into group therapy sessions.

SCOFF's founder Sam Weller says: 'Nearly all our members are people who fly frequently. People come with heart-rending stories of their children in Australia they cannot see. Or their holiday homes which they want to visit for three weeks and find that the week before they go they are so tensed up, it takes a week after they arrive to wind down from the flight. They get one week of holiday, and then the last week of the holiday they are winding up again ready for the flight. Businessmen fly out on a trip and find they are in no state to do any business when they arrive.'

Weller hopes that people who suffer from fear may get special luggage stickers and ticket holders. 'It would help enormously, both at the airport and in the air, if staff could tell at a glance that someone needed special treatment.'

All too often this huge army of the fearful is sneered at. 'We call them caterpillars,' says a captain. 'You know, he looks up and sees a butterfly. "Huh! You wouldn't get me up in one of those things," he says to himself.'

There are more than twenty known cases a day of flight hysteria at a big airport like Heathrow. Others are painfully but quietly coped with by the passengers without being noted. Yet airlines do nothing to help, though they spend millions on reassuring advertising – KLM changed the stripes on its insignia from diagonal to horizontal 'to promote a greater feeling of security'. However, most major airports have medical centres with special travellers' help units staffed by volunteers from International Travellers Aid, a branch of the YWCA.

The symptoms of the phobia are unmistakable. The mouth becomes extremely dry, the hands shake slightly and seem difficult to control. A nervous habit, such as coughing or scratching the head, flares up. There is an acute sense of panic and an inability to cope. Breathing is shallow and rapid and the heart-beat increases. The best antidote is to do something to break the concentration on panic, reading if possible or talking to somebody else. In extreme cases, walking to the toilet, and washing the face with cold water is often effective in switching the mind off panic.

Far from being panicstricken, however, the average passenger tends to be over-optimistic about flying. A test group was asked to choose the number of airline crashes and deaths in one year in Britain, with five sets of figures given. The great majority opted for the lowest figures – four crashes, fourteen fatalities. The actual figures were the highest, nineteen crashes and 214 deaths.

An international survey* of 6,000 passengers revealed an interesting list of their priorities. They put good inflight service first, then public reputation, satisfactory past experience as a passenger, convenient schedules and comfort. Safety was well down the list.

It is difficult to assess which is the safest airline. Airlines never stress their safety records in their advertisements: punctuality, experienced crews, superior engineering, good maintenance and other safety aspects they may mention, but safety itself they do not.

This is partly because it would be tempting fate to advertise an accident-free history, partly because it is thought that it would frighten passengers away, but mainly because IATA forbids it. Airline advertising has to concentrate on the safe trivia of flying, the beauty of the stewardesses, the excellence of the food, or the width of the seats.

But it is certainly possible to see where it is safest to fly, if not always with whom. Research† shows that United States airlines are much safer than the world average. American flights have been four to five times less likely to crash than the world average.

The Western European airlines are right on the average. Those from Africa are twice as bad, from Asia two and a half times as bad. The airlines of South and Central America and of the Middle East are four times worse than average – and those from Eastern Europe, though excluding Russia's giant Aeroflot for which accurate statistics do not exist, are a frightening ten times worse.

One crash can send an individual airline's safety rating slumping far down the table, and individual safety records are thus difficult. *Flight* magazine publishes annual surveys, however, and from these and other sources a rough guide emerges. As of 1977, Qantas and TAP are two of the safest internationals, carrying the flag for Australia and Portugal respectively, though TAP had its first fatal

* By Thai International. It also listed the most popular airlines in the East – Singapore International, JAL, Lufthansa, KLM, Swissair, Pan Am, Cathay Pacific, British Airways, Qantas and All Nippon Airways are the top ten. The bottom ten are equally interesting: Tarom, Iraqi, Aeroflot, Alia, Union of Burma, JAT, Syrian Arab, Ariana, Gulf Air and Bangladesh.
† *Sunday Times*, 24 October 1976.

crash involving passengers in 1977. Delta, American, United, Continental and Eastern are domestic carriers with excellent records.

British Caledonian is well up the European list, with Lufthansa, SAS and Swissair. TWA and Pan Am also tie into the table here. None of the world's major airlines gets into the high passenger-death positions, although some flag carriers are there – CSA of Czechoslovakia, Egyptair, Romania's Tarom, PAL of the Philippines and Garuda of Indonesia.

The safest leading nations, in order, are the Netherlands, Australia, Scandinavia, the US, West Germay, the UK, Canada, Japan, Italy, Belgium and France.

The loss rate of jet airliners at the beginning of the 1980s shows the marked differences between geographical areas. The average loss is one jet per 460,000 flying hours, or 52½ years of continual flight. Above the average are Australia and the South Pacific, with 2,744,000 hours or over 300 years, the US at 761,000 hours and Canada at 469,000. Western Europe is slightly below average with 412,000 hours, although that still represents 47 years. Central and South America are 313,000, and Asia 255,000. Africa, the only area not to have enjoyed a substantial improvement since the 1960s, is 217,000 hours, or almost a quarter-century of non-stop flying. The figures differ from the overall picture because they refer only to pure jet aircraft.

These odds are minute, and the passenger should realize that safety is more a matter of his own conduct than of choosing an airline. In his book *The Safe Airline* (London, 1976), J. M. Ramsden calculates that the odds on a passenger being killed between take-off and arriving at his destination are three in a million, or 0.0033 per cent. Taking a flight a day, a passenger could expect to die once every 913 years – though he could die at any time during those years, of course. Ramsden also lists the smaller air transport countries with excellent safety records. They are, in alphabetical order: Austria, Finland, Iceland, Ireland, Israel, Portugal, South Africa and Switzerland.

A further analysis of Ramsden's figures shows that two countries, the Netherlands and the US, have records that are better than might be expected from their volume of air traffic. Australia, Belgium, Canada, Italy, Japan, Scandinavia, West Germany and the UK are more or less on a par. France, Brazil and India are worse than statistically expected.

A pilot with a major scheduled airline has a one per cent chance of being killed throughout his career, compared with two per cent in coal mining and five in construction.

The passenger should note that flying by commercial jet in the US is now fifteen times safer per passenger mile than driving by car. A holidaymaker off to the Continent might remember that fatal car accidents on French roads have run at 4.7 per 100 million kilometres (and motorcycle accidents at 60). Yet commercial air transport led to 0.08 deaths per 100 million kilometres. Some 8,000 people in Britain were killed in accidents in their own homes during 1980. The odds of being killed in the air are considerably less than being killed at home, although this of course reflects the fact that people spend a lot less time in the air than at home.

Accident liability is an appalling mess. The family of one passenger can receive $3 million or more, yet the man in the seat next to him could be worth only $20,000. It depends on the nationality of the airline, the country of departure and arrival, the eventual destination and even the country where the ticket was bought.

The first attempt to work out liability was the Warsaw Convention of 1929, limiting the airlines to 125,000 Poincaré gold francs. This sounds a lot, but is in fact worth only $10,000 1976 dollars. It was doubled to $20,000 by the Hague Protocol of 1955, but this was still considered too low. The US Government pressed airlines flying to or via the US to sign the Montreal Agreement, which increased the limit to $75,000 for passengers on those routes. In addition, limitless damages can be won if negligence by the airline or aircraft manufacturer can be proved, particularly in the US.

The crash of a DC10 near Paris on 3 March 1974, killing all 346 aboard, gives some idea of the legal complexities. Turkish Airlines, the aircraft's operators, were not even a party to the Warsaw Convention. But the flight was between France and England, both of which are Warsaw-signatory states. And many passengers, who had switched to Turkish Airlines because of a British Airways strike, were on Montreal-based tickets from British Airways.

The aircraft crashed because a cargo door came away in flight and a buckled floor seized the controls. This was variously alleged to be due to negligence by Turkish Airlines, by the US Federal Aviation Authority, which licensed the aircraft, McDonnell Douglas, which assembled it, and General Dynamics, which designed and built the door.

With liability so inexcusably complex and shabby, the wise passenger looks after his own life insurance.

Luggage liability is equally unsatisfactory, with airlines compensating by weight at $10 a kilo. Some travellers thus put bricks in their bags to bring the weight up to twenty kilos. Passengers whose baggage has been lost can claim an 'overnight bag' from the airline, which must contain slippers, shaving kit, scissors, after-shave, soap, pyjamas and towel.

If the general safety of the airline and his redress for liability are not in his hands, the individual passenger can look after his own life by listening to safety briefings on aircraft. Most people assume nothing untoward will happen, and ignore all attempts to get them to listen. But the wise passenger always examines the safety leaflet, primarily to memorize the position of the emergency exits. These exits differ from aircraft model to model* and from airline to airline. Remembering where the exits were on one 747 is no guarantee they will be in the same place on another.

He will also see how they open. Main exit doors may have to be pulled inwards before they can be rotated and opened. This is to prevent them being sucked out in flight, but passengers have died crushing against doors that needed an initial pull before being pushed. Wing exits are simpler, though they may be unusable if wing fuel tanks catch fire.

There is a simple drill in an emergency which much improves your chances of survival. First, remove any sharp or metal objects from your pockets; a pen or comb can cause serious injury on impact. Put them in the seat pocket in front of you. Make sure the seat belt is really tight, and the seat upright. Take off tie and spectacles. Put your feet flat on the floor, not under your seat or the one in front. The seat could collapse and trap you. Work out

---

* There are five types of 747; e.g. a short-range, high-density seating model, a long-range passenger aircraft, a cargo-passenger convertible, an intercontinental freighter and a special long-range version.

exactly what escape route you are going to use, and make sure you have an alternative should the first be impassable for any reason.

When the crash is imminent, try to cover your head with a rug or pillow. Put your arms, with fingers interlocked, over your neck and push your face into your knees, keeping your feet straight down. The aircraft will probably hit more than once in the crash, so don't move from the braced position until the aircraft has stopped. When it has definitely done so, undo your belt and get out of the plane, fast. Once out, run away from it as fast as you can in case it explodes. Do not take any possessions with you, briefcases, cameras, anything. Delay kills.

Obey the crew, but never expect them to rescue you. Rescue yourself. Thus you should work out for yourself how to operate emergency exits, ensure your legs are not trapped, minimize the odds of being knocked unconscious by protecting your head. Never ever inflate a lifejacket inside an aircraft. It will jam you in the exit, stopping your escape and that of the other passengers.

Women, children and the old are particularly at risk. In one crash, 32 out of 37 men got out of the aircraft, but only 15 of 36 women, children and elderly. The aircraft, a TWA Boeing 707, hit a roller at Rome airport and ruptured a fuel line. There was no noticeable impact at all, but the aircraft rapidly went up in flames. Family groups, women and children and the old were tragically slow to leave. Such people should take particular care to rehearse mentally what they will do in an emergency.

Above all, the wise passenger knows that he can make it if he does not panic. Most accidents are on take-off and landing, where the speed is not great and where the impact itself is usually survivable.* It is not the crash in an aircraft that kills, but suffocation or poisoning later. The wise passenger, anticipating a crash, remembers: Impact does not kill. Fumes and fire do. As a rule of thumb he has sixty seconds to get out.

* About sixty per cent of fatal crashes have survivors. An average of thirty per cent of those aboard survive fatal crashes. The percentage would be higher if passengers listened to safety drills and reacted fast and firmly. Even more would live if airlines improved seat fastenings, so that they remained fixed to the floor under greater forces.

A Boeing 707 of Varig Airlines of Brazil was approaching Paris Orly on a flight from Rio on 11 July 1973.* There were 134 aboard. Heavy smoke started billowing from the left rear lavatory. It could not be stopped from spreading with an extinguisher. The smoke penetrated up the length of the fuselage. The flight engineer depressurized the aircraft and opened the rear discharge valve, but smoke still poured into the cockpit.

The flight crew put on oxygen masks and opened the cockpit side windows. They were finally unable to see their instruments and had to put the aircraft down in a field just four miles short of Orly. The aircraft slid for 600 yards, tearing off the undercarriage but not doing any major damage to the structure. Everyone survived the crash.

The number four fuel tank then caught fire, spreading quickly after the plane had stopped. The seven crew in the cockpit got out through the side windows, and three other crew got out from just behind the cockpit. It was left to rescuers on the ground to pull out their passengers, only one of whom survived. 116 passengers died, and most were found still seated and strapped in. The cause of death was toxic gas, breathing poisoned air.

There is a simple moral to this unhappy tale. Passengers who are delighted at surviving the crash impact, and who then sit and wait for the crew to give instructions, die. Passengers who are concerned only to get out of the aircraft, and who know how to do it because they know where the exits are, survive. Ruthless avoidance of poisonous smoke is the name of the survival game in most crashes. Smoke and fumes rise: dropping to the floor gives a chance to breathe and see.

The appalling death toll in the 1977 collision of two Jumbos on the ground in the Canaries was also fuel-fed. It may eventually be possible to use fuel that cannot ignite in a crash. A chemical is added to it which will not mix or react with the fuel if it is kept under pressure. But if the tanks or fuel lines are ruptured in a crash, pressure is lost and the chemical combines with the fuel to thicken it and make it non-ignitable.

An anti-misting fuel is to be tested in the remote-controlled flight and crash of a Boeing 720 airliner in 1984. The FAA, which

---

* International Civil Aviation Organization ICAO Summary No. 54.

will conduct the experiment with the obsolete jet, reports that 'anti-misting fuels could prove to be the single most significant safety improvement to reduce the post-crash fire hazard'.

However, many technical problems remain to be solved and it is likely to be 1989 at the earliest before such fuel could be ready for regular use. A critical factor will be whether the number of lives that might be saved would justify the considerable extra cost involved. The FAA calculates that an average of thirty-two lives a year would be saved on US airlines.

When an airline is involved in a typical 'survivable' crash, large amounts of fuel are ejected from damaged tanks and fuel lines. Shearing of the fuel by the airstream produces a highly flammable mist in and around the damaged aircraft. The formation of the mist can be prevented by an additive in the fuel. One promising candidate is a British-developed polymer with a very high molecular weight.

The flammability of the furnishing materials used in passenger cabins is another important area where safety could be much improved. Apart from the Varig crash, a fire aboard a Saudia Tri-Star at Riyadh in September 1980 called attention to this factor. The aircraft made a safe forced landing at the airport of the Saudi Arabian capital, but all 301 aboard died in the cabin fire that followed, even though the fuel tanks never caught alight.

The UK Factory Inspectorate regards nearly all cellular plastics as being 'highly flammable'. Nevertheless, cellular or foam plastics like polyurethane are widely used for the furnishing and seats of almost every modern airliner. They are light in weight, cheap and comfortable. They are very difficult to light with a low heat like a match or dropped cigarette. Most seats are covered with flame-proof textiles that make them almost entirely safe to the casual hazard of the dropped cigarette.

The trouble comes when they are exposed to high temperatures, such as a fuel fire, or the butane stoves carried by Muslim pilgrims on the Saudia flight.

Once ignited, polyurethane foam burns with great heat and thick smoke. Tests for the Factory Inspectorate showed temperatures so high, above 1,000°C, that the steel-plated floor of the test rig melted.

Polyurethane produces large quantities of smoke and carbon

monoxide. It also gives off hydrogen cyanide and other poisonous gases. The British report concluded that 'although foamed poly-urethane burns quickly its principal danger probably lies in the rapid production of unusually large amounts of hot dense smoke and poisonous gases. Moreover, these high levels are attained very quickly, usually within one or two minutes.'

Once polyurethane does catch fire, it reaches its peak temper-ature of 1,000°C or slightly more in two minutes. The maximum production of smoke and hydrogen cyanide also occurs after two minutes. 'The furnishings in a modern cabin take time to ignite,' says a safety expert. 'But once they go, the cabin will become a poisonous cauldron very rapidly. The passengers should leave it as soon as the aircraft stops in a crash landing.'

It can make all the difference to be seated in the right part of the aircraft in a crash. The only trouble is that it is impossible to tell in advance which is the safest part. Smoke, like the actual crash, is also unpredictable. In theory, the nose and tail are safest in an aircraft with underwing engines, and the forward part of the cabin in a rear-engined aircraft. This avoids fuel lines which may rupture in a crash.

In practice, the only real sense is to sit near an emergency exit or to know where the exits are. It is also sensible never to put anything heavy in overhead racks, or to take up the cabin floor with hand luggage. The restrictions on hand luggage are not for weight reasons, but to ensure the cabin is not so cluttered up as to make evacuation difficult.

Make sure that the seat is firm. Shake it, and if it is loose refuse to sit in it. In a crash you could be hurled forward strapped in a seat that has broken away from the floor fastenings. The seat and belt should hold you firm to an impact of 15g, although US Army Air Force research[*] shows that the body can survive short impacts of up to 35g. Rear-facing seats are the safest of all, but only the RAF insists on them. This is ironic, since the RAF's record is so good, it has never had to demonstrate this. The Munich crash of 1958, when an aircraft with Manchester United footballers aboard

[*] USAAVLABs Technical Report 66/43.

crashed on take-off, showed clearly that more survived in the rear-facing seats than in the conventional ones.

Looking after his physical comfort on the plane, the passenger will keep his seat belt lightly done up throughout the flight, in case of turbulence.* Two people were killed when a BAC1–11 hit turbulence near Grand Cayman Island in the Caribbean. They were not wearing seat belts and they hit the ceiling. It is now standard advice on aircraft to wear loose seat belts at all times. Only a fool would ignore it. However, airlines have not yet put seat belts into lavatories even though there is no chance of a passenger regaining his seat in sudden turbulence.

Soft, large shoes are helpful since your feet will swell in the cabin atmosphere. So will your waist, and casual trousers are best. It is easy to catch cold in the thin, dry air and sweaters and cardigans should be worn. Collars will chafe and so ties are a menace.

The comfort-conscious passenger will also try to avoid jet-lag. This exhaustion can take eight days to disappear after a long flight. Research shows that heart rate, temperature, blood pressure and breathing patterns are affected. The adrenal glands go out of phase, and potassium loss in urine increases, affecting heartbeat.

The Institute of Psychology in Dublin has prepared a list of hints† to cut back on flight fatigue. Before a flight, a passenger should have a high protein meal with a minimum of carbohydrates, animal fats and gas-producing foods. Long sun-bathing should be avoided. A passenger should drink a lot during the flight, noting that milk reduces tension, that wine in reasonable quantities is beneficial, but that tea, coffee, spirits and dry food should be avoided.

Long-distance flying is bad for the body if only because of the long period of immobility. In one experiment, six healthy 'pas-

---

* A colleague on an aircraft flying over the Caprivi strip in southern Africa suddenly found himself flung across the cabin. The aircraft had hit turbulence and dropped 800 feet like a stone. A stewardess hit him in mid-air. She broke her leg when she hit his chest, fracturing his ribs. That, at least, is his story and he is sticking to it.

† *Psychological Aspects of Transmeridian Flying* by Brendan McGann, published by the Institute of Psychology, Dublin, 1971.

sengers' simply sat in a chair all the time they were not in bed. Within four days they were all showing symptoms of dizziness, fainting and circulatory collapse. There was also nausea and vomiting.

No flight should last four days, although hijackings have, but a passenger will begin to show mild symptoms after three hours. The young and fit cope best. The Irish study showed that half the pilots under thirty on transatlantic flying actually showed a sleep gain on arrival in New York, whereas 95 per cent of pilots over thirty-seven showed a sleep loss. Children hardly notice time-zone changes.

What is good for the pilot, in terms of efficiency and a quick return to normal after crossing time zones, is also good for the passenger. There is research into the body rhythms of pilots* which the wise passenger will note. A group of pilots were required to fly in a simulator what approximated a holding pattern in a 'stack' waiting to land. Their ability to do this was tested at various times throughout twenty-four hours.

Two performance factors were measured, deviation from speed, range and altitude and the time needed to correct the error. A curve of performance evolved, with a maximum efficiency from 2 p.m. to 3 p.m. Minimum performance at 3 a.m. was fifty per cent lower than the total average performance.

Two incidents occurred during the simulator run. These were the equivalent of a sudden increase in weight or popping up of speed brakes. The time needed to recover from these incidents varied from 53.4 seconds in the afternoon to 103.3 seconds at three in the morning.

Pilot skill is thus severely diminished in the early hours of the morning. A passenger should also try to avoid these flight times where possible, not simply because the pilot is less competent then, but because the passenger himself will arrive more exhausted.

After a transatlantic flight of five time zones (Europe to India, Japan to Honolulu, or Dallas to Honolulu are similar flights) research shows that it takes eight to nine days for the body to

* K. E. Klein et al., 'Circadian Rhythms of Pilots' Efficiency and Effect of Multiple Time You Travel', *Aerospace Medicine* 41 (2), 125–32.

adapt completely and return to normal. Fatigue is probably worst on the third day,* rather than the first, although thereafter it improves very rapidly.

The research confirmed what many passengers have long suspected. West to east flights on the North Atlantic are more exhausting than east to west. Many passengers who have no problems on other flights complain of restlessness, panic and unease on East coast to Europe flights. 'I go into a cold sweat,' says a widely travelled publisher who normally enjoys flying. 'I panic, and lock myself in the lavatory and splash cold water over my face. The only way I can get myself from New York to London is by getting drunk.'

In fact, what many passengers think is personal weakness is judged by experts to be bad airline scheduling. Brendan McGann, a member of the Aerospace Medical Association, and a former Aer Lingus pilot, blames the airlines for the evening take-off, early morning arrival timings. In his study *Psychological Aspects of Transmeridian Flying* he writes: 'The combination of Circadian effect, sleep deprivation, possible high temperature and humidity, traffic density, night take-off, holding delays, fume inhalation, and many other factors make 8 p.m. New York time the worst possible departure time imaginable, from the point of view of flight safety.'

McGann says that the major cause of exhaustion after flights from North America to Europe is the policy of night departures. The passenger who flies by day, or at least avoids the hours of maximum sluggishness between 2 a.m. and 5 a.m., will arrive less exhausted and be flown by safer pilots.

Research conducted by the Federal Aviation Agency† has proved that it is time zones rather than the length of trip which

* Wegmann *et al.*, 'Effects of Transmeridian Flight on the Diurnal Excretion Pattern of 17-OHCS', *Aerospace Medicine* 41, 1003 G 1005.
† A medically accepted rest formula has been worked out. Devised by the late Dr Lloyd Buley of the International Civil Aviation Organization, it takes actual flight duration as well as time changes into account. The equation is: rest periods (in tenths of a day) equals flight duration in hours divided by two, plus the time zones passed in excess of four, plus the departure time coefficient plus the arrival time coefficient. These coefficients are based on social behaviour patterns, particularly sleep periods. They are:

counts. Passengers flying from Oklahoma City to Rome, across seven time zones, and to Manila across ten all showed marked differences in temperature, pulse, blood pressure, respiratory rate, reaction times, emotional tension and urinalysis. In contrast, passengers flying from Washington to Santiago, Chile, across one time zone were not affected at all (see footnote, p. 145).

The real answer to jet-lag may have been found by Russian Aeroflot crews. Those on the Moscow–Havana run live on Moscow time in Cuba. They eat breakfast at midnight, and supper at noon, and go to bed in the afternoon. This is easy to enforce, since Aeroflot crews normally stay in their Embassies when abroad, with 'constant' discipline.

Period (local time)	Departure time coefficient	Arrival time coefficient
0800–1159	0	4
1200–1759	1	2
1800–2159	3	0
2200–0059	4	1
0100–0759	3	3

The vital factor is to make the combined departure and arrival coefficients as low as possible. The passenger cannot control flight duration. But he can choose a flight that leaves and arrives at the best time for his biological clock.

Thus, the flying time from London to New York is 7 hours, crossing five time zones. These are reduced to 3½ and 1 by the equation, making 4½. Leaving London at 1700 hours, and arriving in New York at 1900 local time adds only 1 to the score, which then gives 5½. This is 5½ tenths of 24 hours, or 13 hours and 12 minutes' sleep. However, a flight that left London at 0700 would arrive in New York at 0900 local time, amassing 7 'penalty' points. Seven tenths of a day gives a rest of 16 hours and 48 minutes.

11 The Flying Zoo

Ten million animals a year travel by air. Many of them are smuggled in – immigrants as illegal as any human. A large cage was consigned to Heathrow from Amsterdam. Travelling in noisy comfort up front were 400 budgies. Wrapped in sacking and hiding in a secret compartment at the back were two king vultures.

This was noticed by a girl at the RSPCA hostel, who called in the Customs. King vultures cannot enter the country legally as they could carry disease and are a protected species. They are part of the large trade in smuggled animals worth several hundred thousand pounds annually.

The RSPCA hostel on the north side of the airport was run by Neville Whittaker, a quiet man with a bitter contempt for smugglers and for many airlines. 'The airlines wash their hands of the animals they carry. They take the money but no responsibility. As for the smugglers, I am amazed at their mentality and greed,' says Whittaker.

The crates can be appalling. 'There was a shipment of five gibbons packed face down in a box five inches high. A gibbon is thirty inches tall. They all died. Squirrels arrive wrapped in chicken wire to stop them eating through the box, starved to death. Coral fish are put in plastic bags. They cut the plastic with their spines, the water drains out and they die. Lions are put in cages with no through ventilation. If the animal turns, it blocks the air holes and suffocates,' Whittaker recalls.

Whittaker has opened cages to find live emerald doves as food for a leopard *en route* from India to the US, starlings to feed falcons and live parrots for eagles.

Other cages break in flight, and Whittaker has had to capture two tigers loose in a 707.* 'I put myself in the position the animals should have been in – in a cage. I shoved the cage along the

---

* Cargo pilots have a standard drill when animals run amok. They go on oxygen, and then depressurize the aircraft. The animals breathe rarefied air and rapidly fall asleep.

aircraft to where they were sitting and shot tranquillizers into them.'

The American Airline Pilots' Association has in its files the case of a 100-lb coon dog which broke loose on an airliner. The dog went berserk when the engines started up, and ripped its way out of its wire cage. It attacked the cockpit door as the aircraft took off, trying to savage its way into the cockpit. The captain reported: 'The crash axe was our only defence if he made it through. I have never been as concerned about the safety of a flight as I was about this one.' He managed an emergency landing. The dog quietened when the engines shut down.

The Association wrote to the Federal Aviation Agency, the American air safety authority. The FAA replied: 'This appears to be an isolated case since the last time we can recall a similar incident was many years ago when a panda broke loose in the cockpit of a DC3.' The aircraft almost crashed before the panda was overcome by the crew and trussed up.

Snakes escape, and Whittaker has been asked by Customs to check a box of snakes, especially spitting cobras, that could contain smuggled goods. Finding cannabis in reptile boxes is not odd.

Animals are sent in whisky cartons and tea chests. A falcon was strapped into a shoebox. Over 100 vervet monkeys and baboons died on a flight to Heathrow from East Africa: four animals at a time had been put in communal containers only eleven inches wide. It is often crucial to recharge the oxygen in water for fish, but no instructions are given.

New legislation has cut the numbers arriving at Heathrow, and New York's JFK is now the major centre. More than a million and a half animals a year pass through JFK. Many are smuggled. A Customs agent heard hiccups coming from a large crate that had arrived from Mexico. He opened the box, took out the false bottom, and came upon a flock of illegally imported parrots. They had been drugged with tequila.

They were part of a trade worth millions of dollars a year: animal smugglers, according to Kenneth Berlin of the Justice Department's Wildlife Enforcement Programme, make profits 'comparable to those that drug dealers make'. The victims include macaws, buffleheads, pygmy and red-breasted geese, and African monkeys. The business is simple and can be hugely moneymaking.

Stashed away in a big room near JFK are racks of expensive fur coats, crates of Calcutta lizardskin shoes, leopard skins and polished tortoise shells. A large moose head and a stuffed crocodile, in which furs have been smuggled, rest on a pile of elephant skins.

They have all been confiscated by the US Fish and Wildlife Service. There are around 1 million* dollars' worth of trophies and souvenirs in the Fish and Wildlife Service offices at 700 Rockaway Turnpike, near the airport. More than 200 pairs of crocodile-skin shoes and furs and skins are stored in Hangar 11, where the products from closed criminal cases are stored.

Individuals or companies who are found in violation of the wildlife laws can be fined up to £8,000 per unit of shipment and a year in prison.

Life has been hectic for the twenty-man team of wildlife inspectors and agents. Examining a live snake, they found heroin stuffed down its throat in plastic bags, and the smuggler was arrested. They caught the exporter and middleman for an operation taking American alligators out of the country illegally, in shipments of £20,000 to £25,000 each.

The agents determine the legality of incoming wildlife and products, frequently confiscating £100 alligator purses and £4,000 leopardskin coats from unwitting passengers. Under the Lacey Act, agents must also block the importing of species that may be dangerous to indigenous American species, like the red-whiskered bulbul bird, the Java rice sparrow and the multimammate mouse.

Two extremely rare spix macaws – they have not been seen in the wild since 1903 – were shipped to JFK via London misrepresented as blue-headed macaws. They were sold for £5,000 the pair. Bird-exporter Gordon Cooke admitted: 'When this shipment of spix macaws arrived at London I told the Customs they were blue-headed macaws. The Customs men didn't know any different. They look very similar. These were little babies still being hand-fed.

'It was a mixed shipment from South America. I was acting for a Dutchman, looking after the shipping. We paid £400 to the man who gave us the name of the customer in the US. The American

* *New York Times*, 3 October 1976.

was willing to pay £5,000; he had set his life on building a collection of rare birds.*

'His wife flew over from the States to Britain and flew them back as pets. They went out with her as blue-headed macaws.' Cooke says he has 'no regrets about the deal, despite a bit of collusion. I could not think of a better man to have them.'

Cooke has had plenty of other US business. He admits to exporting red-headed geese. 'They fetch £300 a pair. They are the most distinctive kind of geese, but the Customs men still don't recognize them. I send them abroad simply marked "geese".'

Birth certificates were forged for two African monkeys of the species *Diana roloway*. When a new private building was opened at the Louisiana Purchase Gardens and Zoo in Monroe, Louisiana, zoo director Jake Yelverton Jr started a search for animals to fill it.

Cooke came up with two monkeys. One was female, fifteen months old, and the other was a four-year-old male. The monkeys were sold to Jake Yelverton for £250 and were shipped by air to New Orleans. When the flight arrived at New Orleans airport, Mr Yelverton was there to clear the animals through Customs. He was disappointed.

The monkeys were seized by Fish and Wildlife officers and placed in another zoo for their safety and health. There were no proper importation documents. Yelverton wrote demanding either a certificate saying the monkeys were born at a specific place and date in Britain or an African export document.

Three weeks later, he had a document which falsely stated that both the *Diana* monkeys had been born in the Wigstone Zoological Gardens in England. This satisfied the Fish and Wildlife officers, who released the monkeys to Mr Yelverton. They are still thriving attractions at the Louisiana zoo.

The document was a forgery, although Cooke denies all knowledge of it. Jake Yelverton was acquitted in a Louisiana court in October 1978 of a charge of entering two monkeys into the US by means of a false statement. Although a British Customs officer testified that no such place as Wigstone Zoological Gardens existed, the prosecution was unable to prove positively that the monkeys were not born in England.

* *Observer*, 14 January 1978.

A diseased parrot imported into the US in 1971 caused an outbreak of Newcastle disease that left 12 million chickens dead, slaughtered to control the deadly virus. Chicken farmers were paid £11 million in indemnities.

This illicit airport trade is not confined to birds and monkeys. In one month alone, February 1979, US Customs officials seized £450,000 worth of furs of endangered species from Mexico. The growing market for bobcat pelts, at £175 apiece, is savaging the populations of those small cats. Reptile skins, ivory and turtle oil have been seized from air cargo.

Money is at the root of it. Exotic macaws that sold for £12 to £16 in 1970 now sell for thousands in the US: a particularly rare specimen fetched £12,000 in 1979. A Chicago businessman was convicted of trying to smuggle two peregrine falcons to the Middle East, as gifts for an oil sheik he wished to impress.

Animals smuggled into the US through JFK include green tree pythons, Fiji iguana and Johnson's crocodiles. These sell for £300 and upwards, the majority passing through the airport with false descriptions suggesting they are not endangered species.

The growing threat to wildlife from animal smugglers and their collector clients is clear. Many nations subscribe in theory to the Convention on International Trade in Endangered Species. Negotiated in 1973, the treaty divides endangered species into two main classes. It totally prohibits trade in some 400 animals registered as 'endangered', and requires strict licences for the import and export of species 'potentially threatened'. More than fifty plants are also classified as 'endangered'. Air shipments of cacti for foreign collectors are depleting many species of cacti in the US and Mexico, and the once abundant growths of ginseng in the Appalachians have been denuded by people cashing in on the great demand for the supposed aphrodisiac in the Orient.

In practice, most countries are overwhelmed by the size and complexity of the trade – including the US, where importers bring in more than 90 million wildlife items a year. Customs men are often unable to distinguish between a rare and not so rare animal.

False descriptions and hidden compartments are used to get animals through US airports where the trade is heaviest, at JFK, Los Angeles, Atlanta, Miami and Dallas/Fort Worth.

Passengers have been caught at JFK with rare birds tucked in hair rollers with their beaks taped and strapped to their hind legs. Young gorillas are described as monkeys. Orangutans are dyed black.

JFK has a special Animalport, run by the ASPCA. It prides itself on providing 'every type of food from live mealworms for foxes to bamboo roots for pandas, raw meat for lions and alfalfa for elephants'.

It is a serious indictment of the airlines that the ASPCA should have to run the Animalport. The airlines, though happy to take animals to boost their cargo earnings, wash their hands of responsibility for the animals they carry. They leave crating to the shippers, who may well be smugglers with a callous disregard for their stock, and ground and transit operations to the ASPCA.

Inadequate ventilation and extreme temperatures in baggage compartments are often cited. An American stewardess once placed a thermometer in the baggage compartment. It registered extremes of 104°F on the ground and 0°F in the air. Cages are flung in upside down and animals are left in warehouses without food.

Livestock transportation can be a terrible trade, with conditions more like a slave ship than an aircraft. Calves often die through overcrowding, which leads to heat exhaustion, heart failure through extreme distress, or simple suffocation. Sometimes the overcrowding can lead to the collapse of the cattle pens and the animals are literally crushed to death.

On one flight between Dublin and Athens, 450 ten- to twenty-day-old calves were loaded into an aircraft. It met violent turbulence approaching Greece. The upper tier of the pen collapsed, crushing and killing twenty calves in the pens below.

Some aircraft are so tightly packed that even their supplementary ventilation systems cannot prevent a lethal build-up of carbon dioxide from the animals' breath, and they become flying gas chambers. On one flight between Canada and the Middle East, 320 calves were dead out of 720 loaded when the aircraft touched down at Bordeaux for refuelling.

Many airlines that pride themselves on the excellence of their service in the passenger cabins think nothing of letting animals die in the holds beneath them.

Part Three
Ready, Steady, Fly

12 Maintenance

Most of the important services at airports are hidden from the passengers, even one as vital as maintenance. An 'A' check is carried out on airliners every sixty hours. An engineer inspects the landing and anti-collision lights, landing gear, doors, tyre pressures and oil level. The wings, fuselage and tail are checked for visible damage. The water system and the coffe-makers are drained. Oxygen masks, fire extinguishers, life-rafts and escape slides are examined.

The 'B' check is much more thorough. It is done every 400 or so flying hours and lasts a night. Every system on the aircraft is examined, from passenger safety belts to the thrust reversers on the engines.

Full overhauls take a month. The frequency depends on the aircraft type and varies between 14,000 and 24,000 hours. This shows the basic simplicity and reliability of modern design. An airliner need only be taken to pieces after the equivalent of 1,000 days and nights of non-stop use.

Allowable deficiencies are the inoperative systems and faults an aircraft can be flown with. The Americans talk of 'Go and No Go' items, the British of a Minimum Equipment List. It is generally drawn up by the manufacturer, though a great deal depends on the airline. No airline wants to ground a multi-million pound machine because of a minor fault, but some airlines push 'ADs' much too far, flying with deficient windscreen wipers, undercarriage solenoids and radio cooling fans. The pilot can get by on rain repellent, manual undercarriage and the standby radio: safety should be more than just getting by. The faults are not fixed but merely entered in the aircraft's 'squawk book'. After checking out, an aircraft is put through all checks by the 'Run Gang'. The inspections are very thorough. Any suspect part is put 'into quarantine', stamped in red and can only be used again if an inspector signs for it.

There is little mechanical wear in jet engines. But the great heat at which they operate weakens them. Temperatures go up to

2,000°C in the jet pipe and the finely engineered turbine blades can be exposed to 500°C. A turbine has 130 blades or more, costing £300 each, on each stage.

Every component on the crucial turbines and compressors has a 'life limit', which varies between 16,000 and 30,000 hours. Stones damage the blades. The engine starts burning too much fuel as it wears out. Eventually it is dumped. But where the scheduled airline sells it off for £1,000 for scrap, small charter operators pay the scrap dealer five times that, and use the engine as a 'spare'. Sometimes such spares get used.

Tyres cost over £1,000 each and are carefully logged. A card shows the history of each tyre. The main tyres last longer than the smaller nosewheels, even though they take more of an apparent pounding, with smoke pouring out as they touch down. On a twin-jet like a 1–11, 247 landings are possible on the mainwheels, and 202 on the nosewheel. A 707 takes 114 and 82, whereas a VC10 is down to 89 and 51.

Typically, an operator with ten Boeing 707s has two 'inflight shutdowns' (engines switched off in flight) in a month. He keeps six engines at his base. Elsewhere, he has a pool arrangement with other airlines. A big pool will keep spare engines at 160 airports round the world. A member pays a flat rate per hour into the pool for using an engine.

A passenger on a long-haul route, say London to Los Angeles, an eleven-hour distance, will be aboard a 'spanker', as the engineers call a good plane. It means the engines are relatively new, operating at maximum economy. The 'burners' go on the shorter hauls where fuel consumption is less crucial.

Special care has to be taken of aircraft operating to areas with high salt condensation like North Africa, the Gulf, the Bahamas and the Red Sea. It corrodes aircraft badly and rapidly, and is present in the air up to 3,000 feet. The Caribbean also has coral sand in the atmosphere. Flying over deserts, where sand can reach above 15,000 feet, wears out engines.

Dirty atmospheres have an adverse effect on performance, the aircraft itself gets dirty and thus less streamlined. Most UK airspace is designated dirty. It costs £175 in extra fuel to send a dirty aircraft from London to the Mediterranean and back, which is why they are kept clean. The washing bays are just like car washes, with giant detergent sprays. Repainting a 747 costs £40,000 and the paint adds 1,000 lb to the aircraft's weight. This is not far off half a ton, which is why few airlines do a complete paint job on their aircraft.

The cabin also needs maintenance. A single seat may have 1,500 people sitting in it during a year. The carpets take an enormous pounding. Things are found in seat-backs. 'People dump things they have second thoughts about smuggling, like hash. On flights back from the Far East, you get cartons of 200 cigarettes abandoned. They always seem to be State Express, still in the cellophane, but filled with drugs.

'Then you get blue magazines, of course, on the Scandinavian returns, and porno movies. They are a wretched nuisance because people fling them down the toilets and jam them,' says a cleaner.

Air conditioning is a problem. People tend to smoke heavily on aircraft and nicotine jams the air filter valves. Passengers throw bottles into the lavatories, and crew fill up galley sinks with tea bags. They get stuck in so tight that often the drain pipe has to be cut out.

Fuses are blown on ovens when stewardesses, trying to rush through, overfill them. This is an expensive item: the four galleys on a 707 cost £125,000, including the fridges, ovens, electrics, sinks and stowages. On a 747 the galleys cost over £500,000.

The line (or ramp) maintenance man checks before departure and after arrival. He is also responsible for Customs bar seals, and for having the toilets drained and flushed. These have an electric flush, on a centrifugal basis, draining into a thirty-gallon main tank. Wash-basin and galley water goes straight out into the air under pressure, through a specially heated pipe to prevent freezing or icing up.

13 Turn-round

Aircraft can be serviced with astonishing speed. An international flight can be turned round in less than ninety minutes. It needs the same sort of cool urgency as a pit stop in a motor race.

The first warning comes when the plane is seven minutes out, as it comes off the stack. The men with the steps are warned. The caterers, cleaners, fuellers, engineers, apron controllers, Customs and Immigration get ready.

The aircraft is allocated a stand. A system of red and green lights guides the pilot to the correct position; red lights to right and left if he is off course, green if he is not. There are marker boards along the side of the jetty to help him stop in the right place. When the name of his aircraft type is level with his shoulder, the pilot puts on the parking brake. Doors are in different positions with different aircraft, so this is important.

The incoming aircraft is met by fifteen vehicles and thirty people as it taxis to a stop. There is a ground power unit, to run the lights and air conditioning whilst it is on the ground. Two pairs of mobile steps, two baggage cars and a truck are needed to take off the cargo. There are buses for the passengers and crew.

The ground engineers have a maintenance van. Three high-lift trucks carry fresh food, stores, cleaning equipment and commissary staff. Authority is represented by a Customs car and a supervisor's jeep.

As soon as the aircraft stops, it is earthed and chocks are put on the nosewheel. The auxiliary power unit is plugged in. The pilot cuts the engines, and the steps are driven up as the doors open.

Nobody can leave until Customs officers have cleared the plane. The captain tells the engineers of any faults that have developed.

The air freight, mail and baggage are cleared. The water cart arrives to pipe fresh water into the tanks, 99 gallons on a 707, 250 on a Jumbo. The cleaners, called 'groomers', and commissary attendants move into the aircraft. They change the pillow cases and blankets, tidy out the seat-backs, and clean the ashtrays, the galleys and the cockpit.

All the unused food is unloaded, and the ovens and containers and refrigerators are restocked with fresh meals. The surplus food, even smoked salmon and steaks, is thrown away. The groomers also change the spare oxygen cylinder, the medical kits, and the baby kits with their baby foods, evaporated milk, cornflakes, baby powder, nappies and pins and toys. 300 tablets of soap, rolls of lavatory paper, tubes of toothpaste, aftershave are distributed round the toilets.

Red roses and a large basket of fruit are placed in the first-class cabin. Sweet trays, for handing round before take-off, are laid out in the galleys. A van comes out with 300 newspapers: major international airports can supply same-day papers from forty or more countries.

With forty minutes to go, the maintenance men have finished their checks on tyre pressures and treads, the undercarriage and the hydraulic system.

With thirty minutes to go, the sanitary servicing vehicle ('honey cart' to the crews) drains the waste from the lavatories, and flushes and refills them. The pipes cannot be connected until an hour after landing, as the valves freeze in flight.

The cabin maintenance man arrives to check seat lights, call lights, seat-reclining mechanisms, oxygen, refrigeration and air cooling. Seats that will not recline should be replaced from airline stocks. Often, they are not.

It takes half an hour to check the radio, radar, electronics and instruments in the cockpit. The windscreens are cleaned, and the wipers checked.

Every window is cleaned. Fresh supplies of 'seat literature' are put in the seat-backs: maps, postcards, writing paper, envelopes, brochures, menu card, emergency instructions and sickbag. Special vacuum cleaners are used for the carpets.

The four galleys on a typical 707 flight will be loaded with 1,400 Lily cups, paper cups for water and fruit juice, 700 cocktail sticks and 400 swizzle sticks. There will be 140 packets of nuts, 16 lb of sweets, 15 jars of onions, olives and cherries, 600 tea bags and 30 gallons worth of coffee packs.

There will be 100 cans of fruit juice, and 1,000 cans of bitter lemon, tonic water, dry ginger and soda. There are emergency cans of food for the crew: luncheon meat, corned beef, tuna fish and a jar of Bovril. They will eat this if there is a hijack or if the ordinary food turns out to be bad.

In reserve in the hold for use in countries where such things are unobtainable are 300 tea bags, 6 packets each of cornflakes, Rice Crispies and Sugar Puffs, 50 packets of Vita-Wheat, 36 tins of orange, grapefruit and tomato juice, ¼ lb each of Indian and China tea, 100 large and 100 small doilies, 2 packets of Paddi-pads and 6 toilet rolls.

Another emergency round of luncheon meat, corned beef and tuna fish is kept in the hold. There are also, more romantically, two emergency bottles of Angostura bitters, one of Worcester sauce and two jars of Patum Peperium, the Gentleman's Relish.

With half an hour to go, the second officer arrives to supervise the refuelling. He also checks instruments, emergency oxygen cylinders, cabin oxygen pressure, emergency hatches and life-rafts. A 707 has seven fuel tanks, and a pilot has to be on board to control the inflow from the two tankers. The aircraft can take 15,000 gallons or 65 tons of fuel, and it is an important part of flying to keep it flowing from the right tanks to preserve trim.

Fifteen minutes from start-up, the crew bus drops off the cabin staff. They check that all food and stores are aboard. Loading with freight, mail and baggage starts. With ten minutes to go, the crew bus returns with the captain and flight crew. They have already had a briefing on the weather, and have filed their flight plan.

The tankers go. As the passenger buses swing up with eight minutes to go, the air starter vehicle arrives. It supplies the compressed air that starts the engines by running up the compressors and blades. The doors close, and are checked for pressure leaks. The captain radios for start-up clearance. The turn-round is completed.

14 Cabin Confidential

Like a hotel or a liner, an airliner has its own safes, its own secret recesses. On a 707, a special part of the freight hold is used for diplomatic mail. Valuables are stowed in a lockable container just behind and to the left of the cockpit door.

On a Jumbo, the Queen's Messenger or the Diplomatic Mail courier boards first class before anyone else. He sits unobtrusively in a front row seat. In front of him is the 'nose lowboy', a fitted table.

It looks unobtrusive enough, with magazine racks on it and a vase of flowers on the top. Indeed, at take-off it may well have a child in a cot strapped on to it, since this is where infants are supposed to travel at take-off and landing.

Inside, on the right-hand side, is a special locked and sealed compartment, the 'dip-locker', for the world's diplomatic secrets, or drugs, or duty-free whisky or stolen blueprints or illicit love letters or whatever else still travels diplomatic, accompanied by the man in the front seat in the neat grey suit. The chief steward has the key if there is no courier.

At the back of first class on many airlines there will be another man, whose jacket will remain on throughout the flight, and who will show keen interest in his fellow passengers. He is the security guard.

Besides the 'dip locker', the Jumbos have a precious cargo compartment, a simple cupboard next to the lavatory at the head of the stairs in the first-class lounge. The chief steward will take passengers' jewels and cash and place them in its rather flimsy care.

An aircraft can have up to fourteen toilets, and each one will cost some £12,000. They get well used. Studies show that more than ninety-eight per cent of all passengers on a flight of more than four hours will spend over three minutes in a toilet, a figure only explicable by the fact that it is the only place to relax and get away from the claustrophobia of the cabin.

But toilets are not the sanctuaries they seem – they are designed to be easy to open. A British Airways manual for its well-bred stewardesses states firmly: 'A locked toilet door can be opened easily from the outside by inserting a pencil, nail file or similar object into a slot in the OCCUPIED sign. Slide the sign diagonally to the left.'

The toilets come expensive because they are fairly complex arrangements of plumbing. The power for heating the water has to be taken from a generator whirling at many thousands of revolutions per minute from the outer right (number four) engine. The flush has to be electric, since there is no gravity feed to help. The hand basin water is pumped in, but taken out under heavy suction and left to stream out of the aircraft's belly in a 580 mph stream of instantly iced spray – the only thing that deliberately leaves the aircraft in flight.

The toilet water system has three large pressurized tanks, situated far away in the forward cargo compartment. Each tank holds 110 gallons of water, giving 300 usable gallons in all. This water is pumped to the galleys and iced water fountains, as well as to the lavatories. Each wash basin has its own individual electric heater, thermostatically controlled to give a temperature of 125°F.

300 gallons of water would play havoc with the aircraft's electrical system if it got loose. Should the shut-off valves in the galleys and lavatories not contain a flood, it is a serious enough emergency for the captain to be responsible, and not the chief steward. Through a special switch in the cockpit, he can depressurize the tanks and cut off the supply. Runaway toilets are part of a pilot's regular checklist.

Whereas water from the basin is sucked out of the aircraft, waste from the toilet is caught in tanks cleared on landing by 'honey carts'. It is therefore quite safe to use the lavatories when the aircraft is stationary at an airport, unlike trains.

The aircraft holds such assorted necessities as 7 gentlemen's wet razors, 20 electric razors, 12 shoe horns, 300 Do Not Disturb labels, 5 packs of playing cards, 25 hand fans, 10 spare baby teats. There is a special Baby Bar installation, that will heat three bottles of milk at a time, with an automatic timer.

The heating is complex. Each oven – and there can be up to fifteen ovens – heats fifty-two plates from frozen to a temperature of 120°F in 45 minutes. Extractor fans remove cooking and lavatory smells along ducts and out of the aircraft. Hot plates boost temperatures to 200°F in 45–60 minutes. Each galley has its own refrigerator, and bar trolleys have dry ice to keep drinks cool.

The lighting system is automatic. There are four phases on the light switch – SLP, TRANSIT, MOVIE and BRD. BRD or Board is full lighting. Transit and Movie cut it further and further until SLP or Sleep leaves only night illumination and the crossover lights between cabin sections.

Passengers pushing the call button set off a low blue light and a low tone chime in the galley. When the flight crew want attention, however, the effect is a lot more urgent: the call light in the galley starts flashing furiously pink to the accompaniment of a high tone chime. Passengers pulling call buttons in lavatories, in fairness, should also get prompt attention: a special amber light goes on together with the high-pitched chime.

The aircraft has a lot of a discotheque to it, with dimming and flashing lights. The cabin staff play taped music – but must remember never to play it for more than thirty minutes at a time, or the airline could be in trouble with the Peforming Rights Society, who look after the interests of live musicians and make sure that 'needle time' (canned music) is limited. The society has not pressed a claim for live music in the air, although the Zeppelins used to carry a folding piano and a pianist. But a musician has estimated that if British Airways handled the same percentage of live music as the BBC, they would have to carry a string quartet on every transatlantic flight for the next two years.

There is an internal telephone service so the crew can ring each other up on a special interphone with push numbers. The set has buttons with numbers from one to five, and also the letter P for emergencies. To ring the chief steward, for example, the handset is lifted and 25 punched. For a non-urgent call to the pilot, his number is 31. But for urgent calls, punching P twice, PP, automatically cuts off any other conversations and gets straight through to the flight deck and captain. This is the 'drunk funk' number in slang, Pilot Alert in officialese. (It is mainly used by stewardesses frightened of drunks, who want the captain and his four gold rings to come down the aisle to impose discipline.)

Nowadays, the announcements that blushing real live girls used to give out in schoolgirl French or stammering English are all prerecorded in an impersonal studio. British Airways have gone so far as to get BBC announcers to record them all. The prerecorded announcement system, bringing that old joke about the 'this is a fully automatic flight . . . this is a fully automatic flight . . .' closer home, is a complex piece of cassette playing equipment. It has twelve punch buttons, each of which releases a different announcement. There is a 'cancel' button and those who believe in live voices will be relieved to hear that 'the activating of the cancel button will cancel the prerecorded announcement, and if necessary, allows an announcement to be made over the public address, using the handset'.

So the lovely crew who welcome you aboard, with a prerecording of a girl who is not on the aircraft, can actually talk direct to you if they want, as long as they first remember to cancel the speaking equipment.

Buttons one and two are red, and have guards over them so that they cannot be set off by mistake – not surprisingly, since number one is the oxygen instruction (the one that is used when decompression actually has occurred), and this cassette should go on automatically when decompression happens.

Number two is the Ditching instruction. The reassuring voice that is saying: 'We are forced to make an emergency landing on water . . . The rescue services are aware of our intentions . . .' was recorded months or years ago in a distant studio. The relaxed 'Do not panic if you cannot swim' belongs to a BBC announcer.

Number three cassette contains the preflight oxygen and lifejackets briefings in English. Other cassettes are in foreign languages and can be changed for different briefings. This has led to worried Dutchmen being assured that they should be preparing for touchdown at Paris when they were about to take off for Stockholm. On another occasion a voice presumed to be the captain, speaking in excellent German, assured the passengers of a British aircraft that if they looked out of the left-hand windows they would see the Alps. The aircraft was over the Channel at the time.

Then there are films, with four independent projectors. (Inflight movies are not new. British South American Airways had them in 1948.) The movies are started by pushing the Movie switch and keeping it depressed until the white light behind the

Off switch changes to (aptly for the medium) blue. It turns itself off automatically when the film is over.

The image of the brutal and licentious soldiery lives on in PA announcements. On charter trooping flights the men are welcomed aboard with this cassette: 'This aircraft is pressurized and it is essential therefore to avoid damage to cabin walls with knives or other sharp instruments. Apart from disfiguring the interior this is extremely dangerous.'

On Eastern and African routes, many passengers have never used a Western-style toilet before, with predictable results. Increasing numbers of illiterates fly, who cannot read safety leaflets. This is not restricted to the passengers. Much of the instruction given to cabin crews and ground firefighting teams from African airlines at the Beirut flight centre has to be presented audio-visually, a chilling thought.

There is no need to panic if fellow passengers tug at the exit doors, thinking they are lavatories. The doors swing sideways and backwards initially, and the pressure difference at altitude would make it impossible to open them even if the handle could be twisted through its stop pin. It would be possible to open it at low level, but it would not matter much unless the muddled traveller stepped out.

Some aircraft cabins are very exotic. Hugh Hefner, the owner of *Playboy* magazine, had a long, black stretched DC9 called the Big Bunny, a temporary victim of an economy drive. The ordinary version carries 109 passengers. Hefner's carried just 33, in a series of chambers or caves. There was a boardroom with space for ten directors, a disco and dance area, a master hi-fi system, a games room and a kitchen.

The focal point was the master bedroom. It was dominated by a huge, elliptical bed six feet by eight. Sixty-eight racoons gave their skins for the bedspread. By Hefner's fingertips was a complex of buttons. These controlled all the entertainment systems on board, enabled him to talk to the crew, darkened his polarized windows so he could watch a film, beamed in FM/AM shortwave radios and connected him by phone to whoever he wanted to talk to.

At the foot of the bed was a chair. It was motorized and could be rotated to face a typewriter ledge. Here Mr Hefner wrote

165

articles for the next issue of his magazine, or examined the colour transparencies of his next Playmate of the Month on a lightbox. There was a shower.

The $5 million aircraft was designed by Dan Czubak. 'Basically, Mr Hefner said, "I want to take my mansion and put it in the aircraft." Well, it's a big mansion, but he wanted the same sort of environment. He said he wanted first-class service all the way, and not airline first class. He wanted it the same as he had at home, at the mansion – bone china, cut glass, everything,' said Mr Czubak.

'So take the electronic gear he has on board. Seven colour TV sets. Then we found a problem picking up interference flying from city to city, so we decided to have pretaped shows. We carry fifteen hours of TV tapes right there in the hi-fi cabin, along with the cartridge recorder, tape recorder, cassette recorder.'

Hefner just beats Arab financier Adnan Khashoggi in the television stakes. Khashoggi's Boeing 727 has four sets. However, Khashoggi does have gold taps in his bathroom.

Mr Hefner likes films. So the Big Bunny had a cinemascope screen and storage for ten films. Every seat had channel selectors so that guests could choose whichever of the many entertainments they wanted to listen to – and have a choice of headset, professional for purists, ordinary for others. Naturally, Mr Hefner had master control. He could pre-empt the entire entertainment system from the headboard by his bed.

Dan Dzubak says: 'Normally you get on an aircraft, turn on the overhead light and you have to hold your paper out two feet in front of you. On the Playboy jet, every individual seat has its own light position worked out. The operation in the lavatories is entirely electronic. Water, heat, everything is by button. There are no taps. The nozzle of the faucet is sculptured into the mirror so that the water appears to flow out of the glass.'

The panelling was rosewood carved by German craftsmen. The seats were lined with Himalayan goat. And of course the Big Bunny was serviced by seven specially chosen Jet Bunnies.

Their uniform was a black knitted nylon ciré dress, with thigh-length boots in the same material and a long white scarf with a black bunny on it. The aircraft had a large bar, but the Jet

Bunnies stuck to non-alcoholic cocktails with names like Shirley Temple and Virgin Mary (a Bloody without the vodka).

Only two things disturbed Hugh Hefner as he jetted in his mini-mansion to the outposts of his empire in London, Miami and Montreal. He tended to look slightly absurd strapped into his sybaritic bed when flying through turbulence; and his pilots, in their conventional jackets and caps, looked out of place in this flying dream.

The weather cannot be changed, and neither was he able to persuade the pilots to wear Buck Rogers spaceman style coveralls in fluorescent colours.

King Khaled of Saudi Arabia has ordered a £21 million 747 executive jet. The plane will have a throne room and a hospital section with satellite communications to a hospital in Cleveland.

The Queen of England, by contrast, travels modestly. The first thirty rows of seats on a BA Super VC10, normally the aircraft Canopus, are removed for her quarters. The entourage travels in the back. A lounge area, red-carpeted with a settee and small dining table, is created in the converted first-class cabin. There are two dressing rooms with six-foot-high leather wardrobes for her and Prince Philip.

The royal cipher appears on the cigarette boxes, cutlery, wine decanters and silver trays which are specially kept for royal flights. But the beds, curtained off from the lounge area, are simple divans. Nor does the Queen have exotic tastes in food.

Her favourite is glazed duckling, with a little Nuits St Georges. A stewardess often on royal flights says that 'very often she'll settle for a ham sandwich and a coffee'. The menus are vetted by Buckingham Palace well in advance, and it is quite common to find the Queen has asked for chicken when her equerries at the back have put down for oysters and champagne.

During flights she is briefed on her destination and the people who will receive her by an air vice-marshal or equivalent. Lists of intelligent questions to put to locals, whose photographs will have been shown to her so that she can 'recognize' them and ask after their families and affairs, are drawn up.

If she is flying out to join the royal yacht *Britannia*, forty of her retinue travel in the back – personal secretaries, cooks, butlers.

All ships at sea and other aircraft *en route* are informed of her royal progress. Only the President of the United States equals that.

Unlike the President, however, the Queen is not allowed to travel by helicopter. It is considered too dangerous and she does not like helicopters. The sole exception was a royal tour of Ulster, where terrorists on the ground were considered more dangerous than a fragile helicopter in the sky.

15 Haute Cuisine

or *cooking in the clouds*

The dull crackle of meat on a spit competed with the whine of the jets. A succulent smoke filled the aircraft as the royal servants laid out gold plates with Lebanese hors d'oeuvre, hummus, shrimps, unleavened bread. Khazak carpets were laid in the eating area, so the King could lounge easily with his concubine of the moment, taking handfuls of the lamb and rice with dates and almonds.

Ibn Saud, King of Saudi Arabia and descendant of the Prophet, filled his lead crystal glass with his favourite Montrachet. With the Turkish sweetmeats and the jasmin water ices came Taittinger champagne, and bitter black coffee was made on a brass stove in front of the King. When the King had finished, the spit revolved over the charcoal fire at 30,000 feet as the servants ate.

Such ostentation is no longer politically wise even for oil sheiks. Indeed, there was a plot to blow up Ibn Saud, gold plate, Comet airliner and all.

Mass travel has done away with the elegance of earlier days, when Imperial Airways welded the Empire together with flying boats. The proconsuls and generals ate in special dining rooms from a galley where food was cooked and not merely heated. They relaxed in the smoking cabin, or on the promenade deck looking out of extra large windows with specially provided field glasses as the geography of Empire – Alex, Singapore, Durban – slipped by at 120 mph.

Luxury in airships was even greater. Four times as long as a Jumbo, they had mahogany and mother-of-pearl walls and ceilings, and wickerwork furniture. Each sleeping cabin had a sofa, table, stool, wardrobe and bed. There were gramophones and baby grand pianos for dancing, and special smoking rooms sealed off from the inflammable hydrogen by airlock doors.

The Hindenburg had a dining room 15 feet by 50 feet for her seventy passengers. The chef had five assistants, and he attended each meal. The classic Hindenburg lunch served on the second and last day out over the Atlantic, was Indian swallows' nest soup, caviar and Rhine salmon, lobster, saddle of venison, crème Hindenburg, fruit and cheese. The wines were 1934 Graacher Himmelreich, 1934 Diedesheimer Kranzler Riesling, 1934 Piesporter Goldtropfcher and 1928 Feist Brut. The brandy was 1842 Meukow.

The only things that are cooked on aircraft now are the steaks in first class, and even they must have the surface browned and black grill marks burnt on them before they come on board, since an aircraft oven cannot give this grill effect.

The size of airline catering is staggering. Every year, more than 350 million meals have to be pre-prepared, taken on board in the right numbers to the right aircraft, and served. Pan Am serves over 16 million meals in flight, British Airways 20 million, the US domestic United over 30 million. British Caledonian gets through 320,000 chickens and 80,000 lb of bacon a year.

The kitchens of a large airline are far bigger and more complex than those of any hotel, and much more subject to strain. Because of the vagaries of fog and weather, there may be a sudden and unexpected quadrupling in demand. Aircraft that are going to remote airfields without adequate caterers must have meals specially packed in their holds on dry ice for return flights.

Even politics plays a part. Middle East Airlines found that it was carrying, quite unaccountably, Jaffa oranges on flights from London to sensitive Arab countries. After the embarrassing affair of the oranges stopped, something even worse started. The duty-free Marlboro cigarettes on flights into Cairo started appearing with 'specially packed for El Al Israeli Airlines' on them.

Airlines will go to great lengths to get the right ingredients. British Caledonian flies the long routes from South America to Europe. The airline's catering manager says: 'There is no substitute for a British breakfast. Passengers are entitled to the real thing. So we fly British bacon and chipolatas out and store them specially in Buenos Aires and Rio. We do the same with smoked salmon and caviar and some liqueurs – you can't get them in South America.

'We've tried experimenting with local chipolatas there, and in West Africa. They just aren't up to it, so we fly out our own.'

The same airline makes use of spare freight capacity to fly shellfish and crab from the Seychelles to send out to Los Angeles from London in fish dishes; mangoes, avocados, pineapples and limes are flown in on the African flights; coffee comes in the hold from Brazil, maté tea from Argentina, all to be sent out on other flights from London.

No aircraft leaves unless there is food for all aboard. With an aircraft on the ground costing a company about £1,200 an hour, with a crew that may go out of hours it's expensive to wait for food. It is a catering manager's nightmare, but it happens, despite the twenty-minute-plus-five rule (putting on the food only twenty minutes before take-off and allowing five spare meals above the number on the passenger manifest), and despite the 'meals on wheels' vans that cruise permanently round to top up aircraft.

A strike by catering loaders is often the reason. Airlines are vulnerable to strikes by all the specialized groups they rely on, and pilots, cabin staff, engineers, maintenance men, refuellers, air traffic controllers and baggage handlers have all severely affected international flights in the past three years. If the aircraft is bound eastwards from London, it can pick up food at Frankfurt, Zurich or Rome. But if on a transatlantic route, it must wait until food can be flown in from Frankfurt or Paris. Thus Pan Am always has enough food at Heathrow to last six weeks.

On a flight westbound across the Atlantic to Los Angeles, the aircraft will be taking off around noon, the peak period for the westbounds. Lunch will be served slightly west of Ireland. A typical first-class menu:

Smoked Scotch Salmon

or

Royal Game Pancakes in Madeira Sauce
Consommé Grande Duchesse
Grilled Fillet of Steak Aberdeen Angus

or

Sauté of Chicken Chasseur

or

Turbot in Shrimp Sauce
Green Salad – French or Italian Dressing
   French Beans
   Baby Carrots
   Parsley Potatoes
Strawberry Chantilly

During the previous night, between midnight and dawn, the turbot and chicken will have been cooked, the shrimp sauce prepared and heated. The catering manager will have the manifest giving the numbers and names of first-class passengers, and will have made a subconscious decision on relative quantities. The plane cannot take off with sixty main courses for twenty first-class passengers – the economics would be mad.

It must be refined so that just one spare first-class entrée is carried for twenty passengers. And it must be right. 'You can tell people at a first-class restaurant that something is off and they take it without a murmur – even though you could go out and buy it,' says a steward. 'But if you tell somebody the fish is off 32,000 feet above the Atlantic, they go berserk – they'll say, "I've paid £400 for this meal." And of course if they are travelling first they've got a point – they are whacking out way over the odds for the pure transport, like the people back in economy are paying for, and they're in for a few hundred dollars for a better seat and better food.'

Flight times are an important factor. A 1 p.m. take-off means meat, but every hour before or after that means more fish. Names are examined. Women are more likely to choose chicken or fish; fish on Fridays will increase if there are people with Catholic-sounding names. Children almost always go for chicken; during the 'lollipop flight' periods at the end of term times this is taken into account.

But for a normal London to Los Angeles run, the emphasis will be on steak, with the women listed for chicken, and two fish – one for a 'rogue' who may order it, another as the reserve. The flight crew eat first class. They cannot eat shellfish, so the turbot in shrimp sauce is out. Steak is heavy. They are put down for chicken.

A flight to Africa would mean more chicken; to the Far East and Japan more fish. For the Middle East and West Africa, saddle of lamb would be on the menu – though for Japan, where lamb is not eaten, it would be rigorously avoided.

The manager makes sure there have been no mistakes to these regional rules, makes his guess on ordering patterns, and leaves a note for the chief steward with the amounts of each dish. Thirteen hours later, with the aircraft cruising, the chief steward will already have worked out who to strongly recommend what to.

If the passengers prove awkward, the pilots and engineer will have to eat what is given to them – although the captain and first officer must by law eat different dishes to avoid simultaneous food poisoning.

Whilst the entrées are prepared, another chef makes the strawberry chantilly. An urn is filled with consommé, and left to chill slightly.

The morning shift comes on at 6 a.m. and cuts the smoked salmon and lemon wedges. At 10.15, with three hours before take-off, as the passengers finish packing in their hotels, the chefs cook the royal game pancakes. These will stay warmed and go on board the aircraft warm.

Two hours before take-off, the steaks are browned and seared. Some are part cooked, and marked for well done with black foil. Others are left bloody with red foil. On board the aircraft they will be heated and partially cooked. The green salad is carefully placed in bowls. Like bread, it is easily affected by pressurization and its crispness goes. Cream is also affected, quickly turning sour, which is why airlines use powdered milk sachets.

Vegetables are taken out of the frozen food stores. Twenty minutes before take-off, the meals are taken out to the aircraft by van and stowed in the first-class galley, and packed in the ovens and refrigerators.

The economy menus were prepared and preset on trays during the night: 160 hors d'oeuvre, coq au vin with green beans, diced carrots and small roast potatoes, pineapple cheesecake, cheese and crackers.

Although a first-class menu can be as elaborate as the airline wishes, economy is strictly governed by IATA. The most that can be given is hors d'oeuvre, a main dish with no salad and only two vegetables, and dessert or fruit, not both. These rules are binding, but explain why almost every international airline gives so much salad with its hors d'oeuvre – it can't give it any other way.

The main food course is in wrapped foil containers inside ovens which are then plugged into the aircraft's electrics. The rest is laid out on trays in special containers. All the stewardess has to do is to heat the prefrozen main course, put it on the trays and serve.

Twenty minutes before take-off, the galley closes. No more food will be taken on for late arrivals, but there are already five spare economy meals. If extra first-class passengers turn up, the crew must forfeit eating first class.

The bars are installed and sealed by Customs. A 707 on an intercontinental flight will carry 18,000 cigarettes, 900 cigars, 56 bottles of whisky, 16 bottles of brandy, 8 bottles of gin, 200 miniatures of spirits, 200 quarter bottles of wine, and 5 bottles each of, say, Château Latour-Camblanes 1967, Puligny Montrachet 1964 and champagne for first class.

Thirty minutes before serving the economy passengers, the ovens are switched on to 300°F. These are electric ovens with a fan to give them even temperatures, since the trays are stacked in tight.

For first, the turbot gets twenty minutes at 350°F, the chicken twenty-five. The steaks get ten minutes for rare, thirteen minutes for medium, twenty minutes for well done. Turning on ovens should be in strict sequence, allowing each ovenload to be served before the next one is fully heated up.

The routines are laid down to the smallest detail. Serving 434 passengers on a Jumbo is a military-style exercise, where all ten cabin crew are taught: 'Meal service routine as per "diagrams" and "sequences".'

The task of steward 11 in the aft galley of a 747 is thus: 'Check progress of ovens, prepare meal trolleys 3 and 4. Position meals on trolleys 6, 7 and 8. Pass trolley 6 to stewardess C, 7 to D, 8 to senior steward. Replace meals removed from oven 9 and oven 10 with forty-nine refrigerated meals for second cycle heating for meal service sequence 3.'

There are the regulations for crew meals. Most airlines give the pilots normal first-class menus, except that they prohibit oysters and other molluscs (on medical grounds to prevent food poisoning), and allow other shellfish provided they have come only from the UK, USA, Canada, South Africa and Japan and nowhere else. The crew are not allowed alcohol. Although insisting that 'the chief steward shall see that full service is given in the control cabin', airlines draw the line at caviar for the crew on economic grounds.

Some airlines cling to tradition, still treating the crew as ships' officers from earlier and more gracious days. British Airways provides a white-coated steward on all-cargo flights to look after the crew. He serves their meals on a white cloth on the navigation table in the cockpit.

Such flamboyant touches apart, the food is predictable. Salmon, prawn cocktails and trout travel well, keep their appearance, and so are common. Pâté goes off; melon and green salads have a short life. Poultry and steaks are readily available, easy to prepare, acceptable and thus beat anything else.

There is a world-wide telex and computer code for people whose eating habits are dictated by religion, medicine or fashion. Airlines serve millions of 'religious' meals each year. If KSML appears next to a passenger's name he will get a kosher meal, kept in a separate part of the galley from gentile food, and presented to the passenger with the original seal intact. Most intercontinental aircraft have emergency kosher packs in the dry food stores, wrapped in plain brown paper for going through Arab countries.

On the other hand, a MOML will get a Muslim meal. The airline standard is lamb, goat or chicken with rice pilaff. HNMLs, for Hindus, are the same as a VGML or vegetarian – mushrooms in salad with diced potatoes and cauliflower – but with a curry seasoning.

There are BBMLs for babies with milk feeding bottles, seafood meals for slimmers and WSMLs, salt-free meals. Businessmen get DUMLs, diatetic ulcer meals of grilled lean beef with little salt, boiled potatoes, boiled marrows and fruit compote with fresh milk. All these meals can be produced to identical standards within a few hours at any major airport.

Airlines do get seriously caught out. One of America's largest wine producers was fined a quarter of a million dollars for successfully passing off cooking wine as first class.

But then it wouldn't be an airport business if there wasn't a racket in it somewhere.

Part Four
Airborne

16 Flight

The theory of flight is simple. Drag and weight try to stop an aircraft: lift and thrust have to overcome them. Thrust in a jet aircraft comes from the engines, which push a 'jet' of heated air through the exhaust pipes against the surrounding air. The push propels the aircraft forward. With a propeller plane, the thrust comes from accelerating the air through propellers.

Drag is the resistance of the air to the aircraft passing through it. Streamlining reduces the drag. The lift comes from the flow of air round the wings. Against this there is the weight of the aircraft and the force of gravity pulling it down.

When thrust and lift are stronger than drag and weight, the aircraft can accelerate and climb. The wing develops lift because it is designed so that the airflow over it causes less air pressure on the top surface than on the bottom. The difference in air pressure causes a lift vertically upwards.

The faster an aircraft goes the greater the lift. The higher the aircraft goes, the 'thinner' the air becomes. Air is compressed by its own weight. 100 cubic feet of air at sea level weighs about eight lb, but the same volume at 20,000 feet weighs only four lb. Although there is less lift at high altitudes, there is also much less resistance and drag. This enables jets to fly high and fast without using so much fuel.

The air itself changes greatly with height, becoming colder, less dense or 'thinner', and with a steady reduction in barometric pressure. An International Standard Atmosphere is used to average out its qualities. At sea level, the ISA barometric pressure is taken as 1013.2 millibars. Although the actual pressure may be different, every pilot at height sets the standard 1013.2 millibars on his altimeter to give his height. If different pilots used different settings, collisions would result. The ISA temperature at sea level is assumed at 18°C, and relative density at 1.00.

By 10,000 feet, the temperature is already down to −5°C, the relative density 0.862. At 20,000 feet, it is −25°C, density 0.533 and the pressure has dropped to 466 millibars.

Just above the uppermost reaches of cloud, cruising at 35,000 feet, the air temperature outside the aircraft is −54°C. Barometer pressure is 239 millibars and the relative density 0.311. The jet is at home where the air is cold and very thin. Above this is the lower stratosphere where the temperature steadies but the density goes on dropping.

An aircraft has three basic instabilities that are used to control it (a totally stable aircraft would only be able to fly straight and level). Yaw is the name given to the swing of the nose to left or right. This is resisted by the large surface of the tail fin. A rudder set into the fin gives controlled yaw, so that the pilot can move the nose sideways through rudder pedals at his feet. The fin is large, 1,660 square feet on a Jumbo, which is as much as the total sail area of a big racing yacht.

Pitch is the movement of the nose up or down. It is controlled by the tailplane, or horizontal stabilizer to the Americans. Parts of the tailplane are hinged and can be moved up or down by pushing the control column backwards or forwards. These are called the elevators. Sometimes the whole of the tailplane moves: this is called an 'all flying tail'. Here, the bulk of the tail is used to get the plane in roughly the right attitude of climb or descent, and the elevators are used for sensitive trimming.

Roll is when one wing goes up or down relative to the other. The wings are inclined upwards from the fuselage to prevent rolling. The angle of rise is called the dihedral: on a 747 it is seven degrees. The wings are also swept back to delay the onset of high-speed shock waves, on a 747 by a full thirty-seven degrees.

The wings have hinged surfaces on them called ailerons. They move in opposite directions: if the right aileron is up, the left one will be down. The aircraft will 'bank' towards the aileron that is up – if the right aileron is up, the plane will roll to the right. The pilot controls the ailerons by turning the wheel on his control column to the left or right.

Engine power is controlled by pushing a hand throttle backwards or forwards.

That is the basis of control.

A modern jet airliner has a lot of ironmongery on it, though that does not change the basic rules. Take the wings. On a jet, they are designed for maximum performance at high speed and altitude. They must have low 'drag' to pass cleanly through the air, so they are thin.

What is desirable at high speed is dangerous at low speed. Landing or taking off in a jet would have to be done at a very high and risky speed if the wing stayed the same shape as it is when the plane is cruising six miles high. So the wing has devices built into it which the pilot uses on take-off and landing, but which are tucked away for the rest of the flight.

The most obvious devices are flaps. A simple flap is a section at the back of the wing which is rotated downwards. On a modern aircraft it not only rotates downwards, but it can also be pushed back, which enlarges the size of the wing. Some aircraft have a flap on the back of a flap, called a slotted flap. Other variations are zap flaps, Fowler flaps, blown flaps and split flaps, all of which are on the back of the wing for the same reason. They increase lift because they increase the size of the wing. By going downwards, they also trap the airflow and force it downwards, which pushes the aircraft up.

This means that the aircraft can stay in the sky at much lower speeds.

The flaps are normally fully down for landing, but only partially down for take-off since they slow the plane's acceleration. Thus a high-speed cruise wing is converted into a high lift, low-speed wing for landing.

More lift at low speeds can also be obtained from flaps on the front of the wing. They extend forwards and down. An advantage is that, where flaps on the trailing edge pitch the nose down when they are extended, leading edge flaps counteract this by pitching the nose up. They are called droops, Kreuger flaps, variable camber flaps or slats.

Jet aircraft are so streamlined that it is very difficult to slow them down quickly. Flaps might do this, but they would tear the wings off at high speeds, and on most aircraft they are not safe to use at more than 250 mph.

So the wings are fitted with speed brakes or 'spoilers'. These are panels on the top surface of the wings which can be raised to block the airflow. This cuts the speed very quickly, although it leads to buffeting and noise in the cabin. The spoilers also reduce lift and help the aircraft to lose height. Very powerful spoilers are called 'lift dumpers'.

The passenger's view of a wing whilst an aircraft is landing is impressive. On an aircraft like a Boeing 727, there are six devices used to convert the 'cruising' wing into one that is safe for landing. From the cabin outwards, there are: inboard spoilers, inboard flaps, inboard ailerons, outboard spoilers, outboard flaps, and outboard ailerons. On a 747, there are three Kreuger flaps and ten variable camber flaps on the front of the wing as well.

Hanging all this from the wing creates a lot of drag and wind resistance. The plane tends to descend very quickly, and to have what pilots call a 'high sink rate'. A number of airliners have hit the ground before they got to the runway, because their pilots were used to earlier aircraft which were more gentle in their approach. The Russian Il-62 is so out of balance that it is thought to carry water ballast in the nose, and has a long, low approach pattern.

A jet has to use a lot of power on the landing approach. If the throttles were allowed to idle, it would take six seconds to get back to level flying from even a small rate of descent. So a lot of power is needed, for this and to overcome drag, on the approach.

There are often many changes of engine power and noise during an approach. This is partly because of the sinking effect of the flaps, and partly because if a jet is not set up for exactly the right descent, coarse power changes are needed to get it on to the runway.

The flaps themselves and the undercarriage make a noise when they go down. This worries passengers who have, up until then, been lulled by a near silent cruise and initial descent. It is, however, normal.

Jets have a number of handling problems. One is the high sink rate. Another drawback on the approach to landing is the absence of any propeller wash over the wings to give lift and reduce the stalling speed.

A jet is so streamlined that it can descend at 14,000 feet a minute, though the wings would probably fail if it attempted to pull out of such a dive. The normal descent rate on an approach to landing is only 700 feet a minute. The pilot must not let the plane drop too fast. Once it is allowed to do this, it is very difficult to stop it without losing a great deal of height.

All aircraft will stall. This happens when the lift is so weak that the aircraft falls back towards the ground. The air, instead of flowing over the wing and producing lift, breaks away and the wing becomes an area of turbulence without lift. This 'tired' air reaches the tailplane, and has too little flow for the controls to work. Stalling on propeller aircraft is straightforward. It happens when the forward speed is too low to maintain flight. The aircraft gives plenty of warning by buffeting and shaking. When it stalls, the nose drops straight down. The pilot increases power, or simply waits as speed builds up during the descent, and then pulls the nose back to recover. Some height is lost. It is obviously a dangerous manoeuvre when close to the ground, but it is predictable and straightforward.

The early jets had the same good stalling characteristics. But most modern jets are capable of 'super-stalling', or 'deep stalling', and sometimes it is impossible to recover. Rear-engined, high-tailed jets are the type most at risk. The problem started on civil aircraft with the Caravelle. A stage comes with the nose lifted by about thirty-five degrees, when the aircraft is as stable and immovable as a rock. The drag is so high that no amount of engine power is of any assistance. There is complete lateral control but the aircraft comes down like a lift.

As this type of aircraft stalls, the nose pitches up. This puts the tail into the wash of the wings. The airflow has already stalled over the wings, and so both tail and wings are stalled. Because the tail is stalled the aircraft cannot be pitched nose down, even though only with the nose down can speed increase and the aircraft recover. The wings are stalled, so the pilot cannot bank or roll the plane to an angle that will free the tail from the stalled wing wake.

The aircraft thus drops very rapidly. It will hit the ground slightly nose up, its wings dead level and with almost no forward speed. This is exactly how a British Airways Trident crashed at Staines on 18 June 1972, shortly after take-off. The pilots withdrew the droops on the front edges of the wings at too low a speed, the nose went up, and the aircraft slammed into the ground with all the 'locked-in' stability of a runaway lift.

183

Aircraft like this would not be allowed to fly unless they had an advance warning system to make sure the pilot never gets into a stall. They stall without the buffeting that warned the pilots of earlier planes of imminent danger. This is largely because, as wing design has improved, the air does not separate from the wing so easily, and the aircraft goes into the stall suddenly and without warning.

So the aircraft have 'stick shakers' and bells to warn the pilots of an impending stall. The angle which would induce a super-stall is calculated, and if the angle is coming dangerously close the column control automatically shakes. A motor starts up an out-of-balance weight on the control column, shaking it. Some types, such as the Trident, go even further. They have 'stick pushers'. When the aircraft is near a stall, the control column is automatically pushed forward to get the nose down. The pilot can, however, override the system, and this happened with the Trident crash.*

Some jets are prone to 'Dutch roll'.† The nose yaws from left to right, and this starts the aircraft rolling as well. If the rolling gets bad, the plane will start to sideslip and go out of control.

This is countered by 'yaw dampers' which automatically adjust the rudder to stop the nose-swing. The pilot can deal with it himself by using his ailerons to check the roll, or he can lose height rapidly. Dutch roll is most dangerous at high altitude in thin air where there is less resistance to rolling.

Modern aircraft also suffer from 'jet upsets'. These are high-speed dives, often at a high angle of bank. A jet cruising at high speed is a delicately balanced machine. If it is upset, it will go out of control very rapidly.

This is normally caused by turbulent weather. It can also hap-

* Test pilot D. P. Davis, in *Handling the Big Jets*, published by the Registration Board, Redhill, Surrey, England, points out that tactile warnings are best in aircraft. Of the five senses, two (taste and smell) are useless in the air. Pilots respond best to touch, like the shaking control columns in their hands. Sound, the shouted warning, is also powerful. But visual warnings, such as flashing lights, can easily be ignored. Thus visual warnings of real emergencies, such as fire, are often accompanied by bells and hooters.

† This curious term has been inherited from the sea, and is based on the walk of inebriated Dutch sailors.

pen if an autopilot slips out, if there is a 'runaway stabilizer' where the tailplane starts moving of its own accord, or if the aircraft goes out of trim and stability. The nearer to the speed of sound, the more unstable some aircraft become. The rudders on all jetliners get less effective as the sound barrier approaches. On some the effect is reversed so that pushing right rudder yaws and rolls the plane to the left. Thus, no rudder is used when Concorde is flying supersonically.

Jets use huge amounts of fuel. As it is burnt, the weight of the aircraft gets less and the centre of gravity alters. A pilot has to make sure that the aircraft does not creep out of balance as the flight progresses. A four-engined jet like a 707 or DC8 can 'lose' sixty tons of weight on a flight through fuel consumption and this has to be allowed for in trimming the aircraft. A Jumbo can burn 140 tons of fuel. On Concorde the fuel is pumped around during flight to keep the plane in balance.

Speed is, of course, the essence of flight, the sole justification for jets and particularly Concorde. The indicated airspeed the pilot sees on the clock in front of him has less and less relation with the airspeed as he climbs. The airspeed indicator, or ASI, like the altimeter, is affected by the density of the air. The higher the aircraft climbs, the lower the density of the air, and the more the airspeed indicator underreads. An aircraft with an indicated airspeed of 200 knots at 20,000 feet, for example, will have a true airspeed of some 275 knots.

This is an advantage to the pilot in actually handling the aircraft. The forces of lift and stress on an aircraft also depend on the air density, and so the indicated airspeed is a reliable guide to how an aircraft can be manoeuvred in terms of stallspeed, flap limiting speeds and so forth. In other words, an aircraft behaves much the same at 275 knots at 20,000 feet as it does at 200 knots at sea level.

True airspeed must be known for navigation in order to work out the speed over the ground. To obtain it, the pilot feeds the indicated airspeed, and the height and air temperature, which affect the air pressure, into a mechanical computer which produces true airspeed.

Pilots talk and think in terms of indicated airspeed, and most of the speeds given here are IAS, not true. In general, the higher the altitude, the higher the true airspeed. On a normal day, when the world exactly corresponds in air density to the averaged out International Standard Atmosphere, 160 knots IAS will be accurate at sea level, but will really be 220 knots at 19,000 feet and 323 knots at 37,000 feet.

Height also affects the speed of sound. Above 24,000 feet pilots fly more off the Machmeter than the airspeed indicator: the higher the aircraft flies, the closer it gets to the speed of sound, and this becomes more important than its simple airspeed. A Machmeter shows the speed the aircraft is flying at in relation to the speed of sound, the Mach number.*

The speed of sound or 'sound barrier' is important because of its relation to shock. An aircraft moving at less than the speed of sound sends out waves in front of it that warn of its coming. The airstreams then begin to divide to make way for it, and there is little change in the density of the air as it flows over the aircraft. The waves are similar to sound waves and they travel at the speed of sound.

If an aircraft flies at or near the speed of sound, no warning is sent out in front, and so the air hits the aircraft with a shock. Shock waves form over the aircraft and affect the wings and tail. Shock waves are accompanied by a sudden increase in the air density, a rise in temperature and a decrease in speed.

This causes a sudden and very large increase in drag, resulting in a loss of lift, and severe 'buffeting'. The aircraft's balance may be thrown off, and lead to serious pitching of the nose. These symptoms are very like a stall and severe shock wave effect is called a shock stall.

Shock stalls are highly unpleasant. There is a sudden change of trim, usually slamming the nose down, but sometimes leading to the nose pitching up and down. Very large forces are needed to move the controls. The aircraft will buffet, the ailerons will vibrate and the whole machine will start pitching and yawing oscillations which may go out of control. These may be 'snaking', yawing from side to side, 'porpoising' up and down, or roll and yaw combined in 'Dutch roll'.

* Mach is named after the Austrian scientist Professor Ernst Mach, a nineteenth-century pioneer in observing shock waves.

The control problem can be very severe. If the elevator is in the turbulent air behind a shock wave on the tailplane, the forces on it may be so great that it becomes almost immovable. To avoid this, an all-moving, power-operated tail must be used. (To guard against power failure, modern aircraft have several control surfaces. Concorde, for example, has two rudders, one above the other, and six elevons, combined elevators and ailerons.) Wings are fitted with vortex generators, small metal wedges projecting an inch above the wings and set in lines, which weaken the shock waves.

However, the only way to avoid shock stalls is to fly slowly enough to avoid them – or fast enough to get through the transonic difficulties of the sound barrier and into the less complicated supersonic world. Shock stalls can occur whenever any part of the aircraft is at the speed of sound. The airflow over certain parts of the aircraft, particularly the wings, can reach the speed of sound even though the aircraft itself is travelling well below this.

The speed at which this happens, with its inherent risk of an uncontrollable shock stall, is called the critical Mach number. Each aircraft has its critical Mach number, known by the diminutive of MCr. The simple stall is the critical speed below which the aircraft will go out of control: MCr is the same at the other end of the speed range.

The speed of sound varies with air temperature, and thus with height, and the Machmeter takes this into account. On the basis of the International Standard Atmosphere, in average conditions, the speed of sound is 661 knots at sea level, 640 knots at 10,000 feet, 614 knots at 20,000 feet, 589 knots at 30,000 feet and 573 knots at 40,000. The true speed at which a shock stall will occur on a large modern jet, with a typical MCr of Mach 0.9, is thus 595 knots at sea level, 552 knots at 20,000 feet and only 516 knots at 40,000.

Supersonic aircraft are designed to pass through the sound barrier, and to minimize the effect of shock waves. Concorde does this so well that it is only by looking at the Machmeter that the pilots can tell they are going through the sound barrier.

The double curve, or 'ogee', of Concorde's wings give a very thin wing with low drag. The large wingspan also reduces drag, and the stalling angle is so large it cannot be reached in normal flight. The wings do not need the normal mass of flaps, spoilers and air brakes: the shape means they are good for speeds from 127 knots to 1,260 knots. Flaps are not needed because of the high lift of highly swept back wings, and the cushioning effect of a large delta wing when near the ground. The complex engineering required, however, made it necessary for Concorde to be tested for 5,800 hours before being granted a Certificate of Airworthiness. The subsonic 747 needed only 1,500.

A slim body and thin wings, together with limiting the top speed to just over Mach 2 (twice the speed of sound), have kept Concorde's temperature rise down. It has thus been possible to make most of it from aluminium alloys instead of heavier and more expensive stainless steel or titanium alloys. The relative lightness also reduces the sonic bangs, since these bangs – in fact, the shock wave as the sound barrier is broken, just as with a cracking whip or a bullet – increase in intensity with weight and volume.

Cosmic radiation increases with altitude and Concorde has a radiation meter to warn of high solar-glare conditions, although the radiation doses are substantially less than the limits for industrial workers.

17 Engines

A balloon will fly without power, apart from gas or hot air. Men first crossed the English Channel by air in a balloon in the eighteenth century. But an aircraft needs an engine.

The first engines used were piston engines developed for cars. The ultimate high performance piston engine on aircraft makes Formula One racing-car engines look like power packs for mopeds.

The engines run up to twenty-four cylinders, set in four banks with six cylinders each. At 6,000 rpm they develop over 3,500 horsepower. A single crankpin can have six pairs of connecting rods set on it. Six-throw, seven-bearing crankshafts have to be perfectly machined over months.

Fuel injection and superchargers are used to increase performance at altitude. Automatic controls sensitive to changes in pressure and height cut in the supercharger and prevent the pilot from pumping in too much fuel.

The propellers themselves are geared. At low forward speeds, when taking off or landing, the blades are most effective when they are full on to the airflow. They must force back as much air as possible over the wings to improve lift. Since the airflow is slow, the propellers meet little resistance from it. The full-on attitude is called 'fine pitch'.

As speed picks up, the blades are twisted to give less resistance to the air. The angle to the airflow is 'coarsened' as the blades twist into it. On the most modern of the great piston engines, the pitch is automatically varied at different heights and airspeeds.

If an engine breaks down in flight, the propeller is twisted beyond the coarse position. Only the edge of the blade is into the airflow. This is called 'feathering'. An unfeathered propeller would windmill in the airflow and drag the aircraft off course as well as slowing it.

Beyond fine pitch, the blades can go into reverse. This spins the air forwards and slows the aircraft down on landing. Most prop and propjet aircraft have 'constant speed' propellers. They adjust automatically, twisting to coarse pitch as speed increases and back to fine as it drops off.

Piston engines cannot produce enough power for fast flight. They are easily the most efficient engines at speeds below 300 mph. Over 400 mph, their efficiency tails off quickly. Jet engines bisect propeller engines at just over 400 mph on efficiency graphs.*

Getting more power means increasing the number of cylinders. Simply making larger cylinders is not possible, as they could not be cooled. Valves have to be cooled with molten sodium which splashes between the head and stem to transfer the heat. The pistons are cooled with oil: cooling the oil in radiators and large sumps is difficult.

More cylinders mean more oil. A typical piston aircraft, the DC4, carries twenty gallons of oil for each engine, plus a forty-gallon reserve for topping up. Oil is a harsh master for piston engine crews. Riding on no more than car engines beefed up to the ultimate, permanently going through extremes of temperature, vibration and stress, the crews spend nervous hours watching oil temperatures and oil reserves. A jet engine carries just six gallons of oil – and crews worry if it burns two pints an hour.

Even the sparking plugs are hammered hard. If they are large enough to withstand the pitting caused by sparking, they may not be hot enough to burn off oil when the engine is idling. If they are small and heat up quickly, they will explode the charge before sparking. The heat has to be conducted away from them. ·

Pilots call piston engines 'hot engines'. They are very prone to breakdown. They have reached the limits of design at 12,000 rpm. More power means more massive reduction gears to slow down the revolutions between crankshaft and propeller.

More height means less air for the blades to bite on. At 40,000 feet, where a jet comes into its own, a propeller can only deliver a quarter of the power it has at sea level.

Superchargers can only compensate for a fraction of the loss in rarefied air. Discs in casings on the engines drive air at increased speed into the engine, or feed gases from the exhaust back into the engine. But the faster the propeller blades revolve, the less

* As a rule of thumb, a propeller engine is at peak efficiency at 300 knots, a jet at 1,100 knots and a rocket at 4,300 knots.

effective they are. The tips whirl faster than the speed of sound, and the air buffets off them without producing thrust.

Think of a car engine, driving a propeller instead of wheels. On a typical flight, the outside temperature will vary from 70°F to −40°F. The altitude goes from sea level to 20,000 feet. The rpm reach 12,000, 6,000 is maximum on most cars. It is as if a car was regularly driven up a 20,000 foot mountain, went along a 1,500 mile plateau, and then down again. The propeller pitch is the gear lever, constantly changing. The accelerator has to be adjusted to the height to feed in rich or lean mixture.

Not surprisingly, a classic piston engine like the Wright Cyclone needs a major overhaul lasting six weeks every 2,000 hours. Because the ultimate is squeezed out of a basically crude power plant, the whole is far more complex than a jet.

Flight engineers are needed to nurse them along, playing with fuel mixtures, taking the strain off sick engines by altering oil flow and pitch, listening to the beat of the engines to pick up rough running before it becomes breakdown.

'You have to be a good listener on a piston plane,' says a flight engineer now on Boeings. 'The art is noise vibration, tuning like a mechanic in the pits at Monaco. In a jet you can't hear much, and if you feel any vibration it means the disaster has already happened.'

The reliability of modern jet engines is shown vividly by the maintenance schedules. On a piston engine, 35 days in the air meant 42 days of overhaul on the ground. Turboprops need one day on the ground for every 166 in the air. With pure jets, major overhauls are only needed after 1,000 days in the air.

Piston engines are subject to complaints familiar on cars: piston wear, carburettor icing, crankshaft failures, broken push rods, scoured cylinders. Jets have very few moving parts to go wrong.

Simple turbo jets suck air in at the front through a compressor which impels air in. This raises the pressure of the air three and a half times. This compressed air passes into a combustion chamber where fuel is poured in and ignited in a flame tube. As the hot air expands, it accelerates rapidly through a turbine and out of a propulsion nozzle. The turbine is linked by a shaft to the compressor blades at the front. This is the only major moving part.

The power comes from the rush of air through the propulsion nozzle at the back of the engine. This is, in fact, a 'jet' of air pushing the aircraft along. The faster the aircraft is moving, the more air is forced in by ram effect, and the engine becomes more efficient – quite unlike the piston engine. It is best to give a small increase in velocity to a large amount of air: a large increase in velocity cannot be contained in thrust and is dissipated in the slipstream.

The jet comes in various forms. The 'propjets', Viscounts, Electras, Friendships, Vanguards, seek to make the best of both propeller and jet worlds. They are very efficient at speeds under 425 mph, where the pure jet is still not at its best.

On a propjet, most of the power from the expanding air rushing through the turbine is fed to the propeller. Less goes out through the propulsion nozzles as thrust, although the aircraft is to some extent pushed forward by the jet of air as well as pulled forward by the propellers.

Simple turbojets do not use all the power that is available. 'Bypass' engines, like the Conways on VC10s and some 707s, are more efficient. Part of the air from the compressors goes through the turbines and combustion chambers as normal. But some by-passes this heating stage and pours into the combustion nozzles, where it mingles with the hot air to give additional thrust.

'Fan jets' do not mix hot and cold air like the bypass engines. A large fan is made to work like a propeller at the front of the engine, where it is housed in a special duct. The fan blades are short enough not to break the sound barrier like the tips of ordinary propellers. But they increase the thrust. Also, because the jet velocity is reduced through having to spin them, they are quiet for the amount of power they produce. The DC10 is only half as noisy as the DC8.* They are also very economical.

---

* Frank Tucker of Ontario, Canada, took the most original action of the millions of householders affected by aircraft noise. He decided to frighten off aircraft flying over his house to nearby Buttonville airport. He played a recording of anti-aircraft gunfire through a loudspeaker, and trained a searchlight on aircraft landing at night. Alas, Mr Tucker's wit was not appreciated and he was found guilty on two counts of confusing and distracting the pilots of aircraft. *Globe and Mail*, 9 July 1977.

Both bypass and fanjets can be called 'turbofans', because they use the blades of the turbines like fans (or propellers) to increase the thrust of air from the propulsion nozzles, or 'jet pipes'.

Jet engines are small and light, for the power they produce. The control systems are also simple. Cold air is used to cool them, instead of oil and water. The quadrant at the front of the engine guides the air into the compressors, with their many blades. The speeded air is then partly ducted straight through to the jet pipes, and partly via the combustion chambers and turbines. The basic principle of the jet is that air that has been compressed and heated goes out faster than it came in. The air is accelerated and pushed back.

Heat and stress are the main enemies. The heat in the combustion chamber can reach 2,000°C. Turbines spin at 20,000 rpm in heat of 500°C. They can have 130 blades, all individually shaped and fixed, and all balanced so that they do not vibrate. Compressors come in twelve stages and more, with twenty blades all subjected to great centrifugal stress in each stage. Turbines and compressors do fail, although the engine housing should contain the disintegration.*

'The real problem now isn't ordinary engine failure. The engines themselves rarely go wrong. It's the stuff that's hung on them to feed the plane – the hydraulic pumps, the heating systems, the thrust reversers, the dynamos and generators,' says a senior engineer.

At £700,000 for a new 707 engine, and up to £2 million for 747 engines, they should be good. They are checked every 3,000 hours and have major overhauls only every 24,000 hours, or 12 million miles.

---

* Eighteen million man hours of engineering safety checks went into the 747. Besides being able to contain engine explosions, it has fifty structurally independent control surfaces. It has two rudders, four independent hydraulic power systems and four separate ailerons and elevators. Even the undercarriage is designed to rip off in a crash landing without cutting into the fuel lines.

A 747 at San Francisco hit the approach lights on take-off. This smashed two of the four main undercarriage bogies, knocked out three of the four hydraulic systems and cut through a tailplane spar. Steel girders pierced the cabin, badly injuring two passengers as they sat in their seats. The aircraft landed safely.

'Life limited' parts on the vital compressors and turbines have to be replaced at ages varying from 16,000 to 30,000 hours. This is a huge improvement over pistons.

But gradually engines do wear out, helped by stones, hail and birds damaging fans, and by dust grinding down the parts. They cope with water well, even though a single engine during a take-off in monsoon rain will suck through water at the rate of an Olympic-sized swimming pool a minute.

Million-dollar engines have been lost to rags, stones, and jackets left by maintenance men. A single large bird can explode an engine, and a flock of birds can affect several engines.

Jet engines can be stalled, just as a wing can. If the airflow hits the compressor blades at the wrong angle, the air eddies and swirls about. This causes serious overheating so that the engine has to be closed down.

These flame-outs are usually found only on start-up or when a sudden surge of acceleration is pushed into the engine. Several aircraft have crashed when pilots opened the throttles too suddenly in an overshoot.* Engine-surges can be caused by flying man-oeuvres. If a rear-engined aircraft climbs at too steep an angle, the airflow is blanketed from the engines by the wings. The engines overheat.

The positioning of engines is important, since there are pluses and minuses to all configurations. Burying the engines in the wing roots, like the Comet, means that the thrust is near the centreline of the aircraft. If an engine fails, the aircraft will not swing much. The engines are also close to the centre of gravity, so there is no need for a large tailplane to counteract their weight.

Against this, the cabin is noisy, the fuselage can interfere with the airflow, and a disintegration in one engine can affect the one next to it.

Engines in underslung wing pods, as on the Boeing 707, 737, and DC8, leave a clear wing profile. They are easy to get at for maintenance, and the airflow into them is not affected by the

---

* Auto-reduction sometimes, but not always, prevents this. Safety valves open if sensing devices which observe the jet temperatures, compression pressure and speed show that the safe limits have been exceeded.

fuselage. But an engine failure will lead to yawing, as the plane swings towards the dead engine. Because the engines are slung low, the nose drops when power is reduced, and the engines are prone to swallowing stones from the runway. They are easily scraped if the aircraft lands with one wing low.

Three-engined aircraft have one engine built into the back of the fuselage, like the Boeing 727, DC10, Trident and Tri-Star. The other two engines can be mounted under the wings, or also at the tail.

Other rear-engined aircraft are the twin-engined DC9 and Caravelle and the four-engined VC10.

Rear-engined jets have quiet cabins. There is little yaw if an engine fails. The wing is clear of engine mountings. However, passenger capacity is restricted since some of the rear fuselage is taken up with engines. The intakes can have their airflow interrupted by the fuselage and wings.

The aircraft is naturally tail heavy, so the wings have to be set well back. This in turn leads to a large tailplane which has to be put up high as a T-tail to be clear of the engines. And that gives the aircraft a natural tendency to deep-stall, which has to be overcome with automatic stall warning devices.

A jet engine rated to have 16,000 lb of thrust produces only 42 horsepower when it is stationary before take-off. But this soars with speed: one lb of thrust equals one horsepower at 375 mph, and two horsepower at 750 mph.

So the horsepower of a typical engine varies between 42 on the ground and 25,000 horsepower when cruising at 580 mph. Fuel consumption goes from 738 gallons per hour during a descent to 4,500 gph on take off.

The higher and faster it goes, the more efficient a jet engine becomes.* Speed itself helps by ramming air into the engine. All the air that goes through a jet when it is sitting on the ground has to be sucked in by the compressor, which labours to get it. As the aircraft speeds up, air is pushed into the compressor at a great

---

* The maximum fuel efficiency of the propeller engines in the 1950s was 0.9 kg/kg/hr (or 0.9 kilograms of fuel per kilogram of engine thrust per hour). The first jets used only 0.8 kilograms of fuel for the same effect. Modern jets are below 0.6.

rate. Thus an engine that is idling on the ground goes through three times as much fuel as one that is idle in flight.

Jets really need to suck in air at low speeds. Concorde has an auxiliary door underneath the normal intakes to let in additional air at low speeds. Supersonically, the ram effect of air being blown into the engines at 1,400 mph is so great that a special 'dump door' lets out excess air from the intakes. The jet pipe, which can be narrowed to give maximum velocity to the exhaust as it rushes through, is opened wide. Methanol can be injected into the engine, which cools the air in the compressor and gives added thrust.

A Boeing 707 on a 1,000-mile trip at 18,000 feet will use 900 more gallons of fuel than one at 35,000 feet, and take forty-five minutes longer. Fuel is important: a 707 on a trip from London to Los Angeles will burn up 17,000 gallons.

Fuel management is a vital part of modern flying. Climbing too fast makes the fuel boil and evaporation losses of up to ten per cent have been known on climbs to 35,000 feet. A pilot who starts a descent twenty-five miles early on his engine/fuel optima chart will lose 225 kilos of fuel. If there are twenty other pilots like him, and they average 500 sectors each a year, the airline will be wasting 616,000 gallons a year. If they put down the flaps too early as well, 2,500,000 gallons could be, as the pilots put it, 'pissed out of the window'.

American pilots in particular are checked on their use of fuel. American Airlines saved two million gallons in one year by introducing more stringent taxiing rules.

Flying slowly wastes fuel. A 747 flying to Heathrow from the stack at Ongar via Windsor (some forty miles) will use 200 gallons more if it approaches at 170 knots instead of 200 knots. A Concorde holding at 15,000 feet burns 65 gallons a minute at 200 knots, 52 gallons at 250 knots and only 50 gallons at 300 knots.

Aircraft are very thirsty. The average male passenger with his cabin luggage weighs 165 lb. He consumes his own weight in fuel every 1,500 miles – every time he goes, say, from Britain to Majorca – on a full plane. If he is on a half-empty plane, he is getting through twice his own weight, or some 41 gallons.

The typical fuel flow on a 707 shows the thirst. The 'burn rate' in gallons per minute is 76 on take-off, 32 on noise abatement after take-off, 45 in the climb, 24 on the cruise, 12.3 on the descent, 32.8 on the approach and back up to 50 in reverse thrust on landing. With such large changes in consumption, fuel management is a very important part of a pilot's job (kilos 280, 120, 165, 90, 45, 120 and 180 per minute).

A 747 holds 39,000 (47,000 US) gallons of fuel (177,294 litres for the metrically minded), enough for a good-sized swimming pool. It gets through 3,250 gallons an hour at its cruising speed of 580 mph. That is 0.18 miles per gallon, or five and a half gallons to the mile. The machine can weigh up to 366 tons, and carry a 90-ton payload (the rest is the weight of the aircraft and fuel). It will carry pipes up to 180 feet long with a diameter of eight feet, or 73 VW Beetles, or up to 500 passengers.

The 747 is not that thirsty, either. When full, it can get over 90 passenger miles to the gallon. A BAC1–11 only gets 60, and Concorde 42, which is worse than the old propeller Stratocruisers. Meantime, even a car gets 150 passenger miles to the gallon, when full and driven at optimum speed. Diesel trains get 800.

By 1981 fuel economy had become the biggest problem facing the airline industry. IATA calculated that its members had paid £3 billion more for fuel in 1979 than they did in 1978. British Airways alone burned an average of twenty-six gallons of fuel every second during 1980, spending more than £1 million a day on fuel. Where fuel accounted for twelve per cent of airline costs in 1971, in 1981 it was taking more than twenty-two per cent of total expenditure.

Fuel conservation techniques are an essential part of a pilot's value to his employers. British Airways pointed out to its flight crews that one minute shaved off the time between engine start and pushback, when the aircraft is first moved by the ground tug, saves £500,000 a year on its 747 fleet. A similar amount is saved if a minute can be lopped off the taxi time.

Once aloft, two per cent of fuel or £8 million a year is saved if the aircraft is flown within 2,000 feet of its optimum altitude. Cruising four knots, or some five miles an hour, above the minimum fuel speed wastes £6 million a year.

If the pilot retrims the aircraft after speed changes and as the centre of gravity alters during the cruise as fuel weight reduces, one per cent of fuel or £4 million a year is saved.*

There are potential alternatives to oil. Liquid hydrogen is available, but is highly volatile and needs to be stored and pumped at absolute zero temperature. Insulating it at that temperature during a flight would be difficult and expensive.

Synthetic kerosene can be produced from coal. Again, this is expensive and about six tons of coal are needed to make one ton of aviation kerosene. Much research needs to be done. It is unlikely that synthetic fuels will be important until the end of the century. Until then pilots will be expected to increase their role as fuel systems managers.

Fuel management has one side-effect, in letting passengers know how far they are from their destination. The pilots' rule of thumb for economical descent is that they need 300 feet of height for every mile to go. If the pilot has said that the cruising height is 30,000 feet, when you hear the power come off and the aircraft starts to descend, there will be 100 miles to go.

On a short flight the cruising height may be 24,000 feet. The power should be reduced then with eighty miles to go. The guide is to divide the height by 300, giving the miles to run.

On landing, and on some aircraft whilst still in the air, the engines are put into reverse thrust. A jet engine has two 'clam-shells' in the jet pipe at the back. These two are joined when the pilot lifts the throttles over a special gate into reverse, rather like a car gear lever. The jet pipe is now blocked and special ports open so that the thrust is pushed forwards to brake the aircraft.

This saves brake and tyre wear. Brakes are very efficient but they tend to overheat tyres and wear out the tread.

Turbine blades are the most checked part of an engine. On a

* *Flight* magazine, which organized an international conference on fuel economy in 1980, quotes these figures on the British Airways fleet fuel bills. Concorde costs £2,300 an hour in fuel. 747s cost £1,500. The Super VC10, Tri-Star and DC10 all cost £1,000 an hour each. The 707 cost £750, the Trident £500 and the BAC1-11 500 series £375. The fact that a wide-bodied jet like the Tri-Star costs no more to run than a VC10 shows how much fuel economy has improved with modern aircraft. BA, incidentally, was paying around £400 million for its 824 million imperial gallons of fuel in 1980.

transatlantic flight, each blade will have spun 8½ million times, with great centrifugal force and under great heat. There is also a strong pressure loading as the hot air from the combustion chamber strikes them.

Checkers spend their working lives looking at individual blades for signs of cracks or wear. Isotopes and X-rays are also used. Oil is examined on spectrometers where the slightest trace of metal will be picked up, revealing wear.

Engineers have a nice phrase for engine breakdowns, an 'unscheduled engine removal'. (Flying is full of such expressions. For example, a nose dive is never called a nose dive. It is a 'gross height excursion'.)

It takes five hours to change an engine on a 707. Most jets can carry a spare, fifth engine on a special pylon on the wing. Aircraft that break down in out-of-the-way places have to be 'ferried' home – flown without passengers or payload on three engines.

When an engine fails in the air, the first action the crew take is to call out its number. As the nose swings towards the failed engine, the pilots have to put on rudder to keep straight. They also slap the knee that is pushing the rudder, as confirmation of whether the engine is on the left or right.

Aircraft have been lost after crew selected the wrong engine as failed, and the shouting and slapping is an effective if crude way of preventing this. A BAC1–11 crashed at Milan* after the crew shut down the good engine by mistake. This, on a twin-engined aircraft, left them with no power at all.

The next action is to close the throttle. The essential power generator, which is normally run off the number three engine, is transferred if necessary. Engine numbers run from left to right: the number two is the left inboard engine on a four-engined aircraft, the central tail engine on a tri-jet and the right engine on a twin-jet. The essential power generator runs the radios and vital instruments.

The start lever is then cut off, the ignition and generator breakers are tripped, and the aircraft is trimmed to fly on the remaining engines. A modern twin- or tri-jet can maintain height on one

* The British United Airways crew belly-landed the plane in a snow-covered field. It slid for 460 yards before stopping. The crew got the twenty passengers out safely. HMSO CAP 347.

engine alone. A landing is possible on only one engine on a four-engined jet, although extremely hazardous.

The odds of this happening on modern jets are virtually nil, apart from a human error, such as using the wrong type of fuel, or running out of it. As we shall see, this has happened.

18 The Weather

The sky is as varied in its currents and dangers as the sea, and it is charted in much the same way. Areas of severe turbulence and bad weather are plotted. The direction of airstreams is recorded so that pilots can use them or avoid them. These airstreams can go above 350 mph, faster than most propeller aircraft can fly. The charts show the pilot where he is likely to face icing, fog or sudden wind shears.

The most important winds are the powerful jetstreams, found at cruising height from 25,000 feet to 35,000 feet. These winds have been recorded at 375 mph over the Pacific. Most of them are westerly, which means that they blow from west to east. This is why it takes up to two hours longer to fly from Europe to America than it does to come back.

Jetstreams are rarely so aligned to a route that they blow exactly on the nose or tail. They will normally hit the aircraft at an angle, so that the effect is not exactly opposite on outward and return journeys. Nonetheless, some of the differences are considerable.

Westbound flights across North America lose between 60 and 70 nautical miles every hour because of headwinds. The wind gives them an extra 15 to 20 knots on their speed eastbound. Thus, New York to Los Angeles involves a reduction of speed due to headwinds of 63 nautical miles an hour; Atlanta to San Francisco of 61; Chicago to San Francisco of 58; Montreal to Vancouver of 56. The return flights gain, 19, 14, 15, and 16 nautical miles respectively.

The same order of jetstream exists over the North Atlantic, slowing westbound flights by an average of 62 nautical miles an hour, and speeding those to Europe by some 14. The Pacific, however, is not so consistent. A westbound flight from Los Angeles to Honolulu loses a modest 35 knots, and picks up 6 on the return. But a westbound flight from Tokyo to Hong Kong is set back 71 nautical miles an hour by winds at cruising levels, picking up ten on the return.

Australia sees some of the biggest differences, with flights from

Sydney to Perth westwards penalized by 66 knots, but picking up 24 when returning.

Surface winds are not as strong as these high jetstreams. They are slowed to a third of their speed higher up by the friction of the land. But the winds bounce off obstacles, like hills, woods, even airport buildings, and are gusty and turbulent. The effect on aircraft, which are moving slowly as they take off or land, is greater than at altitude.

Differences in the heat of the earth also affect low-flying aircraft. Sandy and rocky areas and cities are hotter than grassland or lakes or sea. Hot air rises, cool air falls, and the result is severe bumping for the airliner. On sunny days, particularly when passing over coastlines from cool sea to hot land, the bumping from these thermal currents of air can be felt at a considerable height.

Flying at night and on overcast days is normally smoother, since there is less variation in temperature.

Sudden strong winds are a hazard, although the pilot will know when to expect them from his wind charts. The Foehn can be a killer of aircraft. It is a warm, dry mountain wind that can spring from total calm to gale force in three minutes. It is normally a spring wind, which gusts down valleys on the lee side of mountains. It brings avalanches for skiers as well as trouble for aircraft.

It is most dangerous in the Alps, particularly at Innsbruck, although it also affects ranges as small as the Scottish Cairngorms. In the American Rockies, it is called the 'chinook' – ironically an American helicopter is named after it.

'Funnel winds' are accelerated by being forced through valleys. One of the most severe of these winds is the 'mistral' which is intensified by passing through the Rhone Valley. It affects several Mediterranean airports.

'Ravine winds' are common in valleys that penetrate mountain ranges, and the tunnel effect makes them strong. The winds stay strong and gusty even in open country after leaving the valley mouth. A ravine wind affects Genoa, the 'kosava' rips along the Danube close to Belgrade, the 'vardar' can make landing at Salonika dangerous.

Fog is widespread in Europe, particularly in the spring and early summer. It is worst where an arid hinterland adjoins a coast. Southwest Africa, Chile, Morocco and California, the experienced pilot will know, are more of a hazard than ever was foggy London town.

Duststorms blot out visibility as brutally as fog. The dust soars up to 15,000 feet, wearing out engines like sandpaper. The danger areas are well marked: Central and Southwest Asia, the Sahara, Southwest Africa and the Kalahari, northern Chile and central and southeastern Argentina, the central and southwestern United States, the interior and west of Australia. Pilots particularly fear the 'haboobs' of the Sudan. These storms toss sand up to 10,000 feet with gusty winds within eight minutes of starting. Like all sandstorms, they are best avoided by flying at night when there is less wind.

Pilots steer clear of cumulonimbus clouds, the distinct anvil-shaped thunderclouds. The turbulence within these is vicious enough to tear an aircraft to pieces. The vertical speed of hot air rising is often more than thirty feet a second – going up at more than 100 mph, strong enough to stop the largest raindrop from touching the ground, and to whip a man on a parachute thousands of feet upwards.

There are thunderstorms on more than 110 days a year in southern Mexico, Panama, central Brazil, central Africa and Madagascar. Java has 220 days a year with thunderstorms – the most in the world.

Britain and northwest Europe in August, the southern Mediterranean in October, India during the monsoons, Hong Kong in September – these are times when pilots are on their guard.

Summer heat causes frequent storms in the central and eastern US. The crash of a jetliner in the summer of 1975 shows the dangers. An Eastern Airlines Boeing 227 crashed when it ran into a thunderstorm whilst approaching JFK airport in New York, killing 113.* The National Transportation Safety Board found that the Eastern pilots had encountered a severe wind change, and that they did not immediately recognize that they were descending faster than normal.

The board added a chilling rider: even if they had recognized

* ICAO Summary No. 7/75. About five minutes before the crash, a Flying Tiger DC8 had warned of a windshear on the runway, JFK's 22 Left. A Lockheed Tri-Star reported a windshear two minutes before the crash. There were eleven survivors out of 124 aboard.

the descent rate, 'the adverse winds might have been too severe for a successful approach and landing'.

Revolving storms are found in every tropical ocean except the South Atlantic. Cyclones in the Bay of Bengal and the Arabian Sea, hurricanes in the West Indies and South Indian Ocean, typhoons in the South China Seas, willy-willies in Western Australia – the names differ, but turbulence and wind shifts are common to all.

Pilots know when to expect them, and where. From June to October they ravage the northern hemisphere, from December to April the southern. They can be detected in the same way as thunderclouds, with weather radar. This reflects the water content of clouds, and an experienced pilot can distinguish thunderclouds, revolving storms, snow and hail.

Areas of 'mountain waves' are charted. Hills and mountains cause the air to form waves on the lee side, the far side from where the wind is blowing. The wind accelerates and lifts as it passes over the top of the obstacle, but can then break downwards in a welter of turbulence like a sea wave as it breaks. Wave effects from mountain ranges like the Andes can be felt as high as 80,000 feet.

Both the updraughts on the windward, and downdraughts on the lee side can be very strong. Even over the Welsh hills, vertical currents can reach thirty feet a second. In the US, the powerful waves of the Sierra Nevada rise at seventy-five feet a second – ten times faster than a lift, and faster than the plane itself can climb.

The waves should be smooth at height over mountains. Only the pilot would notice them through the change in his altimeter. But the waves can break.

When they do, they can have standing crests like a surf wave. In the area under it, called the 'rotor zone', lurks extreme danger and turbulence. It was a rotor zone that hurled a Uruguayan airliner down 2,000 feet on to a snowfield in the Andes. The survivors were forced to eat the flesh of the crash victims to stay alive before being rescued.

There are 'killer waves' which contain huge destructive power. They occur when the cross-section of the mountain coincides with the natural pattern of the wind wave. This greatly exaggerates the effect like a giant tuning fork. Mountains like the Alps, where air flows over a series of ridges, can build up confused wave patterns as one wave runs into another.

Clear air turbulence – CAT to flight crew – is found at cruising heights. It is a strong horizontal and vertical wind shear affecting a jetstream. CAT is probably caused by large temperature changes in the air at high altitude.

The temperatures move in horizontal bands, and CAT lurks where they meet. CAT is normally no more than a high-speed jarring, like driving fast over a cobbled road. But it can damage or destroy aircraft.

Pilots receive a stream of weather reports as they pass along their route. The international weather code, called SYNOP, gives them eight groups of information. It is detailed enough to keep them out of trouble.

A typical message reads: 03772 60110 66022 09410 36202 03001 83830 86075.* It does not sound very inspiring. But this is what it reveals:

The pilot is over the British Isles. Heathrow is covered by six-eighths cloud. The wind is blowing from 010 degrees at ten knots. The horizontal visibility is sixteen kilometres. The cloud cover has not changed in the past half-hour and more than half the sky is cloud covered.

The barometric pressure is 1009.4 millibars, the temperature is 10°C, three eighths of the sky is covered by (harmless) cirrocumulus cloud though some (bumpy) cumulus is present.

The lowest cloud base is between 3,000 and 5,000 feet. There is no medium-high cloud, although there is dense but harmless cirrus above 20,000 feet. The dew point is 3°C. The barometric tendency during the past three hours has been to increase, decrease and increase again, although never by more than 0.1 millibars. There is three-eighths cumulus cloud at 3,000 feet and six-eighths cirrus cloud at 25,000 feet.

Which all means that there will be a couple of small bumps on the way down, and that passengers will get a good view of London and arrive on a day which, by London standards anyway, is not bad.

* Quoted in the *Handbook of Aviation Meteorology*, HMSO, London, 1971. This is the standard work on the subject.

The pilot will also know that the high-flying jetstreams over England are westerlies above 15,000 feet in both hemispheres regardless of what the surface winds are doing. It may, in fact, be blowing very hard from the east on the surface but it is still a westerly at height.

Things are more complicated in the tropics. Away from the equator, the surface trade winds, the easterlies are replaced by westerly jetstreams above 10,000 feet. But nearer the equator, an easterly jetstream stretches in a 1,100-mile belt from Africa to South America across the South Atlantic. It blows from the east at a steady seventy knots, attracting aircraft flying from Europe to South America, but sending those returning to Europe 1,000 miles further north. In West Africa and in India, these easterly jetstreams dominate the southwest monsoons above 10,000 feet.

Where the trade routes were laid out for the sailing clippers, the trunk routes for modern jetliners are also mapped and noted. The greatest trunk route is across the North Atlantic, with over 400 aircraft plying it every day. In winter the jetstreams above 20,000 feet are west-southwest from the United States, becoming west as they near Europe. Winds are frequently 100 knots and sometimes more than 200 knots. They generally add an hour on to a London–New York flight.

The weather is very changeable, and pilots have to use head-wind/tailwind charts to compute a best course and height.

These are based on the frequency distribution of wind strength and direction at various heights along the route.* A pilot must work out a course that uses the wind to best advantage, and also maximizes fuel economy through the right height and speed.

CAT is common on the North Atlantic and so is turbulence over the sea as unstable polar air drifts further south in summer.

---

* Weather hazards are dependent on height. Wind and temperature affect all aircraft, from 0 feet to 80,000 feet. Subsonic and transonic aircraft in the sea-level to 40,000-feet belt meet heavy rain and icing. Transonic and supersonic aircraft can meet clear air turbulence, wave motion and lee waves above 20,000 feet. Supersonic aircraft above 50,000 feet can be preyed on by horizontal temperature variation, cosmic radiation during solar flares and radioactive debris. Hail can be dangerous down to ground level: a Southern Airways DC9 crashed at New Hope in the US on 4 April 1977 after double engine failure in a hailstorm.

It is very cloudy: average cloud cover is six eighths. There is a danger of severe airframe icing in clouds, particularly at fronts. Fog is frequent on both American and European coasts.

Things improve a little in the summer. The Icelandic low of winter is replaced by weak low pressure over northeastern Canada. The Azores high-pressure system strengthens and moves five degrees north. There are fewer gales and the jetstreams are not so strong. However, summer visibility over the Atlantic is actually worse than in winter.

There are predictable problems at airports on both sides of the Atlantic. Heathrow has frequent fog, aggravated by smoke when the wind is from the northeast to east-southeast. Prestwick has good visibility. Keflavik suffers from gales seven days a month in the winter, with frequent drifting snow and drizzle. Montreal is snow-affected and often has a low cloud base. New York has poor visibility when a front is moving through. Bermuda has severe gales in winter, and a hurricane season from August to November.

The subsidiary trunk route in the Atlantic runs on to the West Indies and South America. The West Indies have three hurricanes on average during the August to October season. Recife in Brazil has cloud and rain from March until August. Kingston reaches a thunderstorm high in September, Trinidad in August.

The second great trunk route is from Northern Europe to Athens via Munich or Rome and on to Cairo and Beirut. Europe gradually changes from an oceanic to a continental system as the influence of the Atlantic slowly dies out inland. The westerly jetstreams get stronger with height. Mean speeds of 100 mph at 30,000 feet are common. So too are icing, fog and low cloud. Cloud cover averages six eighths in winter, only improving to five eighths in summer.

The Mediterranean is warmer than the surrounding land in winter. Pilots have to watch out for squalls and showers, though the skies are generally clear. In the summer, with the sea now cooler than the land, light northerly winds set in, with quiet cloudless weather.

There are only light jetstreams in the western Mediterranean, although they pick up further east, reaching 90 mph over Cyprus.

The Mediterranean has some savage local winds which can destroy aircraft. The mistral blows violently from the north and northwest in the Gulf of Lions and the Gulf of Genoa. Marseilles airport is particularly troubled by it. A similar wind, the bora, lashes the eastern Adriatic. At Trieste, the bora can blow at 80 mph, with gusts of 115 mph putting aircraft landing or taking off at hazard.

The sirocco affects the western Mediterranean, with strong gusts and poor visibility. The khamsin, a southerly wind off the desert, brings sandstorms to Egypt.

The trunk route on to the Gulf of Iran is liable to duststorms when the wind is in the south and southeast. The shamal, a northwesterly gale strength wind, often kicks up vicious sandstorms over Iraq. The jetstream blows from the west at a steady 115 mph.

Conditions deteriorate further on towards Calcutta. Severe turbulence rides with the southwest monsoon from mid-June to mid-September. Cyclonic storms lash the Bay of Bengal. The jetstream turns to the east, blowing back towards Europe.

Karachi is subject to duststorms, low cloud in summer and heavy rain in the southwest monsoon. Bombay has thunderstorms and squalls in June. Calcutta is hit by 60-mph squalls in the evenings during the hot season.

The easterly jetstream remains onwards to Rangoon and Singapore. During the northeast monsoon, from December to February, aircraft hug the west coast of Malaya. The east coast is subjected to severe thunderstorms and wild turbulence as the northeast monsoon drives in from the South China Sea. But when the southwest monsoon blows, in the summer, the east coast is the best protected.

Flying conditions are often difficult in this region. Huge thunderstorms rage, particularly in the afternoons. At night 'Sumatras', violent squalls, drive across the Malacca Straits. Singapore suffers from low cloud and strong gusts one day in two throughout the year.

The equatorial rainy climate continues from Djakarta most of the way to Darwin in northern Australia. Cloud, thunderstorms and heavy rain cover the islands, and tropical cyclones veer across the Timor Sea from January to March. In Darwin itself, dust haze cuts visibility to less than 100 yards.

The westerly jetstreams start up again between Darwin and

Sydney and Melbourne. Severe duststorms are blown in with hot, dry air from the interior of Australia. Cold fronts bring 'southerly busters' – cold, strong and violent winds – to New South Wales. Sydney also has the aptly named 'black northeasters' sweeping in with low cloud. Duststorms are driven in front of northwesterlies. By contrast, peaceful Melbourne suffers from nothing more than light fog.

From Singapore to Hong Kong and Japan, the 'crachin' predominates from January to April on the long haul from Cape Cambodia to Shanghai. Siberian air mixes with the warm sea air and produces a low cloud, drizzle and mist like Scottish mist for long periods. Storms in western Japan can be severe.

The westerly jetstream is at its strongest here. One stream reaches from Tibet to southern Japan. Its *average* speed in winter over Yokohama is 175 mph. It can go above 225 mph, bringing severe CAT.

The China Seas are liable to typhoons from May to November. Many curve and move over Japan. Occasionally, one slips the other way into the Gulf of Thailand. The hot, sticky weather brings thunderstorms. Twenty typhoons a season affect the area.

Hong Kong's Kai Tak airport can be weather-affected. A report by 1 IADU of the RAF in May 1978 noted that severe turbulence is usually found when the wind off the hills round Kai Tak exceeds twenty knots. Wind shear and turbulence are particularly expected over the northwest approach area to the runway when the wind is strong and blowing from between northwest and east-northeast. This normally involves a tropical cyclone or a strong winter monsoon.

Typhoons from May to November can exceed sixty-five knots at the terminal, with gusts well over 100 knots. In winter, between November and March, the monsoon from the northeast can blow at gale force. In summer, occasionally, when the southwest monsoon is particularly strong, there can also be mean speeds of thirty- three knots with gusts over sixty knots.

Conditions on the long polar route back to Europe from Japan are surprisingly good. Although ice-fog is a hazard when fog particles freeze, icing itself is not severe. It is mostly too cold for moisture to develop. The visibility, especially in winter, is excellent.

Icing is not much of a trouble on jets. The friction of the speed through the air generates enough heat on the airframe to keep ice away. Jet engines produce large amounts of hot air which can be piped to danger points. The air at the cruising height of jets is so cold that it is dry and cannot hold much moisture (indeed, it is so cold that an early problem with jets was that the kerosene fuel turned to wax. Research came up with a kerosene that only froze at $-50°$ C).

Icing is a most serious problem on propeller aircraft. Alcohol is sprayed on to the propellers to keep ice away. There are rubber tubes on the leading edges of the wings which continuously inflate and deflate, splintering the ice away. Hot air from the exhausts is piped into the carburettors. But the main defence is to climb, as the ice is slung off the propellers and bangs against the cabin, and the controls wallow and the speed drops off, to climb, seeking cold and dry air, and move out of the ice belt.

Some of the smoothest flying in the world is to be had over the wastes of the Arctic. Some of the most dangerous is said to be in the 'Bermuda Triangle'. It is worth taking a look at this claim, and the similar reports of flying saucers and other Unidentified Flying Objects.

The Bermuda Triangle spans an area of the Western Atlantic bounded by Florida, Puerto Rico and Bermuda, where aircraft and ships are said to vanish without trace. Legend has it that they are snatched away by an inexplicable force, possibly from space. Last messages from the doomed crew members are said to tell of Unidentified Flying Objects, spinning compasses, strange surges of power.

It might seem to take a special brand of courage by pilots and passengers to fly in this area. However, the facts are rather different. The air safety record in the Triangle is actually better than it is in the continental US as a whole. Where Charles Berlitz in his book *The Bermuda Triangle* has two KC135 jet stratotankers disappearing 'in strange circumstances' in 1963 with wreckage from each being found hundreds of miles apart, the actual accident report shows that wreckage from both planes was found at one spot. A mid-air collision in turbulent conditions was given as the cause of the crash: the aircraft were flying in close formation at the time.

Again, Triangle enthusiasts say that a US Navy flight, Flight 19, disappeared in daylight in clear weather in December 1945. But US Navy records show that the five Avenger bombers with twenty-seven crew disappeared after dark in stormy conditions after the flight leader, Lieutenant Charles Taylor, had totally mistaken his position. He thought he was flying over islands off southern Florida, when in fact they were off the Bahamas. Navigational error, and not the strange faces of the unknown, was responsible for the flight running out of fuel and crashing into the rough Atlantic.

A plane with thirteen aboard took off on a rescue mission, and is said to have also disappeared, a victim of the Triangle. But a nearby ship saw it explode. It was known as the 'flying gas tank' because of the amount of fuel it carried.

In another incident, an Eastern Airlines jet flying to Miami is said to have been lost on radar for ten minutes. Full emergency services were called out for its landing. But the puzzled crew had no idea anything was wrong – until they checked their watches. All the crew and passengers found that their watches were ten minutes slow.

This would be a tremendous tale, except no date, time or flight number is given for the incident and neither Miami airport nor Eastern Airlines has any record of it.

If the Triangle is slight and suspect, a mass of sightings of Unidentified Flying Objects have been made by pilots and passengers. The term 'flying saucers' itself comes from a pilot, Kenneth Arnold. A 32-year-old businessman, piloting his own plane, he was near Mt Rainier in Washington State when he saw a chain of nine 'saucer-like' objects flying from north to south. That was on 24 June 1947 and there have been many thousands of sightings since.

These were taken seriously enough for the US Air Force to set up a series of investigations beginning in 1948 as Project Sign and followed by Projects Grudge and Blue Book. A contract was also awarded to the Rand Corporation for an independent study of flying saucers. Alas for the saucer enthusiast, all the studies concluded that the saucers were all misinterpretations or inventions and not from space.

The Arnold sighting was put down to temperature inversion,

where 'mirages of moisture' can appear in the sky. An apparently sensational case, where an Air Force captain was killed while climbing to intercept a reported UFO over Kentucky, had a similarly mundane solution. The UFO was either the planet Venus or a US Navy balloon. The pilot died because he blacked out through lack of oxygen in the climb, and the aircraft went into an uncontrollable spin.

It is thought that at least ninety per cent of sightings are in fact of natural or man-made objects, commonly aircraft, satellites, meteors and stars and planets. The crew of a British Airways jet on a flight in 1977 to Faro in Portugal saw 'UFOs' on the outward and return sectors. These were established to be meteorological balloons. The remaining ten per cent are fraudulent, notably from people who claim to have been abducted by UFO occupants. Thus two American shipyard workers who claim to have been seized by visitors from space with lobster-like claws had their lie detector tests, the sole evidence for their story, conducted by an unqualified operator in uncontrolled conditions.

Although pilots and passengers will continue to see UFOs, it is very unlikely that any of them will collect the huge reward offered to the first person who proves that UFOs are from outer space and not natural phenomena. The *National Enquirer* in the US is so confident of the impossibility of this that it has put up its reward from $100,000 to $1 million. Vapour trails, clouds, balloons and planets do not count.

19 Flight Deck

There is a stately progress to a flight. The pilot checks in ninety minutes before take-off. The first call is the duty room. The pilots start collecting the paperwork; airways maps of the route to be flown, flight manual for the aircraft, emergency checklists, forms for the number of passengers and cargo weight.

The meteorological office supplies weather maps, and reports from airports along the route. A weather man gives a brisk briefing on wind, cloud, temperature, pressure and any special difficulties expected.

The papers are in rows of boxes. The pilots go round picking up the sheets they need like guests at a buffet lunch. One set of papers covers most of the major airports. It shows, for example, runway repairs in progress at Frankfurt, a new terminal under construction at Palma, navigational equipment out of service at Malaga.

A map on the wall divides the world up into sectors. Red flags with numbers are pinned on it. The numbers refer to sheets in other boxes: a glider competition over Salisbury Plain, military target practice in southern France, naval gunnery off Malta. It is important that the pilot keeps clear of the military. A French Caravelle flying from Corsica to France was shot down by an accidentally fired missile over the Mediterranean.

The aircraft itself needs documents, its certificates of registration, radio, insurance and of airworthiness, and its log of all past flights.

The paperwork disappears into the battered leather attaché cases that most aircrew carry. Flying involves a great deal of form-filling. The most important is the flight plan. The pilot fills in his expected time of departure and arrival, and the route he wants to take. The details are sent to air traffic controllers down the route.

The pilots wait in a rest room for a crew bus to take them out to the aircraft. The flight crews introduce each other. The crew must be 'airfield qualified', and know the airports *en route*. This can be simply a film of the approach for easy airports. For difficult ones like Hong Kong and Gibraltar, the crew must have flown it with a route captain before tackling it on their own.

Once everyone knows who's who, they set off for the aircraft. The captain walks round it, looking for any external damage, checking tyre pressures on the undercarriage or 'gear'. The cockpit (the 'flight deck' or 'office' as the crew call it) is small. It is crowded with over twenty square feet of knobs, buttons, levers and lights.

The captain's first check is to see that all switches are off. Aircraft switches are down for off and up for on, Continental-style. He looks for the emergency kit, an axe, walk-round oxygen, CO_2 extinguisher, first-aid kit, rain repellent, asbestos gloves and goggles in case of fire.

The captain then reads the log book, in which previous pilots will have noted any of the plane's defaults and snags, from faulty warning lights to torn pillow cases in the passenger cabin.

Slowly and methodically, the captain and first officer go through the checklist of controls and instruments. There are fifty-nine pre-flight checks on a 707. Most of this goes by without any noticeable event, but the checks for the stall warning are spectacular. A light flashes on and off, a hooter grunts, and the control column shakes with the stickshaker.

Fire bells clang, and a strident bell comes from the undercarriage lock control. The cacophony can be intense. Some aircraft have so many audible warnings that they have to use a tape-recorded voice to shout out what is happening. A bell rings, and a voice shouts, 'Fire, fire.' When the height warning device goes off, the voice shouts, 'Pull up! Pull up!'

The chief steward tells the captain the number of passengers. He confirms when they are 'all strapped in and calm'. If they are not all calm, but noisy and boisterous, the captain will go back and talk to them. Any fighting drunk or hysteric who might endanger the flight is taken off at the captain's discretion.

From now on, the pilot will refer to 'people' if he means only the passengers. If he means the total, passengers and crew, he refers to 'souls'. So a flight can have 150 people and ten crew, or 160 souls. Nobody quite knows why.

The captain now computes his take-off speed: the weight of the aircraft should be accurate to the nearest passenger.*

Take-off speed is computed by taking aircraft weight, air temperature, altitude of the airport and wind speed. These are plotted on graphs, which show the speed at which the aircraft will fly, and also the correct throttle settings to get enough engine power. The worst combination is a heavy aircraft, in thin, hot air at a high altitude, with no wind to take off into. The carrying capacity of a 707 is halved at an airport at 7,000 feet compared with one at sea level.

Temperature and altitude are crucial. Concorde can take ninety passengers from London to Bahrein. But she can only bring sixty back: her take-off performance in the hot air of Bahrein is much inferior to that in London. Planes using airports that are both high and hot are very restricted in their loads. Addis Ababa, Nairobi, Bogota and Mexico City are examples.

One knot is added for every quarter degree of upslope on the runway or subtracted for downslope. One knot is also added for every eighteen knots of headwind, to extend decision time. A knot is subtracted for every three and a half knots of tailwind, which should never exceed ten knots.

The captain writes the power settings he has calculated on to a card. Three speeds are written down. There is V1, the decision speed beyond which the pilot must continue to take off even if he loses an engine. VR is the speed at which he rotates the aircraft, by pulling the nosewheel off the ground. V2 is the safe take-off and climb-out speed and also the speed at which the aircraft can fly safely with one engine out.

Speed is calculated in knots, a nautical mile per hour, up to 24,000 feet. One nautical mile is 1.1515 miles, so 100 knots is 115 miles an hour. Above 24,000 feet, the aircraft speed is calculated by the Mach number, its speed relative to the speed of sound.

The speeds are set on the plane's airspeed indicator with white

* Airlines work on the assumption that women average sixty-five kilos and men seventy-five. The pilot adds five kilos for footballers and the like, who tend to be heavy. Ten kilos are added for merchant seamen, who carry a lot of kit.

'bugs' or movable pointers. The co-pilot will shout them off as the speed needle passes each bug.

The speed qualities of his aircraft are vital to the pilot. He must remember them continuously, even though they alter as fuel weight is reduced. These figures must be engraved in his mind; Vms, minimum stalling speed; Vmca, minimum control speed in the air; Vmcl, minimum control speed on landing.

Vc is the cruise speed (Mc if the speed is in Mach terms). Vra is the rough air, or turbulence speed. Vne is the never exceed speed and Vmo the maximum operating speed. Exceed these and the aircraft could break up. On landing, he must check the Vle, Vf and Vt – landing gear extended, flaps down and target on threshold speeds.

Permission to start engines comes from the control tower. The crew work through eleven pre-start checks. The engines are spun with compressed air, and fuel is pumped in and lit. A tug appears at the nose and pulls the plane into position. 'Taxi clearance', permission to move off to the runway, is given.

The pilot needs a lot of power to start the plane moving. The weight of plane and fuel is near the maximum, and he must never taxi at more than thirty mph. Turning corners, using the steerable nosewheel controlled by a steering wheel in the cockpit, he slows down to fifteen mph. A further eleven check items are performed during the taxi: window heat, probe heat on the airspeed indicator, flaps selected, yaw damper, flaps down correctly, radar sweep, attitude stall warning, departure clearance, radios, take-off speeds bugged.

The aircraft has ordinary brakes on its wheels like a car, with brake pedals at the pilot's feet, but they overheat if used too much. There is an emergency hydraulic system with ten brake applications in it if the brakes fail.

If a pilot swings off the narrow taxiways whilst turning, he will almost certainly bog down in the grass. The main wheels can be 100 feet behind the cockpit, so there is a tendency to try to cut corners. Fuel, freight and passengers must be removed before tractors try to drag it free.

Take-off speed on a laden jet on a hot day can be more than 200 mph, which is the normal top speed for tyres. There are special high-speed tyres, good up to 225 mph, with fusible plugs that will deflate the tyre before it explodes.

Overheated and burst tyres can set a plane on fire when they are retracted into the wheel wells after take-off. Most of the inhabitants of a Swiss village died like that when their chartered jet caught fire.

The jet is held at the end of the runway whilst the final nine checks are done. The parking brake is checked 'off' – although the check will not necessarily show if the brakes are sticking. A big DC8 jet crashed when it tried to take off with the brakes on at Anchorage, Alaska, on 27 November 1970. The ice-covered runway was slippery enough for it to reach 120 mph even with the brakes on.

All engine instruments must be in the green sector, not red. All controls should be free: aircraft have gust locks put in the controls to stop the surfaces flapping in high winds when they are parked. Airliners have crashed after trying to take off with the locks still in. Indeed, a Canadian DC8 crashed at Heathrow after the captain, who had 21,428 hours of flying time, throttled back after taking off. He mistakenly thought the gust locks were still in.

The flaps are partly down, at fourteen degrees. Take-off trim must be selected, the aircraft correctly balanced. Fuel must be sufficient and flowing. The 'squawk', a transponder that will identify the aircraft on the controller's radar, is set.

Take-off clearance is radioed from the tower. The pilots check visually that there is no other aircraft in the way. They cannot, however, look backwards to see if another plane is trying to land on top of them.

The pilot now concentrates on his seven basic instruments. The airspeed indicator gives his speed through the air in nautical miles an hour, or knots. He must make sure that the hollow tube on the outside of the plane which measures the thrust of air does not ice up. If it does, the indicated speed will drop and he will put the nose down and increase power in the mistaken belief that he is going too slowly. Eighteen passengers literally hit the roof on a German flight when the pilot pushed the nose down after failing to switch on the pilot head heater swith. A Northwest 727 stalled at 24,800 feet and crashed twelve minutes out from JFK. The pilot head heaters were not on, and the pilots stalled the aircraft through reacting to false indicated airspeeds. The left tailplane was torn off in the stall at 3,400 feet and the three-man crew was killed as it slammed into the ground near Stony Point, NY.*

The artificial horizon shows the aircraft's attitude relative to the horizon. It uses a silhoutte of a plane. If the model plane is below the horizon line on the instrument, it is nose down: if above, it is climbing. If the horizon tilts to the left, the plane is banked to the left, and the same for the right. Without an artificial horizon, most pilots lose control of an aircraft in cloud in forty-five seconds. Unlike birds, man must have a horizon to orientate himself in space. A British Airways Comet crashed at night in Ankara because a small screw in the artificial horizon worked loose and jammed it. On take-off, the captain could not get the right angle of climb on the horizon and continued pulling back on the controls until the aircraft was pointing almost vertically up. It then stalled and crashed, killing twenty-seven.

The rate-of-climb indicator shows quickly how fast the plane is going up or down. It reads in hundreds of feet per minute.

The altimeter shows height. It can be set to height above sea level, or height above an airport. It depends on knowing barometric pressure for its accuracy, which must be radioed to the pilot from the ground.

There is a gyro compass, and a special radio compass which points towards radio beacons.

The instrument landing system, the ILS, has two needles, one showing if the aeroplane is to right or left of the runway, and another showing if it is too high or low. When they are centred, the plane is on course to land.

The initial roll is slow as the throttle settings are pushed forwards towards their targets. The movement is coarse and bumpy as the speed builds up, and the rudder comes in to replace the nosewheel steering at eighty mph. Fairly hard heaves are needed on the rudder to keep the nose straight at low speed.

A warning horn at this stage of take-off means that the aircraft is not safe to take off: the speed brakes are not locked away, the stabilizer trim is not in the green, or the flaps are not at the correct

* NTSB *AAR* 75-13. The crash was on 1 December 1974.

take-off angle. A Lufthansa 747 crashed at Nairobi killing fifty-nine because a wrong flap selection was not noticed during the take-off roll.

Passing through ninety mph, the acceleration builds up much faster. The needle on the airspeed indicator winds up rapidly towards the first white bug, the decision speed. At thirty seconds, well into the roll with the speed over 110 mph, the rudder is much more sensitive. Kicking it too hard can put a wing down and start a cartwheel crash.

If an engine is lost at this stage, only just enough rudder must be pushed on to counteract the swing. The decision must be made quickly. An average decision speed for jets is 150 mph. To stop, the power comes off, wheel and speed brakes go on, and reverse thrust is applied. The skill is keeping straight.

The runway is blurring now, and the nose has to be kept on it by firm forward pressure on the stick. The thousand-feet-to-go boards flash past, and the runway bumps jar less as the wings begin to take some of the weight. V1 is shouted as the needle passes the first bug. Very shortly afterwards comes Vr. The control column is palmed rather than pulled back, although it needs firm movements at these low speeds. The nose lifts and the tyre marks on the runway beneath drop away.

At V2, a steady pull back on the stick and the nose comes up further. Tugging too hard scrapes the tail along the ground: 747s can do this. A last slight bump from the undercarriage and the aircraft flies, almost imperceptibly until a crosswind catches it and floats it across the runway.

Once airborne, typically fifty seconds after brakes off, the full power of a jet is felt. The landing gear retracts, the airspeed indicator winds round and the altitude builds up. This phase is called the 'climb-out'. There is a sinking feeling as the flaps come up in stages, but after edging the nose forward for a few seconds the speed and rate of climb pick up again.

Noise abatement is awkward. After a quick initial climb to put the aircraft and the noise as high as possible, power is reduced when it crosses housing. The aircraft is often in a turn, under air traffic control and in cloud. The rhythm of the flight is not yet established.

The flight engineer leans forward and eases the throttles back.

The steady increase in values – height, speed, crew coordination – is immediately diminished.

As the power comes off, the nose drops, and the pilot flicks the stabilizer to retrim with a loud clatter of noise. The momentary lack of trim at low height and low speed is unpleasant, and the controls, which have been improving steadily in feel, appear to get mushier again.

The pilot has to think ahead. The values of jet flying are high, in speed, height and weight. The factors multiply very rapidly. The aircraft should be in a nicely trimmed climb at 1,000 feet but the pilot must already concentrate ahead on cutting the power for noise abatement.

Otherwise he will be through 2,000 feet before he knows it. He will have to heave forward on the control column, cut back power, perhaps be forced to bring in flaps and then re-extend them, whilst worrying about height. Erosion of concentration on a modern jet is severely dealt with: a new Tri-Star of United Airlines crashed into the Everglade swamps in Florida whilst the crew, unaware of their high rate of descent, chatted about a faulty warning light.*

Once noise abatement is over, the throttles move forward again and the flaps come fully in. The aircraft settles into the climb. The main tailplane keeps the aircraft in the right attitude for the climb, and the pilot gets the precise angle with the stabilizer, flicking it up or down with the knob on the control column. Its rattle keeps the radio company as it clatters on to new frequencies for the different air traffic controllers.

Best climbing speed is normally 280 knots. The rate of climb depends greatly on the aircraft's load and the local temperatures. A lightly loaded jet could get to 30,000 feet in fifteen minutes. It could take forty minutes if it is hot and heavy.

The autopilot is switched on. There is an occasional rattle from the stabilizer as it counters passengers moving about in the cabin: one person going to the toilet makes enough difference in trim for 'George', as pilots call the faithful autopilot, to counteract it.

The cockpit heats up as the sun splashes off the glareshield. The engines seem remote and quiet, the gauges the only proof of

* NTSB *AAR* 73-14.

their existence. The crew drink coffee: in the thin pressurized air, they should take liquids every twenty minutes.

At the top of the climb, at cruising altitude, the crew comes alive again. A knob on the autopilot is turned to 'hold altitude'. The autopilot obeys the instruction by gently pushing the control column forward. As the nose sinks, the throttles come back. The stabilizer clatters again as the aircraft is trimmed for the cruise.

The speed builds up on the Machmeter. The pilot is noticeably gentle with the controls. The aircraft is eased along. The air outside is very thin at this height – if the cabin decompressed so that he had to breathe the outside air, he would be unconscious in half a minute.

There is little air resistance at this height, so it takes time to change the aircraft's altitude. But once the effect starts, there is less to slow it down and a slight change can be greatly exaggerated.

Pulling back on the controls is easy because the thin air makes it easy. But once the nose starts coming up, it will quickly rear too much if the pilot is not gentle, causing a 'jet upset' after the sudden climb.

The sense of isolation and beauty is at its height in the cockpit. Apart from the throbbing of air on the windshield, it is very silent. The earth is too far below to matter. The plane is part of the sky, a new world of white cloud and the deepest blue. From the passenger cabin, looking out of the side windows, you see the sky go past. In the cockpit, you are hurled forwards into it – you are in the nose of a great projectile that is penetrating the sky.

The slight sway of the aircraft as it cuts through the air penetrates the soles of the feet, but no further. The feet feel movement, but the rest of the body does not. The eyes run in constant checks over the instruments – altitude, speed, engine settings, temperatures. They are the only proof to the mind that there is movement – they, and the con-trail of another jet, the cloud of frozen water it leaves in its engine wake.*

* A jet con-trail is made of fine ice crystals and not smoke. Kerosene gives off water droplets in the engine exhaust and this freezes at altitude to give the smokelike con-trail. There are other optical illusions in the cockpit. St Elmo's fire is a dancing light of static electricity that glitters on the nose and wings. Electric rain is

This idyllic scene is ruined in a millisecond if the aircraft hits severe turbulence with a harsh jarring that must be countered at once by a reduced speed.

The descent is heralded by the clatter of radio circuits as the pilot gets clearance to go down. The throttles are pulled back and the engine whine drops away. The altimeter starts unwinding and a degree of concentration that can almost be touched comes into the cockpit, as sharp and fresh as the smell of lemon.

The initial descent speed could be the Mmo: the maximum Mach speed. But the pilot would normally stay ten knots below this so that he does not edge over it when talking to ATC or otherwise busy. If he does exceed it, alarm bells are set off.

The aircraft seems to stop and hang in the air when the speed brakes go out. It lurches and buffets, and a push on the control column puts the nose down to counter the sharp reduction in speed.

The descent is regulated in steps, the pilot getting permission to descend a certain number of thousand feet at a time. One thousand feet before the height he has been cleared to, where he must level off, he pushes the throttles forward and the plane slowly levels out. Unexpectedly speed is regulated through putting the nose up or down, and the rate of descent is controlled by the throttle, and not the other way round.

The crew check fuel reserves, altimeters, radar, landing lights, flaps, speed brakes, gear, anti-skid on the wheels. Throttle settings are worked out in case the landing is aborted and the aircraft has to go round again.

There is a clatter and sinking feeling as the stages of flap are unrolled. The undercarriage locks with a bump. The speed drops and the undercarriage warning lights between the two pilots turn from red to green. The pilot banks and turns the plane on to the approach path; as he turns he gives it a burst of power, since stalling speed is higher in the turn.

---

charged drops of rain that hit the windscreen like phosphorescent beams. A lightning strike is a sudden explosion of light and noise. And on the transatlantic there is the Aurora Borealis, the northern lights that dance on the horizon like a glowing halo of snow.

A typical approach would see 18 degrees flap at 230 knots, undercarriage or 'gear' down at 220 knots, flaps 20 at 190 knots, flaps 45 at 180 knots with a flare out and touchdown between 118 and 138 knots.

The navigational instruments flick into life as the plane connects with the ILS glide path, the path of radio beams leading down on to the runway.

The runway appears. The approach speed is calculated like take-off speeds, from graphs. The tower gives the pilot wind speed and temperature. He adds weight – now considerably less than on take-off since tons of fuel will have been burnt – and computes the safe speed, putting it on the airspeed indicator with a bug.

The Vref, or keep above speed, on a 707 weighing 100,000 kilos is 129 knots: but if the pilot has lost the use of his flaps this shoots up to 189 knots. If there is a gusty wind, the pilot will add up to 23 mph to his speed to ensure maximum control in the gusts. The pilot uses occasional rudder to keep straight, controlling his height with the throttles and speed by raising or lowering the nose.

As he passes the start of the runway, he throttles back and begins the landing 'flare' – putting the nose up so that the plane sinks on to the runway instead of flying on to it. He will angle the plane into any crosswind to stop himself drifting away from the runway.

As he pulls the nose back, he kicks the rudder so that the aeroplane is facing down the runway and not at an angle that would strain the undercarriage.

As the main wheels touch, he pulls the throttles out of the gate and into reverse thrust. The lift dampers flip up to kill the lift on the wings. The wheel brakes must be used smoothly. The pilot pushes the control column slowly forwards to get the nosewheel firmly on the ground. He is still moving at 120 mph.

The aircraft slows down through 100 mph. It is kept straight with the rudder. There is a temptation to relax. A final burst of reverse thrust, and the plane is slow enough to go on to nosewheel steering.

As he turns off the runway, the pilot brings the flaps in to save them from damage by stones. The ground controller or a 'Follow Me' van brings him on to the right taxi stand. The pilot cuts his engines. The gyros on the instruments spin slowly to a halt. Needles sink back to zero.

He enters the flight in his log book, and notes any deficiencies in the aircraft's log. Another few hours in the air.

A British Airways 747 with 239 passengers aboard suffered total engine failure whilst cruising at 37,000 feet over Indonesia. The aircraft dropped 25,000 feet before the crew got power back. The incident, in the summer of 1982, happened when the aircraft ran into a cloud of volcanic ash on a scheduled flight from London to Sydney.

'It was blacker than a badger's backside when we ran into the ash,' said the captain, Eric Moody. 'The cloud, like heavy St Elmo's Fire, was how I imagined tracer fire would be. Suddenly the engineering officer called out that the number four engine had failed. We managed to get through the fire drill when he said the number two had also failed. Before we could look he called out, "So has number three – we've lost all four".'

Control of the aircraft was difficult because the dust affected the airspeed indicators. The ash from Mount Gallungung off Southern Sumatra reached well above 40,000 feet. The airliner was down to 13,000 feet when the crew got the first engine started and was down to 12,500 feet before the other three engines were going and it started to climb again.

Captain Moody set his passengers a truly phlegmatic example. He told them over the address system: 'Ladies and Gentlemen, this is your captain speaking. We have a small problem and all four engines have stopped. We are all doing our damndest to get them working again. I trust you are not in too much distress.'

20 Getting from A to B

Jets rarely get lost nowadays. Navigation is so straightforward that most aircraft no longer carry a navigator. Most twin-jets and some three-engined jets fly stages of 1,500 miles and more with two pilots as the only crew.

The captain sits in the left-hand seat, the traditional seat of aerial power. He looks to the handling side of the aircraft, monitoring the autopilot, checking the basic settings of the altimeter to ensure the correct height, heading the aircraft on the right course.

The navigation log work and the setting of radio aids is done by the co-pilot. He checks each aid and identifies the beacons he has tuned to the captain.

The captain has overall responsibility for the flight. If a ground controller gives him an instruction which he thinks is dangerous, he will override it. This is very rare, and most of the navigation is really done by the ground controller and the co-pilot.

The major airports of the world are linked by systems of airways ten miles wide, and extending from a base of 5,000 feet up to 25,000 feet. Above 25,000 feet the whole of the sky is controlled, not just the airways.

English is the international language of air control. This has led to near disaster. A Brazilian pilot on an approach to a European airport was told: 'Set altimeter to 997.' He took this as '2997' and set his altimeter at 29.97 inches of mercury instead of the 997 millibars meant by the controller. The altimeter thus showed the aircraft to be 500 feet higher than it actually was. Fortunately, visibility was good or the pilot could have flown into the ground.

The airways are very like the block system on a railway, where no train can enter a block until the one in front has cleared it. A system of navigational beacons, transmitting on VHF, radiates a series of bearings. These are picked up on the aircraft's radio compass, which points towards them.

The beacons are normally sixty or seventy miles apart. Every time the aircraft crosses a beacon, the co-pilot reports the time it was crossed, his height and the estimated time for crossing the next beacon. The controller who is sequencing the aeroplanes from the ground will not let the next aeroplane cross that beacon until ten minutes after the previous one has left, if it is at the same height.

There is a separation of 1,000 feet between levels, and there are alternate eastings and westings, or north and south. Imagine a series of layers on which aircraft go about their business, criss-crossing each other. That is what you see from the cockpit. Aircraft from the opposite direction pass 1,000 feet below, those on the same course 2,000 feet below.

The aircraft makes its way flying from beacon to beacon. Controllers on the ground watch it as a small white blip on their radar screens and check its progress against the flight plan filed by the pilot. As the aircraft leaves one sector, the controller simply passes it on down the line.

The controller has to make sure that the aircraft sticks to the airway, and that it does not conflict with other planes. This can happen when several aircraft converge on a beacon. An airway has only a given capacity. The airways also converge on to beacons, and the controller has to coordinate several airways flowing into one beacon. The result is sometimes aerial traffic jams, with aircraft having to 'hold', circling round in oval patterns.

The amount of sky that can be used is limited. Huge chunks are reserved for military use. There is only one cross-Channel airway between Bognor in Sussex and Berry Head near Salcombe in Devon. The rest is used as a Royal Navy gunnery and missile range.

Civil aircraft are restricted over northeast Italy and west of Marseilles. The traffic is funnelled through a narrow gap between Nice and Marseilles. The sky over Nice is like a flying railway junction, intersected by airways Amber 2, Red 16, Green 7, Amber 24, Red 34 and Red 46.

The co-pilot can tell when he is over a beacon, because the pointer on the radio compass swings round and he has an audible warning in his earphones. He simply changes radio frequencies for the next beacon, and homes in on that.

The controller also has to get the aircraft from the airways system on to its terminal airport. A transatlantic jet inbound for

London will start its descent from its cruising height of 33,000 feet or so over Bristol, about 100 miles out. The controllers look for clear enough airspace to bring it down through the lower levels of the airways.

If he has an outbound at 20,000 feet, he will clear the inbound to 21,000 feet, asking the co-pilot to 'call passing 25,000 feet' to check on how fast he is coming down. The controller waits for the blocking aircraft at 20,000 feet to get clear: he can see its height and position on a secondary radar screen.

When it is out of the way, he re-clears the inbound jet to carry on down. He wants to get it to an 'entry point' where it can join the flow of landing aircraft. There are two entry points to London from the west – Bovingdon, just north of Watford, and Ockham on the A3. The controller juggles his traffic to get an even flow of inbound traffic over the two entry beacons.

The aircraft may be cleared at once right through to land. But if there is any hang-up at lower levels on the run-in – as there usually is at busy airports – the aircraft has to circle over the beacon. This is called the 'holding stack', where aircraft wait until they become the bottom plane of the stack and are cleared to land.

Aircraft fly a race-track pattern or oval round the beacon whilst they are stacked up. It takes four minutes to get round, and there are 1,000-feet intervals between each aircraft. As each plane is cleared off the bottom of the stack, the ones above all move down 1,000 feet.

A different controller takes over as the plane leaves the stack. His aim is to put it about twelve miles from the runway and four miles behind the previous plane.

The approach radar shows a line of dots moving at four-mile intervals.

When he lines up with twelve miles to go, the pilot should be at about 3,500 feet. He prepares for an ILS approach, using the instrument landing system. Radio signals are sent by a beacon beside the runway to the ILS instruments in the cockpit. The instruments tell the pilot to fly right or left, or up or down, to maintain a smooth glide path on to the runway.

The ILS gives the pilot visual guidance. By keeping both the height needle and direction needle in the middle of a dial, he brings the aircraft down in line with the runway and at a steady three degrees of slope.

The ILS is sufficiently accurate to give most of the information for a plane to land automatically. The ILS, coupled with the autopilot, takes over with a mile to go and the height at 250 feet. Some sophisticated systems enable a totally automatic landing to be made in thick fog, but there are still very few aircraft or airports which have been fitted with the equipment.

A passenger jet of a major airline landing at a big airport will probably adhere to the 'category 2' weather minima. To land, the pilot must break out of the cloud base at not less than 200 feet, and must be able to see at least 800 metres in front of him. Otherwise he must go round again or divert to another airport. A handful of aircraft at only the biggest airports are cleared to 'category 3a', where the equipment is so good that the pilot can land if he has a mere 270 metres forward vision at an altitude of only twelve feet.

Taking off is the same system in reverse. Aircraft take off and land into the wind, to cut back on ground speed, so the choice of runway is dictated by the weather. Major airports have parallel runways, one for take-off and one for landing.

To regulate take-offs there is an international system of standard instrument departures, known as SIDs. These are printed diagrams showing the route the pilot should take after take-off. A pilot going to the Continent from Heathrow, for example, is given a Dover departure and follows the set route of heights and intermediate beacons from his standard departure book.

When the aircraft is taxiing out, the tower acknowledges the route: 'B201 is clear as filed to Frankfurt, Runway 28 Left, Dover 22 SID, Squawk 1022.' The pilot looks up the airways in his book. This clearance is to Dover and a height of 4,000 feet.

Without further clearance, the pilot can go no further than that. The course will take him south to Epsom and then east to Dover. The controller must ensure that there are no problems with crossing traffic: an aircraft heading south for Palma with tour passengers from Luton, or north from Gatwick to Glasgow.

At Dover, he will be cleared to a higher level, and will then pass on down the airways from beacon to beacon.

In essence, there are three types of control. Aerodrome control is situated on the top floor of the control tower. Its controllers regulate aircraft on take-off and landing, and give permission to start engines. They also control taxiing and pier allocation, and check runway surfaces and lighting systems.

Approach controllers order the safe positioning of inbound aircraft in the right sequences, and separate inbound, outbound and transit traffic in the airport zone. They also work in the control tower although from behind darkened windows, since they work off radar and have no need to look at the outside world.

Air traffic control centres, ATCs, are so remote from the take-off and landing of aircraft that very often they are not even situated at an airport. They control the airways, where the high-flying jets are a spot in the sky and on their radarscopes. They have to separate aircraft in the airways and keep in touch with the pilots as they progress along them.

The amount of air each ATC centre controls is huge. Each zone is called an FIR, a flight information region, and there are only three FIRs in the whole UK, London (at West Drayton), Preston and Prestwick. The controllers are also responsible for handing pilots on from one centre to another as a flight proceeds.

Control is a high-pressure job. Controllers have to cope with aircraft speed differentials where a turbo prop may be dawdling along at 270 knots with a jet at 500 knots behind it; with aerial snarl-ups; with safe separations. Occasionally, they blow it, steering two aircraft together. Controllers need personal stability and the gift of coping under tension, as well as good hearing, good eyesight and a good education. To make sure they understand the pilots' problems they are trained to obtain a private pilot's licence, and also 'fly' on jet simulators.

The control sequence starts when the pilot files his flight plan thirty minutes before take-off. This is a statement of his intentions – where he is going, and the speed, height and route he would like to take.

The control tower passes on the flight plan to the outbound controller at the air traffic control centre. He sets up a route for the aircraft to follow, specifies which beacons it must cross and at what height, and the airway the aircraft must follow after leaving the terminal area.

He also allocates a height (or 'flight level') to the aircraft, and gives the time and place at which the aircraft should start climbing to this height. The aircraft's expected speed and route are fed into a computer, which works out the time at which the aircraft will be over the beacons.

The outbound controller then gives the aircraft its basic airways clearance, say: 'Flight One is cleared to Los Angeles via airway Red One, to cross Beacon One at 3,000 feet, Beacon Two at 4,000 feet and Beacon Three at 4,000 feet and then climb to flight level 300.' (Height is given in hundreds of feet, so flight level 300 is 30,000 feet.)

The aerodrome controller then clears the aircraft to start engines, and to taxi to the holding point on the take-off runway. If there is already a queue waiting to take off, the aircraft will not be cleared to start engines until the snarl-up has eased.

The pilot gets the airways clearance at the holding point. The aerodrome controller gives him take-off clearance after checking with the outbound controller that the skies are clear.

Once the aircraft is airborne, the outbound controller correlates the time with the computed speed and route. He writes the times and height that the aircraft is expected over the beacons *en route* on to flight progress strips.

The airways controller at the ATC centre now checks the aircraft down the beacons, altering the progress strips if the aircraft does not run to schedule. He passes the aircraft over to the next ATC centre as it passes out of his zone.

When landing, the ATC inbound controller starts the aircraft descent, and then hands it over to the approach controller. Once the aircraft is well established on the approach and is closing on the runway, it is passed over to the aerodrome controller, who gives it landing clearance and then controls it along the taxiways to the terminal pier.

Controllers also try to cut down on noise annoyance by routing aircraft round towns. Video maps show towns and cities and the controllers keep noisy aircraft, like Concorde and 707s, away from them for as long as possible.

The controllers deal with emergencies. A typical Heathrow emergency: an aircraft with a hydraulic fault on a flight from Amsterdam. Landing may be difficult. The plan is given an immediate, 'straight in clearance'. The controller rearranges the other aircraft waiting to land. The pilot advises that he does not need a foam landing, where he would be diverted to an RAF aerodrome. It is a 'Green Alert' only.

Then he reports that he is on half power. The status changes to Red Alert. Eight fire engines roar out of their bays towards the runway. The plane is eleven miles out.

Local fire brigades and ambulances are informed. The runway is cleared. There are fire engines at the point of touchdown, more halfway along and another group at the end of the runway.

The controller relays weather conditions, temperature, pressure and wind, to the plane. The undercarriage is lowered, and the aircraft comes in rather fast and a little unsteady, because the hydraulic fault has robbed it of full flap. It uses a lot of runway but stops.

The fire engines return to their bays, the ambulances depart, the airport chaplain relaxes, and the Red Alert is cancelled. The controllers settle down to unblock the jam of circling aircraft that has built up. At Heathrow, they average two emergencies like this a day in summer.

It is the great accuracy of navigation, and control on the approach and landing, that has made flying so much safer.

Navigational aids that plot an aircraft's position from its own movement are available. LORAN has a receiver and indicator accurate to a millionth of a second to measure the difference between ground stations. This gives a number read-out, which is transmitted on to a map print out in the cockpit, showing exactly where the aircraft is as it moves.

Inertial navigation systems, INS, are precision-based on gyros. An intertial platform is equipped with two accelerometers, one exactly north–south and the other east–west. The pilot punches in his original position on the departure airport before take-off, remembering that it can take forty minutes for the gyros to spin up to the required degree of accuracy. Every acceleration as the plane moves from its taxi stand is recorded and mapped.

INS is accurate to one mile times the hours flown. After ten hours it will be good to at least ten miles. It is highly accurate westbound, giving a biggest error of only five miles on flights from Europe to the US East Coast. The counter-rotation of the earth affects it eastbound, and that five miles could become ten. During its introduction, however, the maximum recorded error was twenty-seven miles on a nine-hour flight from Seattle on the US Pacific coast to England. Besides position, INS gives the track, the course the aircraft is making and groundspeed.

Three INS are normally carried on a big jet like a 747 or DC10, and two on a 707 – the third on the bigger planes are 'hot spares'. INS is sophisticated – positions can be updated in flight by feeding in VOR and DME from beacons – but also simple enough to ensure its general acceptance everywhere.

The first instrument landing was made in 1928. The equipment used by the American James H. Doolittle (later the first man to bomb Tokyo) is still the basis of finding a runway. A simple radio beam guided him towards the runway, and radio markers on the approach told him how far he had to go.

The simple radio beacon is still the most common landing aid. It works on exactly the same lines as an ordinary radio station like the BBC. The pilot tunes his radio receiver to the right frequency for the beacon he wants. He can tell when he has got it because it plays an identifying Morse code signal through his earphones. A needle on his instrument panel then points towards the beacon.

In fact, transatlantic pilots can pick up and home in on BBC Radio Two from 1,700 miles out to sea. It could get them to within ten miles of Heathrow.

But these systems are badly affected by static and thunderstorms. They can only be used as a homing beacon, and not as a reference for other courses. VOR, very high frequency omnidirectional range transmitters, get round some of these problems. Being VHF, they are not affected by static. Together with DME, the bearing can be fed into a small computer which will give an instantaneous position on a map.

It is easy to tell when the aircraft is passing over a VOR station: a small pointer on the cockpit instrument changes from flying 'to' the VOR to 'from'.

Some VOR transmitters also have distance measuring equipment. The pilot reads off the exact distance he is from the station on an instrument.

This combination can be used for landing as well as *en route* navigation. The VOR needle shows the correct heading for the runway, the altimeter shows his height, and the DME shows the distance to go from the runway. This makes it simple to work out the correct angle of descent. With five miles to go he should be at 1,500 feet, three miles out at 900 and so on: the rule of thumb is 300 feet for every mile.

Take a VOR/DME approach at Tokyo's Haneda airport, on Runway 33 Left. (All London's runways are on the more sophisticated ILS.) The aircraft begins its descent 120 miles out over the Pacific. The VOR is tuned into the Kisaratzu beacon, across the deep bay from Haneda. The pilot keeps well to the south to avoid the Kawasaki refinery: as with most oil refineries, overflying is prohibited. The DME shows the distance to Kisaratzu ticking off.

As the aircraft passes over Kisaratzu, the 'to' slides over to 'from' on the instrument and there is a clattering on the headphones. The co-pilot now sets his VOR on to the transmitter on Runway 33 Left. The crew know from their airways map that it is 10.3 nautical miles from the Kisaratzu beacon to the runway threshold. The map also tells them that at their groundspeed of 150 knots it will take them four minutes and seven seconds to the threshold. They start a stopwatch.

As the distance to go diminishes on the DME equipment, the crew check the altitude. They were at 2,500 feet at the beacon.

The VOR needle has to be kept centred. If it drifts left, it means the aircraft is easing away from the airport towards the refinery. Right, and it is off towards the heavy industry plants at Shinagawa. Centred, it is heading straight down the runway.

As the DME shows two miles to run, the pilot looks out of the windows for the runway lights. The co-pilot scans the instruments, particularly altitude against distance to go. He must ensure that they do not get too low, because a jet engine takes time to correct errors.

The captain is helped by the runway approach lights. They will show red if he is too low, and be invisible if he is too high. He must keep on the white lights. When he has all white lights and the runway well in sight, he goes on to land visually.

The VOR/DME system is the most commonly used at airports. But it gives only heading and distance to go. It does not give any height indication, and so can only be used in fair visibility.

Runways with ILS can be used in everything but the worst

conditions. Yet only twelve per cent of the runways used by commercial jets in Europe are equipped with it. In North America the figure is ten per cent, and for the rest of the world six per cent.

ILS tells the pilot a great deal more than VOR, and it does it in much simpler form. It has four essential ingredients. The 'localizer' is a radio transmitter placed at the far end of the runway. Its beam is picked up by a needle in the cockpit, which shows the pilot where to head the aircraft. By keeping the needle centred, he will stay on the right heading.

ILS also gives him 'glide path' information. This tells him whether he is descending at an angle that will bring him down gently on to the beginning of the runway.

It consists of another transmitter, about 1,000 feet down the runway, which sends out a beam which indicates a three-degrees slope in the air. The pilot can tell from his instruments whether he is above, below or on this ideal slope.

The 'outer marker' is a beacon which tells the pilot how far out from the runway he is. It is normally six miles from the beginning of the runway. As the airliner flies over it, a blue light flashes in the cockpit and there is a buzzing in the pilot's earphones.

The 'middle marker' is 3,500 feet from the start of the runway. An amber light flashes in the cockpit as it is crossed. The pilot should now be at the right angle of descent, distance and speed to touch down 1,000 feet along the runway. Landings can be made even when the cloud base is under 200 feet, and the visibility less than half a mile.

The ILS system is also used with precision approach radar. This reads an aircraft's height so accurately that the ground controller can warn the pilot if he strays as little as five feet below the glide path.

Most of the smaller airports, including many of the busy holiday airports around the Mediterranean, are not even equipped with VOR on all their runways. The American Airline Pilots' Association has found that deaths at airports lacking precision approach aids are ten times higher than at airports with fuller control aids.

Pilots very occasionally become lost. A Korean Air Lines 707 drifted hundreds of miles off course on a flight from Paris to Seoul over the North Pole. The crew blamed their poor navigation, which took them deep inside Soviet airspace, on a faulty gyro compass. Unfortunately, they strayed into the militarily sensitive Murmansk area.

Soviet Su-15 fighters were scrambled to intercept the airliner. The Russian pilots, who were not using the international distress frequency, failed to make contact with the 707 crew. They attempted to shoot it down. The 707 was hit by a missile. Despite the loss of cabin pressure at 29,000 feet, and the explosion which killed two passengers, the captain made a perfect crash landing on a frozen lake.

A navigational error, compounded by 'white-out' flying conditions where it was difficult to judge the horizon in cloud and snow, caused an Air New Zealand DC10 to crash into a volcano in Antarctica in November 1979. It was on a sightseeing trip from New Zealand to the Antarctic. The high point of the trip was the view of the 12,000-foot volcano Mount Erebus. The course in the aircraft's navigational computer had been subject to a last-minute change.

To give the passengers a better view, the captain went well below the minimum safety altitude of 16,000 feet. Flying visually the crew became disorientated by the combination of snow, cloud and haze. The aircraft descended below 2,000 feet. The captain mistook his position and turned towards the mountain instead of away from it. At 1,500 feet the captain said: 'We'll have to climb out of here.' He put on full power but the aircraft hit the volcano at 1,467 feet, killing all 257 aboard.

The worst accident in British aviation history was also due to a navigational error. A Dan-Air Boeing 727 on a holiday charter flight to Los Rodeos airport in Tenerife crashed into a mountain ridge in April 1980. All 146 aboard were killed. After overflying the VOR beacon on his approach, the Dan-Air captain was given instructions by the air traffic controllers to switch from the published airport procedures to an unpublished one. Another aircraft was already on the approach, and the 727 was ordered to follow an approach pattern that was not on any charts. The crew flew south of the airport instead of north and crashed in cloud.

Confusion between controllers and crew was a feature of what was the world's worst air tragedy, in March 1977, at the same airport. The accident took place in foggy conditions. A KLM Boeing 747 with 248 aboard had been diverted to Tenerife after a bomb had closed the airport at Las Palmas. So had a Pan Am 747 with 396 on board. Both aircraft prepared to depart from Los Rodeos when Las Palmas was reopened to traffic.

The KLM Jumbo positioned itself for take-off at the end of the runway at the same time that the Pan Am aircraft entered the runway to taxi down it. The KLM captain, believing that he had clearance, released his brakes and started his take-off run. He hit the taxiing Pan Am 747 with full take-off power. A total of 583 people were killed.

Control is not infallible. In a typical year, 1968, 2,230 near misses were reported in the US alone, with thirty-eight mid-air collisions. Since most near misses take place in cloud, where the pilots could be unaware of them, the true figure is perhaps double this. The official definition of a near miss is when two aircraft are close enough to be in danger of colliding. Some pilots say they should be rechristened 'near hits'.

The US has highly sophisticated control systems, but the FAA has called for the maximum penalty for civil flying violations to be raised from $1,000 to $25,000, with criminal penalties for the worst offenders. The FAA's administrator, Langhorne Bond, also proposed a new rule to make it easier to 'track down the shadowy figures who hide behind multiple leases and sham corporations'. He said that regulations would help the FAA to expose 'cockroach corners – those unsavoury operations conducted at Miami International airport and elsewhere'.

The FAA move was prompted partly by the fatal crash between a Pacific Southwest Airlines 727 and a private plane over San Diego in September 1978. The airliner was approaching San Diego's Lindbergh field and the Cessna pilots were practising instrument flying from nearby Montgomery airport.

A conflict-alert alarm, a warning that two aircraft are close, sounded in approach control, but the controllers were not unduly worried since the alarm sounded eight to ten times a day when there was no real danger.

The cockpit recording from the 727 shows how easy it is to lose track of a light aircraft.

'Are we clear of that Cessna?' asked the PSA first officer.

The flight engineer responded: 'Supposed to be.'

The PSA captain: 'I guess.' Sounds of laughter.

Another PSA captain, one of two riding as passengers in the cockpit: 'I hope.'

The PSA captain: 'Oh, yeah. Before we turned downwind. I saw him about one o'clock, probably behind us now.'

About ten seconds later the first officer added: 'There is one underneath.'

'What have we got here?' the captain asked.

'It's bad,' replied the first officer. 'We're hit, man. We are hit.'

In all, 165 lives were lost in the air and on the ground.

Langhorne Bond said the FAA would change an aviation safety reporting programme which provides immunity to pilots and controllers who report violations of safety rules. 'No longer will a violator be able to draw a clak of immunity around himself by simply turning himself in – even if the violation was witnessed and subsequently reported by others.'

Bond noted that, in Spokane, Washington, 'a DC9 on a missed approach almost hit a DC10 taking off from the same runway at the same time. Both the DC9 pilot and the controller were in serious error – and we knew all about a near miss as soon as it occurred.'

But both men filed a report on the incident, thus blocking any action being taken against them.

'The guarantee of immunity, I'm afraid, can be too easily corrupted into a licence to endanger hundreds of lives with no fear of punishment,' said Bond. Under the modifications, 'airmen will no longer be able to claim immunity for violations – witnessed by others – of safety regulations. And controllers will no longer be able to shield themselves behind a claim of immunity if they direct an aircraft into another's airspace, runway or taxiway, or if they give or accept an inaccurate briefing when changing control positions.'

The American Airline Pilots' Association said modification of the immunity policy 'will without question substantially reduce the number of reported air traffic system errors'. Clearly, the near-miss position in the US is dangerously lax. The primary cause of an unnerving series of incidents in a three-week period in 1979 was air-controller error.

The frequency of close calls around New York is due to the absence of altitude information on controllers' radar sets, the heavy volume of traffic at La Guardia airport because of its nearness to central New York and the workload on controllers.

The first incident involved an Empire commuter service and an American Airlines 727. The commuter plane, a twin turboprop, had taken off from JFK's Runway 31 and was headed northwest. The crew had clearance to turn east after take-off.

Meanwhile, the American 727, inbound to La Guardia, was cleared to turn right into La Guardia's Runway 31. JFK's and La Guardia's runways are parallel. According to the FAA, the Empire turboprop did not turn east after take-off, but continued north, penetrating the buffer zone between the two airports. The JFK controller saw on radar the Empire blip closing on the American blip, although he had no altitude information. He warned the commuter crew.

They passed each other by 300 feet horizontally and fifty feet vertically.

Then an airport-controller error brought two 747s, a cargo plane inbound to JFK and a passenger aircraft outbound to Europe, within 500 to 700 feet horizontally and 300 to 500 feet vertically.

Not long after, an American 727 had just landed on La Guardia's Runway 4 when a controller radioed: 'Traffic rolling on Runway 31. Looks like he's going through the intersection.' The traffic on 31 was a Delta 727 that had been cleared for take-off. The American crew were able to stop before the intersection.

Some parts of the sky are grossly overcrowded by civil and military aircraft. At any time in daylight, there are 5,000 aircraft in the Chicago, Washington and New York triangle. Pilots still call the Ruhr 'fighter alley' because of the number of Dutch, American, British and German fighters roaming the area on NATO business. West Germany recorded a massive 216 near misses in 1976, of which eighty-eight presented an 'immediate danger'. Over New York, a United Airways jet and a TWA airliner crashed and 134 died; four years earlier two planes from the same airlines collided over the Grand Canyon, killing 128.

Military aircraft are a particular danger. Coordination between military and civil controllers can break down. An Italian fighter brought down a British Airways Viscount.* Another Viscount crashed in Maryland after being hit by a jet fighter trainer, and all the passengers died.† A US Air Force F-100 fighter hit a United Airlines transcontinental flight near Las Vegas, and forty-nine died.‡

A US Marine Phantom fighter-bomber took off in California on 6 June 1971. The air traffic controller who was supervising an Air West DC9 that was climbing over Duarte, California, could not warn the flight of the nearness of the Phantom. The Marine pilot was flying visually with no responsibility to inform the controller of his plans, and the transponder which would have shown his position on radar was not working.

As he reached 15,000 feet, the figher-pilot rolled the Phantom. His radar observer in the rear seat saw the left wing and fuselage of the airliner appear. Before he could shout, the pilot rolled to the left again and eighteen tons of fighter slammed into the DC9. Only the radar observer lived out of the fifty-one involved.

Sergeant Yoshimi Ichikawa was on a training flight over Japan with his instructor in another fighter close to him.§ The instructor shouted, too late: 'Climb and turn right!' Ichikawa's Super-Sabre crashed into an All Nippon Airways Boeing 727 and 162 died in a second.

Light aircraft, often flying visually near airports and not under a controller's orders, have crashed into airliners with deadly regularity. Pilots call the area round 1,000 feet, where the light aircraft fly, 'Indian territory' after the Piper range of small planes – Commanches, Apaches and Navahos. In one brief period a Caravelle hit a Beechcraft over Bangkok, a DC9 hit a Cessna at St Louis, and a Convair 580 hit a Cessna at Milwaukee. A student on a cross-country flight from Indianapolis filed a Visual Flight Rules flight plan. This is used only if the pilot becomes overdue, so a search of his route can be made. It is not passed on to air traffic controllers.

The pilot, who had only thirty hours' flying experience, became overdue. The controllers knew instantly. He hit an Alleghany

* CAA 19/58.
† CAA 10/58.
‡ CAA 8/58.
§ CAA 16/71.

Airlines DC9, which disappeared from their radar as it crashed and eighty-two died.*

Another DC9 of Eastern Airlines hit a light Cessna and carried the little plane and its two occupants wrapped round its undercarriage, like a bird of prey with a mouse. The Cessna eventually fell off, killing the pilot and his passenger, and the DC9 survived.†

In Europe, two Spanish airliners collided at 30,000 feet over western France. One made a miraculous landing, the other crashed, killing sixty-eight. French air traffic controllers were on strike, and the airliners were under French military control. Strikes by air traffic controllers have spread in Europe and lethal chaos has resulted. The summer-long dispute of Spanish controllers in 1976 brought congestion over Europe well over the danger level. Also that summer, Yugoslav controllers at Zagreb brought a British Airways Trident *en route* to Istanbul into a fatal crash at 30,000 feet with a Germany-bound charter airliner full of holidaymakers. 176 died.

The pilots of jets are very dependent on controllers to avoid collisions. Speeds are so high that it is very difficult to see other aircraft, even in perfect, clear conditions. Another airliner cannot be seen until it is within five miles. Slim-winged fighters are invisible until 2.3 miles. A pilot flying at 600 mph uses 300 yards whilst his brain registers whether the object is a plane, a cloud or a smudge on the windscreen. Decision time to climb or dive takes another 1,000 yards and 1,900 yards is burned up before the plane responds to the controls.

The margins are in the splits of split seconds. And the controllers are subjected to the same strains as pilots. Psychological tests carried out by the FAA have shown that controllers undergo more stress than combat pilots. At Chicago's O'Hare airport, the busiest in the world, they are only allowed to work for ninety minutes at a stretch during peak hours. A controller may have to land an aircraft every two minutes, whilst keeping track of half a dozen more simultaneously.

About one third of O'Hare's controllers suffer from peptic ulcers and a further one third have gastric or emotional problems.

* NTSB *AAR* 70–15.
† NTSB *AAR* 72–13.

The Chicago branch of the Professional Air Traffic Controllers' Organization has sued the FAA, claiming that the O'Hare unit is understaffed, back-up equipment lacking and training programmes ineffective.

Charles Cacace, a JFK controller, says: 'You don't look at an aircraft as if it were carrying three hundred people. It would affect the way you do your job. Make you nervous. You look at it as though it were a piece of tin needing to be put someplace, but in the back of your mind you always hope that you don't get involved in some mess.'

An American pilot, Captain Power-Waters, interviewed a controller for his book *Safety Last*:*

'Have you ever seen a man panic in the position?' he asked.

'There is one vivid experience I will never forget,' said the controller. 'A man froze on the mike. His eyes rolled back in his head and he broke out in a cold sweat. He keyed his microphone continuously but said nothing. A nervous breakdown right on duty.'

'What happens when the radar or radio goes out?'

'Chaos . . . I have seen radar fail in two or three sectors at one time. This means that approximately 100 planes are in danger of colliding. The only course that the pilots have to take is to try and separate themselves. It's a frightening situation. About all I can do in a case like this is pray the Great Controller will do his job.'

'Who is the Great Controller?'

'God.'

* *Safety Last* by Captain Brian Power-Waters, Millington, London, 1974.

Part Five
Emergency

21 Hijack

Passengers are more likely to be involved in a hijack than a crash. The takover of flights by armed men has soared over the hundred mark in some years. The scheduled flights of major West European airlines are the most popular targets.

These strange odysseys by exhausted crews and passengers, forced over the globe at gun or explosives point by a mentally or politically disturbed person, seem a very modern phenomenon. The word hijack itself was first used to mean the seizure of aircraft in *The Times* on 19 February 1958. Before that it meant the stealing of liquor in transit during the American prohibition.

The first aircraft to be hijacked was a Ford Tri-Motor during a Peruvian revolution in 1930. Six years later, the film *Lost Horizon* jammed the box offices and made Ronald Coleman a superstar. The hero was a Tibetan called Talu who wished to repopulate the isolated Valley of the Blue Moon beneath Shangri-La. An aircraft was the only way to get there. So Talu learned to fly, knocked out the English pilot of an airliner and abducted the passengers to a crash landing near Shangri-La.

Talu would be called a hijacker today. Millions of pounds are spent every year trying to combat his descendants. British Airways alone has an anti-hijack bill of £5 million a year.

Many ideas have been dreamed up to combat hijackers. When Havana was the most common destination, the Americans thought of building a replica of the airport near Miami. During a hijack by Japanese students to North Korea, an airport at Seoul in South Korea was disguised to look like Pyongyang in the north. The students almost fell for the ruse.

There was a suggestion to build a trapdoor just behind the cockpit out of which the hapless hijackers would fall. This would decompress the aircraft however. Nerve gas has been proposed to put them quietly asleep. A drawback is that they could well pull triggers or drop grenades whilst nodding off.

The American Federal Aviation Administration developed a high-frequency ray system to stun hijackers. Labelled 'Operation

Zeke', the system consisted of two 'ray boxes' near the cockpit door. Anyone passing through the rays would be knocked unconscious. But the FAA decided that it was too risky to use on commercial aircraft: there might be more than one hijacker.

Doped food and drink worked until hijackers started insisting that crew or passengers sample everything first. Police dressed as mechanics had a shortlived success. Afraid of concealed weapons, some hijackers will not let anyone near the aircraft unless they are wearing swimming trunks.

The Americans developed a crash course for skymarshals in 1970. A special firing range was built. It was a mock-up of the interior of a passenger jet. The marshals had to be able to fire twelve bullets in twenty-five seconds, at a range of forty-five feet (about twelve rows of seats away), to hit a profile of a hijacker in the aisle.

Marshals carry .38 revolvers, adapted for use inside an aircraft. A normal .38 carries for up to a mile. A 707 has an interior main cabin of just 111 feet and a normal bullet would penetrate through several layers of seats.

The airline version uses a special slug that has a lethal range of only fifty feet. Beyond that it slows down rapidly and will not carry beyond 170 feet. The 'bullet' is a flat canvas bag filled with lead shot, tightly rolled to fit in the chamber.

It comes out of the barrel at 1,000 feet per second, and as it spins the bag opens flat. This slows it down so rapidly that at 100 feet, roughly at the end of the cabin, its speed is down to a dawdling 190 feet per second.

The energy necessary to kill someone depends on the shape of the bullet and the place where it hits, normally between thirty and ninety foot-pounds of force. When it leaves the muzzle, the pancake exerts 125 foot-pounds, well above that needed to kill. But at 100 feet it is six foot-pounds, well below. This means that if the shot misses the hijacker but hits someone further down the cabin, he will survive.

A normal bullet passes through objects leaving holes little larger than itself. The 'pancake', or 'airline special', delivers all its energy into the first thing it hits, and because it is pliable and not solid it makes a very large and ugly hole.

At short range, it is more likely to kill than an ordinary bullet that can pass straight through a man. The danger of ricochet is very small because the pancake loses power so quickly, and because they are pliable, the new projectiles will not penetrate the airframe.

The main danger of piercing the airframe is not, as most people think, depressurization. A bullet hole is much too small to suck anyone out, and the cabin compressors will more than compensate for the outflow of air. All it will do is to make an unpleasant, high-pitched shrieking noise as air escapes. The danger is that the bullet may sever a control line or puncture a fuel tank.

The skymarshal's job is not a romantic one. The best paid, the Americans, get only $15,000 a year – considerably less than a young stewardess. The routine is a month on duty at an airport, then two months flying.

Not that the flying is glamorous. The skymarshal cannot sleep, drink alcohol, watch the in-flight movie, or reveal his identity. Each one is given a separate cover story to use if he gets into conversation with a passenger. He is known only to the crew, and comes under the captain's command, although he can act independently if he feels that he can defuse a situation on his own.

The only known characteristics of a skymarshal are that he will be male, and aged between twenty-one and fifty. Although his main function is to monitor passengers' behaviour continuously, he should be trained to conceal this. On a few airlines, however, the skymarshals stick out like very sore thumbs. On Ethiopian Airlines, four young men board the aircraft at Addis Ababa after everyone else is on board. They wear, despite the heat, identical windcheaters with identical bulges under the arms, and blink out at the passengers through one-way silvered dark glasses.

The airline provides them with identical Samsonite attaché cases with their initials on them. Their cover story is that they are businessmen.

The easiest way to stop hijacks is to stop hijackers boarding the aircraft. This is done partly by machine. Magnetometers can isolate solid masses of metal, like a gun or knife. There are various types of metal scanners, whose sensitivity can be set to pick up a pair of keys but is normally set to record at the density of a .22 pistol. One system has poles that the passenger walks between which will trigger off a light on an alarm box. This is watched by a security guard some way away so that the man actually working the magnetometer will not be overpowered or shot by the passenger, as he might be if he was the person to discover that the passenger was armed.

This system costs around £500. For £16,000 airlines can buy a system that picks up pistols, whisky bottles, gelignite sticks and even heroin stuffed inside plastic dolls. Through sensitive X-rays it shows the outlines of forbidden articles on a screen. But it is too expensive, the airlines say, and slow to operate. Other devices are too sensitive, even picking out women wearing contraceptive coils.

The 'electric truncheon' is another way of searching passengers without having to touch them. The 'truncheon', which looks like a torch with a metal loop on the end, has a dial which registers when it gets close to a metal mass. This costs only £50. And, to be more discreet, there is a system at £120 where the detector is hidden in the searcher's sleeve, giving off a bleep to a 'hearing aid' in his ear.

A new type of lie detector measures psychological stress through changes in voice patterns. A lie alters heartbeats, pace of breathing and upsets the nervous system. Where an honest voice pattern comes out as a straight line on the machine's graph, a lie comes out as a rectangular shape. However, lie detectors rely on a series of questions, rather than a simple 'Are you going to hijack this aircraft?' So that the time needed by this Dekto counter-intelligence and security system is considerable.

Physical searching, 'frisking', is often done as well as checking by machine. It can be highly effective. Not only did British Airways relieve Prince Kalifa bin Ali Al'tani, brother of the ruler of Qatar, of his gold-plated Walther PPK, another brother, this time of Jordan's King Hussein, was in trouble with the same airline within a week. His luggage, on a flight to sunny Bermuda, was found to contain three submachine guns, several pistols and dozens of ammunition clips.

Carrying weapons is not restricted to those of blue blood. In three months at Heathrow, BA passengers alone were relieved of 19 revolvers, several shotguns, 300 rounds of ammunition, 800 pellets, 160 antique and replica firearms and 400 knives. There was also a motley collection of axes, bayonets, cut-throat razors and the Peruvian Naval Attaché's dress sword.

Americans are easily the most common weapon carriers. 'A lot of ladies habitually carry gas guns to prevent getting raped, and the gentlemen carry real guns so as to prevent getting murdered,' says a Heathrow security man. 'Flick knives and comb knives, metal dog combs with sharpened teeth, very nasty, are also common with Americans. Of course, half an hour after we've taken the things off them, they're being given a sharp steak knife at 30,000 feet.'

Security men soon get a feel for what various nationalities carry in their pockets and in their hand luggage. 'For flights to the Far East you almost start getting worried if they aren't laden down with chocolate, Alka Seltzer, masses of Tampax – all the things they can't get in India, or Pakistan. They go in for carving sets, too, so you don't go to panic stations if you find an Indian with a great carving knife. It's quite common.

'And you wouldn't if it was a South American, as long as it was a Georgian silver carving knife. You find half the cutlery from the London Silver Vaults on the Rio and Buenos Aires flights. But you would not expect silver with an Arab. Their things are electric razors, transistor radios and pullovers. Israelis go for suet puddings and cornflakes.'

There is a well-taught pattern to the 'frisk'. Using the standard international method, perfected by American detectives and British troops in Cyprus, Aden and Ulster, it should be possible for six men and two girls to check out a Jumbo load of 340 passengers in under an hour. (Using machines alone would take thirty minutes.)

The searching hands slide in an unbroken pattern down the body. They start round the back of the neck, feeling for anything concealed in the jacket collar. The lapels are lifted slightly so that the hands can feel the weight of the jacket and sense if anything heavy like a gun is in it. Parting the jacket the hands brush the wallet pockets and under the arms, and then run down the back as the eyes check the exposed shirt front.

At the waist, the hands come round the belt feeling for a weapon. Experience has shown that guns are seldom concealed in shoulder holsters. People who want to conceal guns normally strap them to the small of their backs, or to their thighs. Shoulder holsters are too obvious, although the security men keep them there for quick reaction. A police sergeant said: 'Look at that Aeroflot flight engineer', as the Russian airline crewman stood by his aircraft during a turn round to Moscow. 'He's got a very developed left breast and any normal engineer would either be in the crew room or working on an engine. He wouldn't be standing around in the cold.'

The trouser pockets are checked, and the hands slide to the crotch and down the inside and outside of the legs as the eyes check whether the heels are built up enough to have a secret compartment. At no stage should the hands have left the body or slowed down the rhythm of search.

But things go wrong. If the passengers are all wearing overcoats or mackintoshes it can almost double the time. All the coats should be taken off and searched individually. It is very difficult to search through both an overcoat and a jacket. There is too much bulk for sensitive feeling of weight or bulges. So flights on cold or rainy days pose more problems than most. Throw in a charter holiday flight, with passengers laden down with presents and souvenirs as well as raincoats, and the supervisors who have to monitor the flow of passengers for frisking will more than double the time-estimate over a similar load of businessmen in good weather. Hence the choice of a holiday charter flight by the Palestinians who hijacked a Lufthansa Boeing from Majorca to Mogadishu in October 1977.

Despite magnetometers and frisking, some hijackers have got through. The great majority were never searched at all. The number of hijacks in the US dwindled as soon as searching became compulsory.

But searching is not compulsory in Europe. The favourite hijacking method is to board a non-sensitive airline at a non-sensitive airport and to board the target aircraft as a transfer passenger. Thus a hijacker might join his target flight from Paris to the Middle East after being transferred on to it from a non-sensitive Manchester–Paris flight.

A few airlines insist that joining passengers at transit stops should be searched more thoroughly than anyone else. El Al has done this with such success that attacks on it became limited to random machine gunning of passengers in airports, rather than actual attempts to board their aircraft.

Hijackers have got past security with extraordinary ease. Two Palestinians were refused tickets by El Al during the great 1970 desert hijack operation, when three aircraft were taken to a desert airfield in Jordan. El Al had fairly good grounds for suspicion. The men could give no satisfactory reason for being in Europe, let alone wanting to fly to South America via New York on El Al when a direct flight was available. They offered to pay cash. Despite their scruffy clothes, they insisted on first-class tickets.

They thus showed four distinct peculiarities. Normal passengers want direct flights. If they take a roundabout route, they almost invariably want a stopover on the way. They know why they are in the country. If they are poor-looking they rarely travel first, particularly on a 10,000-mile flight. And airline passengers very rarely pay cash.

El Al refused to fly them on their target flight from Amsterdam to New York. (Two others, the notorious girl hijacker Leila Khaled and an Argentinian who sympathized with the Palestinians, did board it and attempted to hijack it. The Argentinian was shot dead by an Israeli security guard and Miss Khaled was captured almost without a struggle.)

The Palestinians booked on to a Pan Am Jumbo instead. The pilot was so suspicious of them that, despite their elevated status in the first-class compartment, he insisted on personally searching them before take-off. He neglected to check their hand luggage under the seat. Ten hours later, after failing to land in the desert because of the Jumbo's size, they blew the plane up at Cairo.

In America, a ramp agent demanded proof of identity from a suspicious-looking passenger. The man indicated that he was deaf and dumb. Pressed further, he produced a (quite valid) commercial pilot's licence. He was allowed on board and hijacked the plane. Nobody on the airline staff had asked themselves how a deaf and dumb person could get a pilot's licence.

'Positive frisking', as the airlines put it, varies greatly. It can be a highly complex scanning machine, or it can be the captain of a Gulf Aviation turboprop, refusing to fly the bodyguards of the Sultan of Oman, with their Lee Enfields and daggers, from Muscat to the other side of the Empty Quarter at Salala. (A compromise was made. The men kept their rifles. The pilot took the bolts and firing pins.)

The airlines have another more secret check, the 'mind frisk'. It is just as efficient. A study of hijackers shows that they behave differently to normal passengers. So a 'behavioural profile' of *normal* passengers was worked out. The profile does not point at the guilty or suspicious: it simply clears the innocent.

The ten-factor profile has been found to clear 99½ per cent of all passengers. The remainder (and that is 2,500 a *day* in the US, with its 500,000 passengers moving daily by air) are checked out with special interviews and with physical frisks.

The profile, for obvious reasons, remains secret. But every time a passenger boards an aircraft of a security minded airline he will be 'mind frisked' by the check-in girl, by the airline security and plainclothes men who always patrol terminals, and by watchers from behind the concealed two-way mirrors that exist in most departure lounges. If he passes the ten very simple requirements, he is considered normal.

What can be revealed is the reverse, the rough Identikit of the hijacker. Research in America has come up with a fair picture of the 'Havana riders', as airline staff call them. Texan psychiatrist David Hubbard interviewed a considerable cross-section of hijackers and found there was much in common.*

The hijacker is likely to be very shy and soft-spoken. So shy, indeed, that the famous parachuting hijacker, Richard McCoy, had to use pre-typed notes to take over the aircraft.

He will probably be small, unathletic and have very poor co-ordination – one hijacker had difficulty in tying up his shoelaces, another in reversing his car.

He turns up at the ticket barrier with all the signs of being a regular flyer. His briefcase is plastered with stickers from recent trips, he has a general air of knowing his way around, and is not at all the lost and puzzled wild man you might think.

The clothing is often absurdly unsuitable for the destination. A hijacker on a Toronto-bound flight from Kansas City in January wore a sports shirt and slacks, but then he knew the flight was

* *The Skyjacker* by David G. Hubbard, Macmillan Company, New York; Collier Macmillan, London.

going to Cuba and not Toronto. Hijackers very rarely bother to bring luggage with them..'It's like prostitutes and hotel doormen,' says a check-in clerk who foiled a hijack attempt on this basis. 'If a man has no luggage on an airplane flight, he's like a girl with no luggage at the Savoy. The sort of customer you think about twice.'

Though both experienced, and shy, the potential hijacker asks a lot of questions. The favourites are: the number of intermediate stops *en route*, the number of passengers, cruising height, location of the engines, distances to cities not on the route. He is probably unsure of the advertised time of arrival, unusual for a passenger.

His general behaviour in the terminal will be odd, even by the standards of the mentally unstable who are attracted to airports. Most like the size and transient nature of the buildings, where they can loiter anonymously and free in the big open spaces. But the hijacker feels trapped and stays close to walls and pillars.

He takes devious routes to cover short distances; he constantly moves round shops, news stands, bars, telephone booths, lavatories, without using any of them.

For many hijackers, travel and particularly flying is their only enjoyment, the only way to cope with upsets and crises. One man who had inherited $350,000 travelled 200,000 miles in two years before turning hijacker. This schedule was getting close to what actual aircrew might do – 200 London–Romes, over eighty transatlantics. But the man never stayed at any airport he flew to. He simply turned round and flew back.

Another man used to drive the long round trip from New Orleans to Houston to Los Angeles and Colorado and back to New Orleans whenever a family row loomed. He took to flying it, and eventually went to Cuba.

Almost all the hijackers Hubbard interviewed were unemployed at the time.

'Mind frisking' these people is not difficult, but it can break down. Richard McCoy hijacked a United Airlines 727 on a flight from Denver. He was last on to the aircraft, but had left a large manila envelope behind in the staging area in his nervous panic. This was his only luggage.

As soon as the envelope – which contained all his hijack plans and pre-typed notes – was obligingly rushed out to him by a United employee, McCoy went straight into the lavatory.

The aircraft's second officer was sent back to ask him to leave the lavatory so that the aircraft could take off. McCoy came out of the lavatory wearing a dark black curly wig, a false moustache, a large blue tie, a blue suit with red stripes, blue shoes and reflector silvered dark glasses.

Also on the aircraft was a recaptured convict, William Coggin, who was being flown back to prison in California by a prison officer. Coggin noticed that McCoy's hair and moustache had changed colour whilst he was in the lavatory. He saw him putting on gloves. When he told the prison officer that McCoy was acting strangely, he was told to forget it.

So even the most obvious hijacker can be successful, although McCoy was later captured after parachuting out of the aircraft with $500,000. He was arrested shortly afterwards, having only had time to spend $30.

Picking up the 'politicals', who hijack aircraft for ideological reasons, is much more difficult. There are no obvious traits to give them away. Even ethnic signs help little – there are plenty of blond, blue-eyed Palestinians, and Christian to boot.

The passports are often diplomatic, forged Jordanian or Lebanese, or genuine Libyan, Algerian and Yemeni. Holders of diplomatic passports can object to themselves and their luggage being searched, even though it is known that arms and explosives for Palestinian hijackers have been smuggled into Europe by Libyan diplomats. When searches are made, diplomats often get very upset. A Saudi diplomat at Heathrow kept an intercontinental jet waiting for five hours and got an official apology after he had refused to be searched.

The US is no longer a haven for hijackers. Special hijack 'command rooms' deal with incidents. They monitor world air traffic and can call up fighter chase planes and special radar surveillance. They are in contact with the Pentagon, the United States Air Force, and the White House. Presidents since Kennedy have all taken a personal interest in hijacks. Kennedy himself ordered the tyres of a Delta jet to be shot out by the FBI to prevent it taking off for Cuba. Resident coordinators, routing experts and psychiatrists are used.

Europe has nothing to compare with this, which makes it all the easier for the hijackers.

★

Pilots react extremely well to hijack. There have been almost no flying incidents connected with hijacking – despite the pressure of flying with a gun in the back for long periods to unfamiliar airports. Three big jets crammed with passengers made flawless landings on an unmarked desert strip in Jordan.

Captain Isaac Risseeue, a fit 53-year-old, was senior pilot of KLM's flight KL861 as it took off from Amsterdam's Schiphol airport at 12.10 one Sunday morning. The giant Jumbo was named Mississippi. (All KLM's big planes are named after rivers, as National uses girls' names, Tammy and Sue, Sabena the towns of Belgium, Air France the great châteaux.)

The flight was routed to Tokyo via Beirut, Delhi and Bangkok. Three Palestinians seized it after it had reached its cruising altitude of 32,000 feet. Captain Risseeue was forced to make an unscheduled landing at Damascus. The Syrians refused to refuel the aircraft, and he flew to Cyprus and then on to Tripoli in Libya.

The hijackers expected a heroes' welcome. But the Libyans ordered them to give themselves up. They refused, and ordered Risseeue to take off again. The 247 passengers were ordered into the rear of the plane, and grenades were held above their heads.

The Libyan army started moving tanks and vehicles on the runways to prevent a take-off. One hijacker pressed a gun into the captain's neck. 'Take off, or everyone dies.'

Risseeue had by now already flown 2,600 miles and made three difficult landings under great strain. But he calmly opened the engines wide and swung the Jumbo towards an unused runway that still had sand smeared across it. There was a tank on it, and Risseeue swerved his plane round it, almost into the sand, before taking off.

He was ordered to land in Malta, the first Jumbo to land there. As the wheels touched down on the lip of the runway, full brakes and reverse thrust were piled on.

Risseeue convinced the hijackers that he could not take off again with any passengers aboard. The weight would be too great, with additional fuel. So he got all his passengers released, and took on 27,000 gallons of fuel.

A relief KLM pilot came aboard. Risseeue declined to hand over control of Mississippi – 'This is my aircraft,' he said.

At dawn on Monday the Jumbo was cleared for take-off and

started the long haul eastwards into the sun. Airports closed as Mississippi approached over the Mediterranean – first Istanbul, then Ankara, then Beirut, then Damascus wanted nothing to do with it. Baghdad airport was sealed. Far down across the desert in the Gulf, Kuwait and Bahrein also closed.

By now the 27,000 gallons were almost gone. Risseeue radioed to the tiny Gulf sheikhdom of Dubai: 'My tanks are almost empty. I need immediate permission to land.' Reluctantly Dubai agreed. But three hours after landing and being refuelled, Mississippi took off again, this time flying through the gathering dusk of Monday night across Arabia's Empty Quarter to Aden.

Aden airport was closed. The Jumbo circled above it in the darkness for three hours whilst the hijackers pleaded with the ground. Risseeue had now been flying the plane for forty-three hours. The dawn of Tuesday broke and went. Aden remained closed.

Mississippi started the long haul back to Dubai. It landed softly although the tyres were burned almost bare. The hijackers were given 30,000 more gallons of fuel. But Risseeue warned them that the tyres were now too stripped to be safe. Another take-off might be possible. But there would be no safe landing. The hijackers surrendered.

Captain Risseeue had been in command of Mississippi for sixty-nine hours and had flown 6,950 miles.

Performances like this, on a hijack that broke the previous record, held by a TWA crew who flew from the US West Coast to Rome, have become commonplace. 'It is curious,' says one pilot. 'You will never be able to stop pilots from reading instruments wrongly and killing people from time to time. But they take hijacks in their stride.'

A major reason is that pilots can play it by ear.

Only in Russia are pilots ordered to resist hijacks at all costs. The results of this policy slip out in small news items. 'Soviet police shot dead two hijackers who attempted to take over an Aeroflot Yak-40 flying between Bryansk and Moscow'; 'More than one hundred passengers on an Aeroflot flight in Siberia are reported to have died after their Ilyushin aircraft crashed during shooting in a hijack attempt': these are two examples.

All American and European crews are advised by their airlines to accede to the hijackers' wishes. They are not ordered to do so, and there have been some cases in the US where pilots have disarmed hijackers, in two cases at the cost of the co-pilots' lives.

The norm is to go along with anything the hijacker wants, as long as it won't jeopardize the safety of the aircraft. Some airlines now have printed hijack emergency sheets, exactly as a pilot carries instructions for engine failure or radio breakdown.

The first action is to quieten the hijacker. The second is to punch the emergency hijack transponder that most aircraft carry. This automatically blips the radar image of the plane on the air traffic controllers' sets. Without the hijacker being aware of it, his presence is known on the ground within seconds as the radar image fades and reforms unlike the constant echoes of other aircraft.

The pilot next selects one radio set on to his company frequency. This is normally used for informing the airline of a late arrival, of special requirements needed on landing such as wheelchairs, or relaying VIPs' messages. During hijacks, using this frequency means that the pilot will not have to wait whilst other aircraft talk to ground controllers – and that he will probably not be picked up on the ground by radio hams who could alert news and television networks to the drama.*

The fourth priority is to make sure the hijacker understands the fuel gauges, the altimeters and has some idea of navigation. 'If you're going to do what the guy wants you to do anyway,' says a TWA pilot who has been hijacked, 'you want to make sure he knows you're helping. Fuel is always vital. If you explain things right off, they'll trust you later when a decision has to be made. With mine, we started running short of fuel and couldn't make the destination the man wanted. But he knew we weren't tricking him.'

A reassured hijacker is a safe hijacker, and if he knows the

---

* An Israeli radio ham picked up messages from German Air Force planes carrying the squad that stormed the Lufthansa Boeing at Mogadishu in October 1977. He passed this on to Israeli papers and the news was soon transmitted world-wide despite German attempts to suppress it. Fortunately the hijackers did not hear it. If they had, the Mogadishu operation would not have been so successful.

height and rough position as well he will get a glowing, if unjustified, feeling of power and knowledge.

The pilot next decides whether to inform the passengers or not. With most 'political' hijacks, this is done by the hijackers themselves at considerable length, as they expound the always complex and often boring motives for their act. But with psychotics, passengers can go through a flight without even being aware of it having been hijacked. 'Passengers do tend to believe anything that comes from the captain. If you say you're diverting from London to Rome on a cloudless day because of "bad weather conditions", it is amazing how many people will just accept it without question,' says a pilot.

Finally, the captain ensures that there are no misunderstandings about routes and destinations. He attempts to keep talking to the hijacker. In many cases, pilots have talked men into handing over their guns without argument in the cockpit.

The hijack drill should be as effortless as an engine failure, reassuringly well inside the safety limits.

Passengers do not react so well to prolonged hijacking. They tend to become servile towards the hijackers and start having bitter rows between themselves. When passengers are released after fairly short flights, they are often amused by it.

Japanese passengers on a KLM flight insisted that the hijackers autographed their airline brochures before they left the plane. An Englishman who found himself hijacked from Rome to Beirut said: 'I wouldn't have missed it for the world. It was a splendid show.'

But those who survived the long desert hijacks came out of their ordeal shattered and exhausted, their physical and mental health deteriorated. Airlines have incorporated some of the findings from the TWA aircraft into the training of their cabin crews – interestingly, the passengers on the British Airways and Swissair aircraft showed much less signs of stress.

There is a pattern of reaction to hijack.

The first real concern sets in at the time when the plane should have been landing at the original destination. Before then, there is a sense of excitement and adventure. But when people realize the aircraft is overdue at the airport they should be going to, and that anxious friends and relatives will be waiting for them, the truth seeps in.

People start swapping notes and addresses with guarantees that survivors will pass them on to the families of those 'who may not make it'. This tension exists during the flying part of the hijack.

Once the aircraft lands, and the passengers are held as helpless hostages, they start going for each other. The hijackers in the desert demanded all passports, and immediately split the passengers by nationality. Some had dual nationality, Israeli and American. They automatically formed a group and protested bitterly when the baggage hold was opened to get medicines for the sick: they were afraid their Israeli second passports would be found in their baggage. By the end of the first day, the sweltering cabin had split into permanent camps along lines of common age and nationality.

Next day food became the focus of rows. The plane's food and water gave out, and only small amounts were brought in by the hijackers. This was rationed. But several passengers immediately started hoarding food and water in plastic cups. When this was discovered, they were accused of stealing.

On the third day, irritation ran right through the plane. Young children were annoying people and were snapped at for playing or laughing.

Their mothers became aggressively protective, and formed a powerful sub-group of their own. Any passenger found chatting with others of a different nationality was disowned by his fellow countrymen, and accused of 'fraternizing with the enemy'. The hijackers were no longer considered the common foe – each group competed for their favours.

Belated attempts by passengers and cabin crew to establish order never got under way. Most people simply sneered, 'Who gave *you* any special rights?' Arguments became more commonplace, and self-discipline started to slide. Some people began to crack up, sobbing without reason.

The health of young children and men of military age was markedly low. The children had less natural resilience than girls and boys above ten. The older men and women accepted the situation better than younger men, who may have felt guilty at doing nothing.

By the time the passengers were taken from the aircraft, shortly before it was blown up, paranoia had set in. Every move by the hijackers was seen as the prelude to being blown up. And each group, Europeans against Americans, old against young, mothers against everyone, thought that the others were trying to make a deal at the expense of their own lives.

Typical passengers appear to have breakdowns after four days. Where a group has a lot in common, this can be extended enormously. But where there is no such family feeling, people split into small groups and fear persists. And it does not apply to airline passengers alone. Immediately after the desert hijackings, and as a direct result of them, 100 or so reporters were trapped in a hotel in Amman as a battle between troops and guerrillas who supported the hijackers raged outside and occasionally inside.

All were journalists or television men, with war-reporting experience. Many of us knew each other from previous stories round the world. Yet we reacted in almost exactly the same way as the TWA passengers. There was an instant split by nationality. English and French journalists, as befits their countries' history, were exchanging insults within two days and punches in three.

Hoarders were common and created ill-feeling – one French TV crew was found to be keeping a bath full of beer bottles stolen from the Americans.

Every time a photographer was seen by the troops taking pictures, long volleys of machine-gun fire were poured into the hotel. So journalists split from photographers, and rumours went round that particular cameramen were trying to get everyone killed for 'political reasons' to outrage world opinion.

After five days, with the hotel a bullet-pocked mess, a serious breakdown was narrowly averted when an elected committee enforced PoW camp style rules and regulations. By this time there had been a complete nationality breakdown. The English and Americans automatically combined against the French and Italians, the Germans sided with the British. The Scandinavians kept neutral, to the contempt of the other two sides. There was only one non-European, a Japanese, and his welfare was totally ignored by all. King Hussein personally intervened for the French, sending armoured cars to get them out of Amman. The King was afraid that his troops would turn on them. In fact their 'colleagues' were on the point of doing so.

That complete strangers, of different professions, ages, nationality and sex should break down in the far smaller confines of an aeroplane seems inevitable, by comparison.

Some airlines give training on hijacks. Stewards are taught how to identify the sub-groups, the little knots of like-minded travellers which will inevitably form. They are told to make sure that none of them is left out of any arrangements or consultations. The PA system is used to prevent the cabin becoming a rumour factory. Food and water must never be hoarded. And if passengers can be told that there is a known pattern of how they are expected to deteriorate, and that it is quite natural if they do, the edge of their fear and hostility towards others will be blunted.

Captain W. H. Davidson of CP Air, a member of the Canadian Air Line Pilots' Association security committee, has published a detailed study of terrorism.* He is worried by the spread of high-technology equipment. Terrorists have obtained RPG-7s, portable anti-tank grenade launchers. The Russian-built fin-stabilized grenades were used in an abortive attack on a taxiing El Al jet at Paris Orly. The terrorists missed the El Al aircraft but damaged a parked JAT airliner.

Intelligence officers estimate that there are 200 sophisticated SA-7s in terrorist hands. Code-named GRAIL by NATO, this is a Russian heat-seeking missile with a passive infra-red homing guidance system and a high-explosive warhead. It has a range of 2.25 miles at heights between 150 and 5,000 feet. Being supersonic, it can be fired after the target passes. Two SA-7s were found in a flat at Ostia close to the departure flight path from Rome Fiumicino airport.

Captain Davidson gives a profile of terrorists. Age: twenty-two to twenty-five and decreasing. Sex: male, but female increasing and often violent. Marital status: single. Lifestyle: urban, middle class to upper class. Education: student/professional. Recruitment: university. Politics: anarchist/Marxist. Philosophy: nihilist. Davidson accuses these countries of providing assistance to ter-

* *Pilot*, CALPA.

rorists: Libya, Cuba, USSR, China, North Korea, Algeria, South Yemen, Tanzania, Congo, Zaire, Syria, Iraq and Lebanon.

He lists points that pilots – and passengers – should consider if they are hijacked or held hostage. Comply quickly and without protest to orders and directions. Express serious, non-contentious interest in your captor's political beliefs. Attempt, wherever possible, to persuade your captors that alternative means exist for achieving their aim. Where several victims are involved, meet whenever safe to discuss your own strength, weakness and capacity for self-help, and your impressions of the captors' characters and susceptibilities.

When troops or police come to the rescue, continues Davidson, take cover and do not engage your captors unless you have to for your own safety. It is likely that some passengers at some stage will show the 'Stockholm syndrome', after a Swedish bank hostage incident when captives identified with their captors and sided with them against the police.* Davidson stresses that pilots should be prepared for this and should realize that a passenger may easily give them away to the captors.

A reason why pilots cope so well with hijacks is that they have to concentrate on flying the aircraft, relaying messages and so forth. Passengers have little else to do but brood, unless they find they can concentrate on crossword puzzles, cards or books.

Physicians at Harvard Medical School have devised a simple relaxation technique. Breathe in. Breathe out again. Before re-inhaling, inwardly say to yourself, 'One.' Breathe in again. Breathe out. Inwardly say, 'One.' Continue for twenty minutes. If you find your mind wandering away from the word 'one', particularly in a way you find uncongenial, refocus it. The results are said to be similar to transcendental meditation. The technique should help a passenger to keep his cool during a delay in a terminal just as effectively as in a hijack.

Prevention is better than cure, of course. Avoiding certain airports can minimize the chances of being hijacked in the first place. The German Ministry of the Interior ordered a report on security

---

* A woman hostage in the bank later married one of her captors. The average airline passenger is not likely to go as far as that.

at foreign airports following the hijack of a planeload of German holidaymakers from Majorca to Mogadishu in Somalia.

It came up with a list of thirteen dangerous airports. Bombay, Dakar, Istanbul and Tripoli were classified as 'very unsafe'. Accra, Algiers, Baghdad, Barcelona, Jeddah, Karachi, Lagos, Palma de Majorca and Toronto were considered 'unsafe'. The Germans reckoned that security measures at a further thirty-seven airports were 'inadequate'.

Hijacking, like so much else in flying, is largely a matter of fashion. It snowballed so rapidly in the US that one man seized a United Airlines plane and ordered the pilot to fly to Detroit. The aircraft was on a scheduled flight already – to Detroit.

Post-war hijacking started with refugees from Eastern Europe forcing aircraft to the West. On a single day in 1950, three airliners were hijacked from Czechoslovakia to West Germany: something that was not to be repeated until the height of Arab hijacking in 1970. The hijackers, former Czech RAF pilots, were treated as heroes in the West and few thought more about it.

But with the arrival of Castro in Cuba, hijacking entered a semi-permanent relationship with flying. During the fighting against Batista, guerrillas of the famous 'Column Six' hacked an airstrip out of the jungle and hijacked two DC3s of the national airline Cubana to it.

Once Castro was in power, Cubans used his old methods to escape, this time hijacking Cuban aircraft to get to Miami. Castro was the first political leader to have to enforce rigorous security checks at airports. Then Cubana pilots themselves started absconding with their aircraft. Castro was forced to put armed guards aboard to watch over the pilots – the first skymarshals.

The traffic soon started going the other way. On 1 May 1961, a man checked on to a National Airlines flight from Miami to Key West. He gave his name as Elpirata Cofrisi. The pirate Cofrisi had scourged the Caribbean in the eighteenth century but the airline missed the joke. Cofrisi pulled a knife on the captain and a gun on the co-pilot, and told them to fly him to Cuba.

The pilots agreed, and the first hijack of an American aircraft began. It lasted just forty-five minutes before the Convair airliner landed in Cuba. Cofrisi was arrested, and the aircraft and passengers were safely on their way back to Key West before anyone in America knew what was happening.

Since then hijacking has blossomed almost into an industry. Two thirds of the world hijackings have taken place in the US. But they reflect troubled politics elsewhere. Palestinians have been using hijacking as a political weapon since July 1968, when they had their first and only successful attempt to seize an El Al 707. The Israelis promptly put highly effective guards on their planes, and since then Palestinians have only succeeded in hijacking and destroying the planes of other nations. The list of victims is bewildering – British, American, German, Japanese, Dutch, Greek, Swiss, Belgian, Turkish, French and Jordanian aircraft or airports or both have been attacked.

Other, more private but equally bizarre, hijacking wars go on. An SAS aircraft was hijacked in Sweden by extremist Croatians, who also hijacked a jet in the US and flew it to Europe to drop leaflets on London and Paris. Ethiopian aircraft became battle-grounds for citizens opposed to the Addis Ababa regime. In one gun battle, fought 30,000 feet above Madrid in a 707, one would-be hijacker was shot ten times by a skymarshal, and the plane's skin was pierced six times. Extreme right- and left-wing Japanese students seize their country's aircraft: the same happens in Argentina.

Nations themselves indulge in hijacking. A British Airways VC10 was forced down by Libyan Air Force fighters over Libya, and two Sudanese removed. The Israeli Air Force diverted a Middle East Airlines Caravelle. They thought that Georges Habash, a prominent Palestinian hijacker himself, was aboard. He had cancelled his flight that morning.

Money has gradually become as important a motive for hijack as politics, or simple mental instability on behalf of the hijackers. The first man to attempt to steal an aircraft for money was a former Nationalist Chinese pilot called Chio Tok. He was tempted by the Catalina flying boats that flew daily between Hong Kong and Macao.

They carried rich British bankers, dealers from Hong Kong, and gold for the smugglers in Macao: a promising mixture of ransom and precious metal. Chio Tok planned to take over the Catalina, the 'Miss Macao', and land it in a hidden part of the estuary of the Pearl River, safe from the police and the pirates who still infested the area in 1948.

With a gang of four, Chio Tok tried to hijack the plane immediately after take-off from Macao. The pilots resisted, and the captain was shot in the back. His weight was forced forward on to the controls and the plane went into a fatal dive into the South China Sea. Chio Tok died, together with passengers and crew. He had been unlucky. Half a million dollars was found on the body of one bullion dealer passenger.

Twenty-three years later, in Washington State on the West Coast of America, another man, almost certainly also an ex-pilot, planned his own updated version of Chio Tok's bungled effort. Nobody still knows whether or not he was successful, although he has become a folk hero:

With your pleasant smile
And your drop-out style,
D. B. Cooper, where did you go?*

Like Chio Tok, D. B. Cooper knew aircraft. But he did not plan to hijack it to a ground destination. He planned to jump out of it, with a ransom of $200,000. He chose a Boeing 727 – like the DC9, BAC1–11 and Caravelle, it has an exit downstairs in the tail, perfect for jumping clear of the engines and tail of the plane. He bought his ticket in the name of D. B. Cooper, had apparently no disguise apart from dark glasses, and was so quiet that none of the other passengers knew the plane had been hijacked when they left it in Seattle, Washington, after an apparently normal flight from Portland.

He hijacked the plane simply by giving the stewardess a note, and showing her some cylinders connected by wire. His note demanded four parachutes and $200,000 in $20 bills. This went into a manageable parcel for a parachutist, two feet long and only eight inches thick. The money was picked up at Seattle.

He ordered the pilot to fly at 7,000 feet, with fifteen-per-cent flaps and the gear down and the rear stairs extended. He jumped half an hour after leaving Seattle on a course for Reno, at night into the wooded Cascade Mountains. No body or parachute was found – but neither has any of the numbered money been spent.

* Copyright Fremont West Music.

The fashion spread. Shortly afterwards, five other Americans jumped out of airliners with over a million and a half dollars. All were caught, but $303,000 is still missing. Extortion hijacks have been most common on Fridays because hijackers thought it easier to get large sums of money at the end of the week.

One sprained an ankle on landing, another dropped half a million dollars into the slipstream as he jumped, another was picked up after a perfect night jump into the Nevada desert because he had left his car waiting for him – and the police had been keeping an eye on it as a suspicious vehicle. Another virtually hitchhiked home; he jumped only five miles from his house.

Today radio bleepers devised for locating shot-down pilots in Vietnam are placed in the parachutes, chase planes follow close behind, and crews can tell from a slight jolt back on the control column when and where the hijacker jumps.

Extortion is out of fashion, but the threat of political hijacks remains. The odds of a passenger being injured in an attempt are low – out of 15,000 hijacked up to 1974, twelve were killed or injured.

But the fear and helplessness of a political hijack, and the difficulty of arranging deals for prisoners to be released instead of just collecting money, come out vividly in this transcript:

The pilot of a Lufthansa Boeing 737, hijacked from Rome after five Palestinian gunmen had killed thirty-two people on the ground with phosphorus grenades, said to Athens control tower: 'For God's sake, do something. These people are not joking. They have already killed. Get someone there who speaks Arabic.'

Control: 'We are doing our best. We are getting the Syrian Ambassador.'

Pilot: 'Rush him there.'

At 5.44 p.m. a shot is heard over the radio. An Italian policeman, seized as a hostage in Rome, is reported shot dead. There is another shot fifty-one minutes later.

Hijacker, in Arabic: 'We will wait half an hour. That's the end. We've waited too long already.'

At 7.26 p.m., Lufthansa reported a third hostage shot.

Pilot: 'We are already past the deadline. They've already killed four and they're not joking. Now they've got three women outside and their guns are pointed at them.'

Control: 'All right, hold on a minute, take it easy . . .'

Pilot: 'Come on. Bring their Palestinian friends to them. They're getting very nervous.'

Control: 'Hold on, we have technical problems.'

Pilot: 'Stop fooling around with them. Get those Arabs on the line. I can't hold off these Arabs any longer. They don't believe me any more. They've gone out to get the women.'

By midnight, the plane was still parked in a dark corner of Athens Hellinikon airport. Greek troops were preparing to storm it, when the pilot again came through on the radio in desperation.

Pilot, above the noise of shots: 'Jesus, there's shooting going on back there.'

Hijacker, in broken English: 'Where are the two men? Stop all talking. No further talk is necessary.'

At 3 a.m. with the Greek authorities still refusing to hand over two hijackers held in Greek gaols, a hijacker came over the radio again.

'Can you hear? This woman will die. Scream!' Control tower reported hearing female screams over the Boeing's radio.

Hijacker: 'If our demands are not met, we will kill all, keeping the pilot and co-pilot for last. Listen to them.'

A woman was forced to the microphone. She pleaded to the control tower in English: 'Come please. Come. Help me. Help me.'

Control: 'Please be patient.'

Co-pilot: 'Christ, they are going to shoot me . . .'

Hijacker: 'If I don't have an answer within a minute, I'm going to kill the co-pilot.'

A shot came over the radio.

Hijacker to tower: 'I'll kill two more within half an hour.'

At 4.50 a.m., with the sun coming up, the jet suddenly rumbled down the runway and took off towards Kuwait. A body was found on the tarmac as the jet hauled past on take-off. A seriously wounded hostage lay nearby. The others, and the crew, were released in Kuwait. The hijackers were never brought to trial.

A new form of hijacking has started. In a classic 'man bites dog' incident, a Filipino pilot attempted to hijack his passengers. The DC3 plane was carrying workers and cash to an oilfield, and the pilot planned to abduct the aircraft to a small island. From there he would make off with the money by boat. It was a Swiftair service to Sanga Sanga in the Philippines.

The flight was on 31 March 1977. He tried to force his co-pilot to alter course for the island by holding an automatic rifle to his head. The co-pilot refused and the passengers tried to rush the cockpit. The pilot opened fire to keep them back, killing four and wounding three before being overpowered. He was sentenced to life imprisonment for murder and attempted piracy.

22 Turbulence

The most noticeable emergency is turbulence. One pilot reports it:

'We encountered the most violent jolt I have ever experienced in over 20,000 hours of flying. It was like sitting on the end of a hugh tuning fork that had been struck violently. Not an instrument on any panel was readable to their full scale but appeared as white blurs against their dark background. From that point on, we had no idea of attitude, altitude, airspeed or heading. Violent buffeting, ripping, tearing, rending crashing sounds. Briefcases, manuals, ashtrays, suitcases, pencils, cigarettes flying about like unguided missiles. It sounded and felt as if the engine pods were leaving and the structure disintegrating. As my briefcase was on the ceiling, I looked up through the overhead window and felt I was looking down on the top of a cloud deck. We applied as much force as we could to roll aileron control to the left. The horizon bar started to stabilize and showed us coming back through ninety degrees vertical to level . . .'

Captain Stephen Parkinson was flying a DC8. He was climbing between two thunderstorms on a flight from Dulles International in Virginia. The aircraft finally rolled right side up and was brought under control only 1,400 feet above the ground.

The pilot had no idea how long the condition lasted. But during it, the 120-ton aircraft and its 109 passengers had rolled completely upside down. Extreme turbulence like this can either pull an aircraft to pieces in mid-air, or it can force the pilot past the limits of his skill, so that he loses control and the aircraft stalls or spins into the ground.

An Eastern Airlines DC8 dropped 13,000 feet in severe turbulence over Texas and had an engine torn off before the crew made an emergency landing. It also was climbing between thunderstorm cells. The co-pilot on this flight was killed when his DC8 and its fifty-one passengers crashed into Lake Pontchartrain, Louisiana, after hitting turbulence.

As Donald Davis, the chief test pilot of the United Kingdom

Airworthiness Authority, a man not given to overstatement, has baldly written in his classic book *Handling the Big Jets*,* in turbulence 'you must fly the aeroplane properly in order to survive'.

Few passengers will ever have come across this degree of turbulence – after all, it took the pilot quoted above 20,000 hours, or more than two years permanently in the air, to meet up with it. When it does come, it is unmistakable. It's not the sort of nasty bumping that may spill coffee or spray it over the ceiling. Nor is it the kind that will throw standing passengers around. It is when coffee floats in mid-air as the cabin revolves around it and where passenger who are standing are killed.

The most common cause is a storm, particularly of cumulonimbus clouds. These towering, anvil-shaped clouds can soar to 40,000 feet in Europe and temperate climates. In the tropics, they can get to 60,000 feet. A jet cannot get above them at that height, but it makes little difference since flying over them is as dangerous as flying through them.

They have enormous energy. Air currents can be rising and falling at 5,000 feet a minute very close to each other. Between them, in the 'mixing area', are extremely violent sharp-edged gusts which can destroy an aircraft. Particles of moisture can be hurled down from 30,000 feet to 10,000 feet, then be shot up again in a rising current, getting larger and larger until they freeze, become too heavy to stay in the cloud and fall as hail.

Each cloud can be thirty miles wide. They can appear, grow to 40,000 feet, produce five-inch hail on the ground, and then decay, within fifteen minutes. At the base, there is heavy rain and hail up to five inches in diameter. Sleet, rain and hail go up to 30,000 feet, and above that there is snow and ice crystals.

The friction between the air currents as they rise and fall whips up static electricity as the whole cloud mass is charged and lightning flashes to earth, to another cloud or flickers inside the same cloud. The storm systems are often large, and line squalls can stretch for several hundred miles. Gusts of 100 mph have been recorded, but since they strike the aircraft as it is also being thrown up and down at high speed, this is far more serious than a hurricane at ground level.

* Published by the Air Registration Board, Redhill, Surrey, England.

It is frightening in the cockpit. 'St Elmo's fire starts dancing around the windscreen. The static builds up so most of your radios and direction finders go on the blink, and your communications. There's so much interference you can't talk to the ground any more,' says a pilot who flew through a severe storm in the South China Sea. 'Lightning strikes give a great flash, bang and a burning smell. The compasses go off. You get shocks from the controls, static again. And all the time there's the noise of the hail, battering on the windscreens to get in.'

But the roughness is the worst. 'The whole aircraft is thrown around so much you feel it is going to slide out of control. The instruments seem to go mad. The airspeed indicator and the vertical speed indicator keep going up and down like yoyos. You think you are about to stall, and you heave on the power and the next thing is that you're rapidly approaching the maximum dive speed and you get the engines back to idle.'

Storms can be picked up by weather radar. A black centre with a white line round the cloud cells spells danger, although the radar cannot distinguish between rain and hail, and a storm can be hidden by great areas of moist but innocent clouds. When a water concentration comes up on the radar, the rule is to reduce airspeed and avoid it by fifteen miles, or twenty miles if flying above 30,000 feet. A typical turbulent, or 'rough airspeed' on a 707 is 280 knots or .80 Mach.

No pilot should ever fly into one, or try to work his way through on radar. There can be severe gusts between clouds and large, dry hail which will not show on the moisture-seeking radar. A cloud can develop in a previously clear bit of sky, to a height of more than 30,000 feet, in two minutes. As the pilot slips between clouds, he may come to a dead end as the gaps fill in.

Severe storms must be avoided if possible. No take-off should be attempted in the area of a thunderstorm. These are the rules. They are sometimes broken.

Heavy thunderstorms were approaching an American airfield. The captain of a Martin 404 airliner decided to take off.* Not only that, but he ordered his first officer to fly, and from the captain's normal seat, the left-hand one. Hail, heavy rain and

---

* CAA 12/63.

winds gusting to fifty mph had already hit the airport as the aircraft taxied.

The co-pilot took off into a wall of heavy rain, shifting winds and hail. The left wing dropped, and the aircraft was severely buffeted by turbulence. The right wing dropped, followed by the left. The airliner hit the ground, cartwheeled and caught fire.

The inquiry found that the captain's 'attempt to take off into a severe thunderstorm raised serious doubts as to his judgement'.

The pilot of an American Airlines 707 over Texas ran into severe hail at 26,000 feet. It ripped off the radome section of the nose, severely dented the airframe sections, crazed the cockpit windscreens to complete opaqueness and damaged the wings so severely the flaps could not be used. In the flapless landing at 240 mph, the pilot slammed the nose forward because he couldn't see through the windscreen properly, and the nosewheel collapsed.

Yet a tornado had been forecast on this section from Dallas to Los Angeles. A 'severe' weather forecast had been made and the pilot turned down a suggestion from ATC of the smoothest ride in preference to a more direct route.

Clear air turbulence is another killer. CAT is unseen and cannot be picked up on radar. It is normally a by-product of the jet-streams, the currents of fast moving air at high altitude. CAT is the turbulence where two different streams meet. Flying through CAT is normally like shooting the rapids. There is a series of hard shocks and bumps, frightening to the passenger since it comes out of a cloudless sky, but not worrying to the pilot. The aircraft is not being thrown around, merely bumping over an uneven surface, and the pilot can easily descend to get out of it.

But when CAT combines with the turbulent waves thrown up by great mountain ranges, the results are more savage. A high chain lying broadside to strong winds, and particularly to jet-streams, will throw up a wave on its windward side to very high altitudes, 40,000 feet and more.

Aircraft can be severely buffeted by these killer waves, particularly if they are in the downdraught area on the lee side. An Egyptair 707 on a night flight from Cairo to London was flying over the Alps at 31,000 feet at over 500 mph. It hit a rapidly descending pocket 'like a brick wall'.

The eighty-ton aircraft dropped vertically for 200 feet. Fortunately, 124 passengers were strapped in, as glasses and bottles shattered on the cabin roof. But one man was out of his seat, coming back from the toilet. He was hurled round the cabin and died later of multiple injuries.

Turbulence is worst in the tail. It is furthest from the aircraft's centre of gravity and can buck more. Most injuries in turbulence are thus to stewardesses in the rear galleys, and next to passengers waiting to use the rear lavatories.

Killer waves can rip a big jet to pieces. A British Airways 707 took off on a flight from Tokyo to Hong Kong in 1966 with 124 passengers, mostly Americans on a package holiday, and crew.* Visibility was excellent and the elegant, 12,000 feet sacred cone of Mount Fuji was visible seventy miles away.

A proverb says: When the sky is blue, Fuji is angry. And indeed the meteorological report confirmed that vicious Force Nine winds were stripping the clouds from Fuji's slopes. They were blowing from the northwest, so that the aircraft would be in the dangerous lee of the mountain on its route.

The pilot decided he would fly VMC, visual meteorological conditions, meaning that he was not under strict control but could choose his own route, until he was past Fuji. He would then fly on to Hong Kong on the more normal IFR, instrument flying rules, sticking to a controller's orders.

A cine film taken by a passenger survived intact. It showed the aircraft climbing over Gotemba City into the turbulent area, fourteen miles from the top of Fuji, until at a height of 15,000 feet and a speed of 400 mph, the film showed a whirl of seats and carpet. Then it stopped.

First the starboard wing and then the front of the plane broke away as the aircraft disintegrated in mid-air. The turbulence was too great for the stress to be taken. All on board were killed. The inquiry reported that 'the aircraft suddenly encountered abnormally severe turbulence over Gotemba City which imposed a gust load considerably in excess of the design limit'. A strong mountain wave situation existed over Japan. Wave clouds were detected by satellites three quarters of an hour before the accident to the west and southwest of Fuji.

* HMSO CAP 286.

If the aeroplane stays in one piece, if the pilots do not become disorientated so that their vision gets tunnelled on to a single instrument, and if they do not lose their sense of the aircraft's attitude and become dizzy – then severe turbulence should be merely frightening.

The first thing the pilot does is to switch on the seat belt and No Smoking signs: unstrapped passengers can be killed, and in bad turbulence it is very difficult even to hold on to a cigarette. He checks his weather radar through the storm. He must not try to climb over it, for the turbulence extends higher than the aircraft can fly. He removes the height and speed locks from the autopilot, which will try too hard to keep the height and speed that it is locked into. If the plane is caught in an updraught, the autopilot will immediately stab the nose down and increase power to lose height. This mechanical overreaction could destroy the aircraft, and so planes are normally 'hand flown' in bad conditions.

The cockpit lighting is turned up to full brilliance, even by day. One pilot will normally wear dark glasses. It prevents temporary blindness after lightning strikes – modern aircraft are bonded together, so lightning should run harmlessly through to discharge wicks at the tail, although one jet is thought to have been destroyed by it.

The speed will be cut back to the 'rough airspeed', so the engine note changes and the air brakes may go up on the wings. Radios spoiled by static are turned off. Deicing equipment is switched on. Ice dislodged from the air intakes can damage engines and cause flame-outs, so engines are deiced singly or in pairs.

All loose equipment in the cockpit is stacked away. When the storm hits, the pilot simply tries to 'ride' it. He ignores even large 'height excursions', as he calls the sickening drops and rises of thousands of feet. He only maintains a rough height and course. All the concentration goes on to the attitude indicator, keeping the aircraft fairly straight and level in attitude. Even if the storm makes the aircraft drop, the pilot will keep it straight and not climb. It takes some eight seconds before the thrust from the jets is effective, and by then the aircraft may be rising again.

Only in mountain wave turbulence, where there is a danger of being sucked down on to the mountains, will the pilot pour on full engine power to fight for height.

Even that may not be enough. The Uruguayan plane that crashed in the Andes was on full power but the downdraughts still sucked it down into the mountains. The Andes and the Sierra Nevadas are the most notorious mountain wave areas, followed by the Southern Alps in New Zealand and the Pyrenees.

If the crew try to do too much, all of them can eventually be trying to fly the plane at the same time, with the power going straight from idle to full, and with elevators, ailerons, speed brakes and rudders being used in a totally uncoordinated way. Control must be positively in the hands of the captain alone.

The passengers may notice the engines being eased off as the aircraft hits turbulence. The speed brakes may also be used, as they are very efficient in cutting back speed rapidly. But from then on, there should be few power changes. The rudder will not be used. At high speeds, the rudder is ineffective, and may reverse its effect, leading to violent yawing and the danger of structural damage.

Aircraft can also suffer from jet upset in turbulence. This is due to the speed and clean design. Because a jet develops a huge amount of thrust and yet has very low drag, it can fly far too fast. This is called 'gross overspeed potential'. It means that an aircraft which is designed never to exceed 650 mph could reach 1,500 mph in a dive.

Turbulence is the main initiator of an upset. A jet has reduced manoeuvrability in the thin air at altitude and can become unstable in rough weather. If it stalls it has poor lift and will lose a great deal of height before it can recover.

Thus a jet at cruising altitude can be 'upset' and start losing height, either at runaway speed, or in a stall. Once an upset starts, it will very rapidly escalate because of the bulk of the aircraft. Jets have lost 25,000 feet in pulling out of upsets.

In a stall, the pilot will be warned by the stick shaker. He pushes the stick full forward to get the nose down and airspeed up. Full power goes on the throttles to keep the height loss to a minimum. The nose has to be kept down in a deep dive for some time for the speed and clean air flow to build up.

If the plane goes steep nose up, the pilot pushes the stick forward and puts on full power. This is a very unpleasant manoeuvre, as it brings temporary negative g or weightlessness as the aircraft noses forward. However, when the nose goes up over fifty degrees, the elevator is probably not effective enough to get the nose pushed down. So the pilot has to put the plane into a 45-degree bank – the wing pointing directly down – and let the nose fall.

Recovery from a large angle of bank takes time, because the nose drops as the aircraft turns. If the pilot tries to pull the aircraft straight too quickly, it will sideslip and tend to roll. He must ease it level with ailerons.

A high-speed dive is counteracted by full-speed brakes, and then pulled out of the dive. It will buffet badly as the nose comes up and speed begins to drop off. In a typical upset, an aircraft could dive from 35,000 feet to 22,000 feet. Its speed would increase greatly. As it pulls out of the dive, it will try to get back to its lower speed by lifting the nose. The pilot must counteract this by pushing firmly forward on the stick to keep the aircraft level. The speed will gradually drop off. When he is back to cruising speed, the pilot can start climbing back to altitude.

In fact, there are recovery drills from even the most severe positions. If the artificial horizons collapse during an upset, for example, recovery is still possible. A spin can be recognized by sloppy controls, noise and a low airspeed, and a high rate of turn. Rudder is put on in the opposite direction to the spin, the ailerons centred, and the stick pushed forward. As the aircraft steadies in the dive, the nose is eased up.

A spiral also sends the turn indicator haywire, and the airspeed rapidly increases. Aileron is used against the turn, and again the aircraft should settle down in a dive.

It is even possible to survive an upside-down dive without an artificial horizon. The pilot tells he is upside down by hanging in his straps and having pencils and briefcases flying around. The aircraft is rolled for eight seconds – that being the rule of thumb for a jet airliner to roll through 180 degrees. It should then be right side up, in a spiral.

A total failure of all attitude information can be coped with – for a short period. The pilot steers straight by the compass and the turn indicator. He keeps level by checking the airspeed and altimeter for height.

If he does not get his instruments working again within a few minutes, he is not likely to live to talk about it.

Turbulent and gusty conditions can be dangerous on take-off as well as at height. A 727 of Continental Airlines was taking off from Stapleton International airport at Denver. The aircraft was expected to have a headwind on the take-off runway of twenty knots. The aircraft started its roll with a slight tailwind, which then changed to gusting headwinds of twenty knots. But as the aircraft started to lift off, the winds changed to violent ninety-knot tailwinds.

No aircraft is designed to cope with such a tailwind on take-off and the 727 stalled and crashed, overwhelmed by a wind-shift of 180 degrees and over 100 mph in seconds. Although the aircraft was seriously damaged, there was no fire and all aboard escaped.

23 Ditching

Another emergency that passengers brood about on flights across the sea is a forced landing on water, 'ditching' as pilots call it. It is reassuring to know that even heavy modern jets can ditch without harm. Indeed, one did it by mistake. A Japan Air Lines DC8 was making an approach in bad visibility to San Francisco airport.* The pilot thought he was close to the airport when he was still over the bay. Calmly and with great precision, he let the aircraft down through the murk to a pillow soft landing in the Pacific. All the 107 passengers and crew clambered out and sat on the wings as the tide went out and the aircraft settled on a mudbank.

If this can be achieved accidentally, think how much better it should be done if the pilot is doing it on purpose.

With the reliability of modern jet engines, ditching is now extremely unlikely: most aircraft that get into the sea have overshot runways or aborted take-offs at airports close to the sea. This is why a few aircraft each year wind up in the sea at Hong Kong and Tokyo.

But it still happens with propeller aircraft, and many ditchings are survivable – a DC3 with engine failure went into the sea off Majorca, and only one person, an old lady who could not swim, was drowned.

An Olympic Airways prop jet was put in the sea off Athens after extreme turbulence, with survivors. And forty-eight out of seventy-six survived when a Lockheed Constellation ditched near a ship 560 miles west of Shannon in the Atlantic. Any aircraft flying 400 nautical miles or ninety minutes' flying time from the nearest land must carry life-rafts and lifejackets.

Much depends on how the pilot touches down in relation to the surface of the sea. If there is a swell running, the pilot must land parallel to it, preferably along its crest. Ditching into the face of a swell would break up the aircraft. So pilots aim to land along

* NTSB *AAR* 70–2.

the crest, just as in the desert they land parallel to sand dunes. Ditching has much in common with desert landings. During the Yom Kippur war, sophisticated fighters like Russian Mig 21s and American Phantoms were landed with little more than scratched paintwork and sand in the engines.

But when wind speeds are between twenty-five and thirty-five knots, the aircraft will drift so much that it will need correction. There are also medium-size waves with long foam crests, and a welter of white caps. Here the pilot compromises: he heads partly into the wind, landing across the swell tops but avoiding rising waves. He keeps the nose almost into the wind to stop drift before yawing away from it with a heavy kick on the rudder just before touching the water.

Above thirty-five knots the wind and waves have to be faced straight on if there is enough space between the waves. The wavecrests have broken into spindrift and large streaks of foam cover the sea. This is miserable weather for yachts, let alone Boeings, but by firmly landing into the wind, which cuts the speed and thus impact of landing and down the back of a large, clearly defined wave, there is a good chance of survival.

In more normal weather, a landing along the crest or on the windward side parallel to waves or swell is the drill.

As soon as the emergency starts, the pilots are drilled to immediately put out a mayday. Typically, this would be 'Mayday, mayday, Flight One, 24 west 21 north estimated, course 140 degrees, speed 220 knots, altitude flight level 300 (30,000 feet). Fire on number four engine. Ditching on present course, descending immediately. Please intercept . . .'

The transponder which identifies the aircraft on radar screens at air traffic control is set to the emergency code, 77. If possible, the nearest ship is located and course set for it. The example is rather charitable, because the aircraft is about halfway between New York and London and is very near a weather ship. Pilots get to know weather ships and their crews well, becoming 'postmen' to them and passing messages on to them. The amount of chat in mid Pacific or Atlantic is vast.

A famous British Airways captain, O. P. Jones, tried to get through to weather ship *Charlie* in the Atlantic one night. But an American stewardess on another aircraft was already talking to it.

'I'm twenty-two, five feet four, 35–22–35, blonde hair, blue eyes. My flat is in 16 Brooklyn Park, my telephone number is . . .' 'Can you cook?' asked the sailor on *Charlie*'s radio. 'Everyone says my apple pie is something,' said the stewardess.

Captain Jones finally got through in a gap in the conversation. 'I'm fifty-one years old,' he said, 'five feet nine, 42–32–35, blue eyes, a torpedo beard . . . I'm interested in breeding bulldogs and I live in Sussex, England. My cooking is well known. Do you want my telephone number?'

The sailor gasped, 'No-o.' 'Then,' said Captain Jones, 'can I have the wind at 19,000 feet?'

To get back to a situation when its engines go quiet and stay quiet.

The cabin staff and passengers are warned. The passengers are moved forward as far as possible, brought into first class, and strapped in away from the tail because the tail is where the captain is planning that the first thump of water will be felt. As the passengers move, he retrims. The cabin staff should be getting food, water and blankets tied down round the exits. Life-raft positions are assigned.

This preparation is vital. An Overseas National DC9, operated as Dutch Antillean Airlines flight 980 from JFK to Juliana airport, St Maarten, was diverted to St Thomas after three attempts to land in poor weather. It was low on fuel, and made for St Croix. It ran out of fuel and ditched. Although a Pan Am flight confirmed the ditching site on radar, and Coastguard, Navy and Marine helicopters were quickly on the scene, one crew member and twenty-two passengers of the sixty-three aboard drowned.

The National Transportation Safety Board found that 'the probability of survival would have been increased substantially if there had been better crew coordination prior to and during the ditching. The Board has recommended that action be taken to improve passenger safety through adequate warning, proper briefing, standardized seat belts and more accessible stowage of life-vests for emergencies.'

The engineer starts dumping fuel if he can. With Flight One he cannot, because there is a fire on the right wing – but enough fuel has been used so that the aircraft will float.

As the aircraft comes down from 10,000 feet to 3,000 feet, the engineer methodically goes through his emergency checklist. The crew work out the landing speed after estimating weight.

On the approach the captain determines sea conditions and his final ditching heading on the sea. Life-vests are put on. Landing speed will be normal.

The first officer transmits a final position. The emergency exit lights go on. The captain checks that the landing gear is up – if down it would drag the aircraft nose down, puncture the belly and let in water through the undercarriage doors. The flaps go to fifty degrees.

At 500 feet, the first officer warns the passengers that ditching is imminent. The captain keeps the rate of descent at 200 feet a minute, a gentle approach, and makes sure he does not stall.

At fifty feet, the co-pilot warns passengers, 'Brace . . . brace.' The throttles come fully back. The pilot pulls firmly back on the stick to get the aircraft 10 degrees nose up. Like this, it hits slightly tail first – not too much, or it will bring the nose crashing into the water as the plane pivots, not too little or the aircraft may bounce and then plough in nose first. The wings must be level as he goes in; if one wing tip is down it will dig into the water and drag the aircraft round.

If most of the fuel has been used, the aircraft will float indefinitely. During the late 1930s a Lockheed twin, the 'Stars Special', which carried Hollywood stars over the Atlantic, had its wings filled with ping pong balls for buoyancy. A Junkers which ditched off Newfoundland in 1931 floated for a week before the crew were rescued.*

If there is a ship the aircraft will land ahead and to one side of it: even a 5,000-ton steamer needs half a mile to stop, and if the chosen saviour is a supertanker it will need six miles.

The rafts are complicated affairs: a thirty-seater life-raft costs

---

* In the film *Airport 77*, a 747 sinks to the seabed with the passengers and crew still alive in the intact cabin. It is technically feasible, just, for a modern aircraft. A 747 freighter, with a small passenger section that stays intact, could sink in shallow water if the freight holds fill with water. At any depth, pressure would implode the fuselage. In practice, however, there is easily enough air in a 747 cabin to keep the aircraft afloat – unless it is holed, when it will flood and sink with predictable results to the passengers.

several thousand pounds. It comes with heliographs for flashing at search aircraft; radio beacons that transmit automatic positions on 121.5 and 243 MHz, the emergency frequencies, and that have a duration of forty hours; rocket flares; compasses; insect repellent and seasick tablets. Aircraft flying over desolate land with snow and ice, such as the polar routes between Europe and the US West Coast and Japan, must carry sleeping bags for a third of those aboard, polar suits for the crew, a stove for every seventy-five aboard to melt snow, and snow shovels and icesaws.

It has taken months for airliners to be found after they have crashed on land, but wartime pilots have survived for fifty days in very small rafts. Fish always follow dinghies: brightly coloured fish, fish that 'puff up', fish with human-looking teeth or mouths like a parrot's or fish covered with spikes or bristles should be avoided as they are poisonous. Protein absorbs a lot of fluid, so people should not eat much if there is little water. Wastes should only be thrown overboard at night if there are shark or swordfish around.

The experienced ditcher will also be up with such tricks as avoiding 'immersion foot' by removing his footwear, drying and loosely wrapping his feet with cloth and exercising his feet and toes. He will reduce thirst by sucking a button and make sure he eats very little so as to preserve digestive fluids.

When he drifts to land, he will know the Search and Rescue signs to stamp in the sand or snow. I means that he requires a doctor, II that he needs medical supplies. F will get him food and water, L fuel and oil. LL means that all is well; N is no, Y is yes. W means an engineer is wanted, ⩔ that firearms are needed. A triangle, △, means that it is probably safe to land. If he leaves his camp, he leaves an arrow, ↑, pointing in the direction he has gone.

24 Pilot Error

The three-engined Boeing 727 took off from Frankfurt half an hour after midnight. It was on a scheduled flight to London Gatwick from Kabul, Kandahar, Beirut and Istanbul. Estimated flight time to London was one hour.

The weather over Northern Europe was mainly brilliant: a cold and very clear night with almost unlimited visibility in the frosty air. Here and there patches of freezing fog stubbornly refused to shift. One hung over Gatwick airport. It was not thick, perhaps only 250 feet. People on the ground at Gatwick could see the halo of the moon through it.

But it had cut the visibility on the runway to 100 metres. Nothing had landed there, and the controllers did not think anything would. They had reckoned without Ariana Afghan Airways Flight 701, and its Captain Rahim Nowroz.

There were fifty-four passengers aboard, and eight crew – Captain Nowroz, co-pilot Abdul Attayee, a flight engineer, a ground engineer and four cabin staff.

The aircraft was virtually brand new, and, apart from a warning light on the autopilot, was to perform perfectly that January night.

Captain Nowroz had 10,400 flying hours. He had been trained in England, with Boeing in America, and in Beirut and Brussels. He was reckoned a thoroughly satisfactory pilot, although his Belgian instructor had noticed a tendency to do routine duties on the flight deck himself rather than ask his crew. The Belgian's report was made three months before Flight 701: it noted that the routine duties were done at the expense of 'handling the controls'.*

Co-pilot Attayee was thought by a Boeing assessor on a training course he had recently completed to be 'weak on instrument cross-checks. Forgets checklist'.

At 1.13 a.m. the Boeing was at 24,000 feet over Wulpen in Belgium. The few passengers who were not dozing had the chance

* HMSO CAP 244.

of a drink and coffee. They could see clear to the Channel coast. Flight 701 passed into the London Airways control zone.

'Gatwick's runway visual range is 100 metres . . . er . . . confirm your point of landing now,' radioed the airways controller. The patch of fog at Gatwick was still refusing to budge. All night the controller had been diverting aircraft to Heathrow.

The weather at Heathrow was sharp and good – the sky was clear and the visibility on the runway 2,500 metres.

'Roger, we are trying . . . er . . . to Gatwick, we'll see later,' Nowroz radioed back from his Boeing.

The controller was surprised: '701. I didn't get that. Again, please.'

Still without much conviction, Nowroz repeated: 'I say again . . . er . . . we are trying in Gatwick, 701.' The controller caught it this time. He asked 701 to maintain height and course to the Mayfield beacon in East Sussex and then on to Gatwick.

To be certain that the pilot knew conditions, the controller repeated: 'Gatwick visual range 100 metres.' He told him to land on Runway 27.

Nowroz acknowledged: 'Gatwick. The Runway 27.' He did not repeat the visibility. It was well beneath limits. He needed a minimum visibility of half a mile and a cloud ceiling of 200 feet before company regulations allowed him to make an approach. The cloud was down on the runway. The visibility was 100 metres.

701 flew on. The controller gave it permission to descend to 8,000 feet. It was 1.20 a.m. The throttles on the Boeing were eased back. The engines hushed a little, and a few passengers stirred in their sleep as the aircraft slipped down over the Channel. The flight was smooth and routine.

The airways controller was still worried. The conditions at Gatwick nagged him. Did the pilot of 701, with that hint of a foreign accent, understand what things were like at Gatwick? He checked with Gatwick for the actual weather at the minute.

At 1.23 a.m. he called up Nowroz again. His voice was conciliatory. No British airport can be closed. Any pilot who wants to try to land, can. If it was of interest, though: '701, London. I just checked with Gatwick. The runway remains . . . the range remains at . . . er . . . 100 metres and there's no sign of improvement at the moment.'

He expected Flight 701 to pull up and divert to starlit Heathrow. All the other flights had diverted – Gatwick was silent and empty as the tomb. Most of the non-essential night staff had taken advantage of the fog and gone home.

But Flight 701 was continuing: 'We'll try Gatwick . . . er . . . if we cannot make it at Gatwick will it be OK if we go to Heathrow?' Nowroz felt a little uncertain. He'd try Gatwick. If it was as bad as the controller said, he could always pull up and make for Heathrow. But it looked beautiful out of the cockpit window. As clear as a bell.

The controller acknowledged and cleared 701 down to 5,000 feet, with a direct course to the beacon at Mayfield. The red warning lights on the beacon flashed brightly over the Sussex countryside. Gatwick was only twenty miles away.

The radio circuits clattered in the cockpit as Attayee transferred to the frequency for Gatwick Approach. London Airways continued to take an interest in the flight, however, checking it on the radar screen. The aircraft had now slid down to 5,000 feet. The passengers were waking up as the warning signs for seat belts and no smoking lit above their heads.

Flight 701 was three minutes away from the Mayfield beacon. It was 1.27 a.m. When Captain Nowroz called up the approach controller, he had hoped for an improvement at Gatwick. It looked so clear everywhere else.

'Gatwick weather – surface wind is calm. Met visibility is five zero fifty metres in freezing fog. Runway visual range is equal to 100 one zero zero metres. Temperature is −3.' The controller dispelled the cockpit hopes. Gatwick lay under a pall of freezing fog bad enough to reduce traffic on the London–Brighton road a few yards away to a crawl.

Nowroz acknowledged the runway number and the barometric pressure, which he set into his altimeter. The controller was puzzled and uneasy. He had thought he would have an empty night, at least until the fog shifted. It was damp and cold. Even planes from the big airline based at Gatwick, now part of the international airline, British Caledonian, whose pilots knew every nook and cranny of the airport, were heading elsewhere without a second thought this night.

'Er . . . 701, do you wish to make an approach?' he asked.

'That's affirmative,' said Nowroz. The Gatwick controller cleared the tri-jet down to 2,000 feet.

The crew settled to the approach checks. The chief steward warned the passengers to put their seats upright, extinguish their cigarettes and tighten their safety belts. They were expecting to land in seven minutes. The steward did not mention the weather, but they could see the lights of Heathfield and the stars.

Altimeters were set and cross-checked. The crew chatted. 'It's ground fog, not air fog,' said Nowroz. 'Yeah, once you get in it you have to be very f——ing slick.'

The engineer was interested in the fog. He had heard the controllers going on about it in his headphones. 'I suppose it'll be known as freezing fog, not moving,' he said.

At 1.28 a.m. the controller turned the aircraft to the right. It had been winding down England parallel to the coast. Now it turned inland towards the runway.

'Alter course,' said the captain. He banked to the right, steadying until the compass was pointing due north.

'What's the minimum?' he asked the co-pilot.

'Minimum?' said Attayee.

'Yeah,' from the captain.

'Gatwick,' said Attayee, flipping to Gatwick Approach in his navigation manual. His finger found the Gatwick minimum, which he was supposed to abide by.

'Er, minimum two hundred (cloud base) and a half mile (visual range),' Attayee reported. They had zero and 100 metres.

'Two hundred and a half,' Nowroz acknowledged. He fretted a little. How high was Gatwick above sea level? 'What's the elevation?' he asked.

'We don't see the . . .' Nowroz was interrupted by the worried approach controller again. '701 . . . er . . . in the event of an overshoot will you be wishing to go back to Mayfield or proceed to London?' he asked.

'Er . . . proceed to Mayfield then proceed to London, 701,' replied Nowroz. He set a cursor on the compass to 270 degrees, the heading he would take if he overshot.

At 1.29 a.m. the controller told the pilot that the flight had thirteen miles to run to touchdown. At 1.29 a.m. and 44 seconds, the captain ordered 'flaps two'. Attayee moved the flap lever low by his left hand to two degrees. The passengers heard the roar of the flap drives and the aircraft sank its nose a little. The speed was 223 knots. It should have been 190.

At half past one, the approach controller ordered the aircraft to turn left to head west-northwest. It would pick up the instrument landing system signals as it closed from the left. It had eleven miles to run.

Nowroz banked the aircraft to the left. As it turned he coupled the automatic pilot to the ILS and selected 'glide-slope auto'. The aircraft would automatically fly down the radio beam being sent out from the runway at an angle of 3.7 degrees.

'Flaps five.' Again the flap drives clattered, and in the cockpit there was a burst of loud ticking as the stabilizer automatically countered the change of altitude as the flaps were lowered to five degrees. The speed was forty knots too high at 200 knots.

The co-pilot saw the ILS instruments come alive as they neared the glide slope: 'Outer marker number one identified,' he called. Nowroz was content. Flight 701 was on the right profile if the speed was a little high.

'Roger, put flaps one five,' he called.

As the flaps came to fifteen degrees, the stabilizer ticked again, as it trimmed the aircraft. The flight was as near to the standard approach as it was to get. Height was almost perfect, the heading good, the speed coming back to 143 knots.

143 knots was the lowest speed to be recorded on the flight.

At 1.31 a.m. and 10 seconds, Attayee told Gatwick that he was established on the localizer. The plane was picking up the ILS properly. The controller cleared him to descend – he had been steady at 2,000 feet, with the automatic pilot on hold altitude. But he added: 'In the event of . . . er . . . overshoot, climb on runway heading to 2,000 feet.' The plane was eight miles from touchdown. There was the normal staccato of pilots concentrating on a blind approach.

'What is the flap?' asked Nowroz.

'Flaps at fifteen . . . Glide slope alive,' said Attayee as the plane flew into the narrow beam of the ILS glide slope.

'Gear down,' said Nowroz.

'Gear is coming down.' A rumble and bump jolted the cabin as the undercarriage started to extend. The speed was high but the flight profile otherwise good.

The throttles came back as power was reduced from forty per cent of take-off power to twenty per cent. The noise in the cabin died away as the undercarriage thumped into place.

'What's that red light?' Attayee had seen a single red light above the fog. 'Yeah, that's the light at the end of 09.' Nowroz thought it was a light at the end of the runway. It was not: it was a hazard warning light on a hill short of the runway. 701 was still flying in clear air, but the fog was under it now.

Nowroz asked the engineer to see if the 'stabilizer out of trim' warning light went on, as it had in Frankfurt, and to set the 'bug points' on the airspeed indicator – 114 knots, the minimum approach speed, on his ASI, and 124 knots, the go-round or overshoot speed, on Attayee's.

'V Ref set at 114 on your side,' the engineer confirmed.

'124 set,' said Attayee.

'Anti-skid five releases.' The engineer checked the brakes of the wheels.

'Gear down and three green lights.' Attayee confirmed that the undercarriage was locked in place.

'Standby for the flaps,' said the engineer. It was 1.32 a.m. and 22 seconds. The plane had five and a quarter miles to run to touchdown.

Height and course were good as the autopilot began to fly the aircraft down the glide slope. Power was at 'flight idle'. The flaps were at fifteen degrees. As the engineer spoke, they should have been going to twenty-five degrees, and shortly after to forty degrees.

Nobody touched the flap lever. Nothing happened.

Little was said as the pilots scanned the fog bank beneath them for a clue, a reference. The autopilot had to push the nose down hard to get the aircraft on to the glide path, since the flaps were not extended enough for it to descend at the normal angle. The altitude hold switches had clicked off.

The increased airspeed demanded more nose-down trim to keep the aircraft on the glide slope. The passengers near the tail felt the upward swing as the nose went down. It was still very quiet.

It was quiet, too, in the cockpit. The pilots were looking out. Gatwick Approach gave final clearance to land at 1.32 a.m. and 42 seconds – 'runway visual range still 100 metres'.

The autopilot had used so much down elevator that it could no longer trim out the load on the stabilizer. The system was overloaded. The 'stabilizer out of trim' light went on. The engineer spotted it at once.

Captain Nowroz punched a button on his control column, disconnecting the autopilot. He retrimmed the aircraft and continued the approach himself. His headphones buzzed as the aircraft crossed the outer marker at exactly 1.33 a.m.

There were four miles to run. Flight 701 was less than three miles away now, at 1,300 feet.

Gatwick acknowledged 701 over the outer marker. There was no further conversation. Gatwick was being called up by a British pilot based at Gatwick, asking, 'I think we'll have to divert to . . . er . . . Luton. Could you just give me your last . . . er . . . RVR, please?' '100 metres.' 'Roger. That clinches the matter then. Thank you very much.' He diverted.

'Flap three zero,' Nowroz commanded.

'Three zero coming down,' Attayee acknowledged. There was a stir in the cabin as the flap drives started to run, and the nose sank. The aircraft seemed to be going nose down but with no lights below it, it was difficult to tell.

There was silence in the cockpit for the next forty-one seconds. That is a long silence on a flight deck during an approach. Both pilots were searching outside the windscreens. The flight instruments ran on their own.

These showed, in the soft red cockpit lighting, that Flight 701 was beginning to go amiss. The flaps moved from fifteen degrees to thirty, without the usual intermediate 25-degree stage.

This caused a marked pitch, which reached an attitude of seven degrees nose down. The rate of descent accelerated. The aircraft sank below the radioed glide slope, leaving it at 1,200 feet with three and a half miles to run.

The plane was coming down at 1,200 feet a minute, twice the normal rate. It was 1.33 a.m. and 10 seconds, and the passengers could hear the increase in engine noise as Captain Nowroz put on a little power.

For over forty seconds, the plane dropped further beneath the glide slope. There was no comment from the crew. The landing lights bounced off the fog now, glistening back at the cockpit. They were still in clear air, descending from 1,000 feet to 500 feet in twenty-two seconds.

They entered the fog.

The crew strained forward, peering out of the windscreens. The runway lights had been switched on to 100-per-cent high intensity, and the red and white lights of the VASIS system, which tells the pilot if he is too high or low, were at eighty per cent. Flight 701 never got near enough to see them. Precision approach radar, which pinpoints height, would have warned the crew that they were too low at 1.33 a.m. and eighteen seconds. There was no precision approach radar at Gatwick. It had been withdrawn eleven months before, on economy grounds: only military airfields normally have PAR nowadays.

The aircraft sank below 500 feet. It moved in the fog across two farmhouses. The nose was still well down at 6.5 degrees and the speed was 153 knots, where it should have been 125 knots for a serious attempt at landing.

At 1.33 a.m. and 46 seconds, Attayee broke the silence. 'Four hundred feet.' Nowroz queried it at once: 'Four hundred feet?' He had not noticed it himself. As his Belgian instructor had noticed, he had been concentrating on other things at the expense of handling the controls. Attayee confirmed: 'Yes, we have four hundred feet.' Nowroz suddenly and acutely realized he was in danger. He had let himself be lured into the fog, and he had not been slick enough. He wanted out.

He tried to get the nose up, but the aircraft was nose heavy. Attayee helped him pull on the control column, but they could only put it back about an inch. Nowroz slammed the throttles wide open.

The passengers heard the roar as the engines opened up to take-off power. In the field below cattle scattered, and a power line slipped by invisible in the fog.

It took Nowroz six seconds to decide to abandon the landing and get up to a safe height. During that time, the aircraft lost another 120 feet.

As the nose slowly began to come up, the horrified Attayee saw trees filling the windscreen. 'We're finished,' he screamed at 1.33 a.m. and 57 seconds.

A second later, Flight 701 brushed through treetops. It knocked a chimney pot off a house. Attayee saw more trees rushing towards him. One or two passengers had noticed the trees below them, but had not had enough time to take it in.

Panic started only when the right wing hit the tree trunks and was severed. The plane began to roll to the right. It broke clear of the trees and the undercarriage touched along a grass field.

It became airborne again, rolling to the right, the nose high now. The crew were shouting but the noises were unintelligible. The engines were still at full power, scorching the field, and the noise was shattering.

The tail of the aircraft, heavy with three engines, slammed into the bedroom of a house. The occupants, Mr and Mrs Jones, died instantly, as the house collapsed. The central engine and the tailplane were trapped in the ruins of the house. They pulled down a ceiling, and the Jones' baby's cot dropped to the ground floor. Rubble covered it, keeping the flames off the baby. The baby lived.

The rest of the plane started to spread itself over two fields. The wreckage trail was 1,395 feet long. The passengers in the back of the cabin were dying rapidly now.

Fire broke out. It was fed by the spray of fuel from the ruptured tanks and started to eat away at the wings and fuselage. Several passengers were thrown clear into the fields. Only seven had been killed by the crash impact, but the fire went through the survivors rapidly.

The crew leapt out of the window exits in the wrecked cockpit. As the flames reached the cockpit, the radio crackled: 'Ariana 701 this is Gatwick Approach. Do you read? . . . Ariana 701. This is Gatwick Approach. Do you read?'

London airways controllers were worried, too: 'I've lost sight of him now at about two miles (from the runway),' said one. 'See if he pops up the other side or stays down . . .' 'I reckon he's either landed or crashed.'

Only eleven passengers and the two pilots and flight engineer survived: forty-three passengers, four cabin staff and the ground engineer, died. It was 1.34 a.m.*

The most common cause of crashes is pilot error. Some of the mistakes pilots make are chillingly simple, like the Ariana pilot forgetting to use his flaps in the correct sequence and thinking that the autopilot was not working properly when in fact it was overloaded.

Three incidents show that the crews of even a leading international airline are subject to make the most simple errors. The airline is British Airways and the aircraft in each case was a 747.

Flight BA 029 was a scheduled service between Heathrow and Johannesburg, stopping at Zurich and Nairboi.† It had a three-man flight crew, the captain, co-pilot and a flight engineer. There were fifteen cabin staff to look after the 281 passengers.

The flight went smoothly until the aircraft was 172 miles from Nairobi, about half an hour out. The captain briefed the co-pilot and engineer for the approach and landing. He noted the airport's height. Nairobi is 5,327 feet above sea level.

At 4.45 a.m. on 3 September 1974, the aircraft started its descent. It levelled off at 12,000 feet twenty minutes later, with thirty-six miles to run. The sky was clear and the Ngong hills spread out beneath the crew. Beyond the hills, the plateau surrounding Nairboi airport was covered by low cloud. The big plane slipped down to 10,000 feet.

At 5.08 a.m. and 59 seconds, the Nairobi radar controller called them again: 'Speedbird (the BA call-sign) 029 . . . descend seven five zero zero feet . . .' Neither pilot heard this right. The co-pilot called back without hesitation: 'Roger. Speedbird 029 cleared to five thousand feet . . .' The radar controller did not remark on the error.

Flight 029 was now headed for disaster. The pilots thought they had been cleared down to 5,000 feet – which, given Nairobi's

---

* Captain Nowroz was grounded after the crash, and now works as an operations training superintendent for Ariana on the ground in Kabul. A. Z. Attayee, the co-pilot, is still flying Ariana 727s and the flight engineer M. H. Formuly is on Boeing 720s.

† *AIB Bulletin* 16/74.

height, was 327 feet *below* the runways. The clearance was to 'seven five zero zero feet', 7,500 feet.

The aircraft was losing height at 1,900 feet a minute. It entered the bank of low cloud which obscured the Nairobi plateau. The crew could no longer see the ground, nor would they expect to until they were almost at the airfield.

At 5.10 a.m. and 38 seconds, the aircraft 'captured' the instrument landing system. But Flight 029 was flying far below the ideal glide slope. The ILS deviation light flashed on. The flight engineer noticed that the glide-slope pointers on the ILS were pointing 'up' so much they were out of view. 'We have no glide slope,' he said. 'We have,' said the captain – who thought the engineer meant that the system had failed.

At 5.11 a.m. the aircraft was ten miles from touchdown, and was cleared to land. It was still sinking at 1,650 feet a minute. At 5.11 a.m. and 42 seconds it was only 270 feet above the ground and the 'decision height' warning began to sound automatically.

The engineer called: 'Two hundred feet decision height.' Normally it comes immediately before landing at the height at which pilots must be able to see the runway if a landing is to be continued.

Almost at once, the aircraft broke out of cloud. The captain saw dark rocks and the ground. He pulled back on the controls and put on power. It was 5.11 a.m. and 50 seconds. The aircraft sank to within seventy feet of the rocks and thornscrub as it struggled for height. It was eight miles short of the airfield.

299 souls poised on the edge of eternity. Then the engines bit into the air, and the captain took her back to a safe height and on to a correct landing. He remained convinced that the controller had cleared him to 5,000 feet until the tapes of the conversation between the plane and the ground were replayed. The controller was heard to say: 'seven five zero zero feet'. In any event, the captain must have known that 5,000 feet in this area was below ground level.

Experience is no guard against this type of error: the captain had been with the airline for thirty-two years and had over 18,000 flying hours.

(British Airways have been singularly lucky at Nairobi: On 2 February 1964 a BA Comet was approaching the airport when the pilot set his altimeter at 938 millibars instead of 839. This made the aircraft appear 3,000 feet higher than it was. The error was not checked, and the aircraft touched down in Kitengele game park, nine miles from the runway. Miraculously, the pilots managed to fly it away.)

In the second incident, a BA 747 was on a final approach to Bahrein when the captain levelled off too high. The aircraft came down tail first, banging the tail on the runway. It was night, and the aircraft took off for Bombay without the tail having been properly inspected. On arrival, having crossed the waters of the Indian Ocean, it was found to be damaged. Such damage to the tail could lead to rapid decompression of the cargo and passengers' cabins.

The third accident was at Kuala Lumpur on 12 May 1976.* Flight BA 888 left Heathrow on a Monday night bound for Melbourne with three stops on the way. Shortly after midnight on Tuesday it started its approach to Kuala Lumpur airport, Malaysia. It was a fine calm night and when the Jumbo was within fifteen miles of the airfield the runway lights were clearly visible to the pilots. The captain, in the left seat, decided to make the landing himself from the northwest.

From this direction the airport has no ILS. Instead, pilots use the less accurate kind of radio beacon, VOR, which is sited to the north and not exactly in line with the runway.

This means that the pilot must calculate his own rate of descent from the airport landing chart. As he passes over the VOR beacon he starts his stopwatch and monitors the times and heights until he reaches the final beacon, called NM, which lies four and a half miles from the runway.

The normal angle of descent is three degrees. Pilots use a rough rule of thumb to check their height on the slope at set points on the approach – by simply multiplying the distance from the runway (in nautical miles) by three. This gives the correct height in hundreds of feet.

When BA 888 was six miles from touchdown it should therefore have been at a safety height of 1,800 feet. But it was at only 980 feet and its sink-rate was too fast and steep for a three-degree slope.

The pilots still had a full view of the runway lights ahead and

* AIB Bulletin 6/76.

remained unaware of their dangerous rate of descent. As they passed the final radio beacon NM with four miles to run, they were distracted by a misunderstanding about the amount of landing flap that had been selected.

The plane should then have been at 1,200 feet with a speed of 168 mph. Its actual height was 600 feet and travelling at 204 mph – well beyond the safety limits.

A few seconds later the captain called: 'Can anyone see the runway?' Almost at the same instant his co-pilot called '100 feet above ground' – a routine call that normally comes during the last seconds before touchdown. They were still three miles away from the runway and should have been at 800 feet.

The captain applied full power instantly and started to climb. As he radioed to the airport controller that he was overshooting, two heavy thumps shook the plane as it hit the tops of the forest trees 150 feet above the airport level, and two miles from the runway.

When they had climbed to a safe height, the crew checked for damage, particularly to the undercarriage, which had been lowered before impact with the trees. Luckily, they were able to land safely eighteen minutes later.

All these incidents took place during the approach and landing. This is by far the most dangerous part of a flight, accounting for up to eighty-seven per cent of crashes in some years, and almost always for more than half. Take-off accounts for a further third or so, with *en route* accidents never exceeding one in ten.

The great bulk are caused by pilot error. IATA's senior safety officer, Lawson C. White, carried out a special investigation.* Of sixty-three jet crashes during landing, forty-four were caused by pilot error, sixteen were for undetermined reasons, two were caused by weather, one by a ground controller, and none resulted from mechanical faults.

Lawson C. White analysed the crashes and pointed out: 'Many of the accidents classified as pilot error I am convinced were the result of another human error other than the pilot's. Someone who forgot that pilots are normal. There is only so much information a pilot can receive and integrate at a given time. Anything in

* 'Safety in the Accident Prone Flight Phases of Take-off and Approach and Landing' by Lawson C. White, *IATA*, November 1972.

excess of this is not conducive to human reliability.'

White noted that most of the accidents followed a deviation from normal operating practices. 'Flying is the type of occupation which encourages free expression . . . There still seem to be a few who cannot resist the free expression and cause so much concern, especially to the other crew members who fly with them.'

He rams down the need to fly by the book: 'Clearances are meant to be adhered to, discipline is all important and accurate flying is essential in order to survive.'

Accidents would be avoided if greater use was made of the flight data recorder, the 'black box' which records what happens on a flight.* White was disappointed by safety exchange information between the airlines. This has been due to the legal problems that could arise if an airline admitted to the cause of an accident in a safety report: 'It seems iniquitous that because of this liability problem, airlines are forced to withhold information which could help to prevent a future and perhaps catastrophic accident.'

White also found that pilots were unwilling to contribute to safety by noting their mistakes. 'Looking through 1,400 or so reports . . . one is also struck by the lack of pilot input, reports on incidents which the pilot knew were only a hairsbreadth away from being an accident. There is a natural reluctance to admit one's failings, nevertheless, the pilot profession demands a high degree of responsibility and this responsibility should be taken to include a requirement to inform others regarding one's own mistakes.'

Pilots literally do not own up to incidents for fear of the sack – even though the transmission of those incidents amongst other pilots would help prevent their repetition. The fear is justified,

---

* The 'black box', in fact red, stores information on steel tapes. It records time, speed, course, acceleration and height. It is normally installed in the tail, which has the best chance of surviving a crash. It is built to withstand fire of over 1,000°C, acceleration of 1,000 g and immersion in sea water for a month. Many are fitted with beacons for underwater recovery: the black box from a Boeing 707 was found 10,000 feet under the Mediterranean four weeks after the crash.

Cockpit voice recorders are standard on most airliners. They record all conversation in the cockpit. Pilots were worried about them as 'spies in the cockpit' so the tapes are wiped clean every thirty minutes and are played back only after an incident.

since pilots have been sacked on the spot after admitting incidents

White's descriptions of landing accidents make dispiriting reading for those who put their faith in gold stripes. The prominent cause is given and fatalities to crew and passengers: 'Pilot failed to arrest excessive descent. Neglected altitude-speed control': United Airlines Boeing 727; nil crew, forty-three passengers killed. 'Aircraft entered steep rate of descent as a result of pilot manoeuvring the aircraft to execute approach at a lower altitude in bad weather. Pilot misjudged approach': CPA DC8; three crew, fifty-four passengers killed. 'Crew failed to monitor altitude of deteriorating visibility': American Airlines Boeing 727; six and fifty-two. 'Pilot attempted night visual approach in deteriorating weather, over a partially lighted terrain without altimeter cross-reference': TWA Convair 880; five and sixty.

The litany goes on: 'Pilot deviated from prescribed track. He was too high for straight approach': Varig 707; seventeen and eighty. 'Premature descent during a visual approach by night initiated from an incorrectly identified point': Air France 707; eleven and fifty-two. 'Lack of crew coordination and inadequate monitoring of aircraft position in space': SAS DC8; three and twelve. 'Pilot miscalculated his position and collided against mountain': Air India 707; eleven and 106. 'Navigation error on the part of the pilot. Premature descent': Alitalia DC8; nine and eighty-five. 'Pilot failed to execute approved instrument safety procedure': Mexicana 727; seven and seventy-two.

White found that take-off accidents were totally different. They are much rarer than those on landing. White computed an accident rate of 0.051 per 1,000 departures, which makes a crash on take-off a two-million-to-one chance. Most were caused by mechanical failure, particularly to the engine or engine-powered systems, rather than pilot error. Other causes varied from detached tyre treads, to an Air India 707 whose undercarriage collapsed after hitting a cow, to a PIA Trident which hit a vulture at Lahore and a Delta DC9 which hit a buzzard at Savannah.

Crashes on small and financially rocky airlines have been caused by pilots flying in poor conditions simply because they needed the revenue. A DC3 of General Airways* took off into low cloud, bad

* ICAO *Accident Digest*, No. 11, p. 79.

visibility, snow, freezing precipitation and icing conditions over Texas. The wings began to ice up and fuel ran low. The captain, who was killed in the ensuing crash, was attributed with 'indifference to elementary rules of flight safety, coupled with severe economic compulsion'. If he had not taken off, the airline would have had to pay board and lodging for the passengers.

Errors in reading altimeters have killed as many pilots as anything by confusing them into fatal error. Altimeters often have three hands on the face, one pointing at hundreds of feet, one in thousands of feet and the other in tens of thousands. Muddle the three and the aircraft is flown straight into the ground when the crews think it is several thousand feet up.

This has happened several times: to the passengers and crew of an Iberia Airlines Caravelle in Sussex; a Lockheed Electra in New York; a DC6 at Acapulco; a Viscount at Prestwick; a Britannia in Hampshire; a VC10 in Nigeria; another Britannia in Yugoslavia; an Air India Boeing on Mont Blanc; an Air France Caravelle; a Pan Am Boeing, and many more. Millions of dollars and hundreds of lives have been lost because altimeters, like watches, have two hands. Like watches, in the dark or when the owner is new to the model, they are misread.

Moreover, the pilot has to juggle with two different altimeter settings. During the cruise, he will use a standard barometric setting. But for greater accuracy whilst landing, he will adjust to the exact barometric pressure of the area. He sets the QNH, which gives his height above sea level, and which at a high airport like Nairobi will read 5,300 feet even after he has landed. For height above the ground, he uses the radio altimeter. He concentrates on this below 2,500 feet.

Pilots, not unremarkably, are prone to the same failings as the rest of us, such as indecision. The only difference is that they are severely punished for this. A pilot spends his working life taking decisions – it is what distinguishes his job and justifies his high salary. Very occasionally, a pilot does not really make up his mind and drifts into an accident.

Captain Nowroz is an example. He never really decided to land at Gatwick. 'We'll try Gatwick . . . er . . . if we cannot make it at Gatwick will it be OK if we go to Heathrow?' He had only decided to have a look, which is a different thing.

Friction between captains trained in the rigorous days of war-time flying, and their young, commercially brought-up co-pilots, can be predictably severe. Some captains refer to their crews as 'milk runners', with their easy and non-combative lives. The crews react by calling ex-wartime pilots the 'bomber buggers'.

The captain of a DC8 at Heathrow, also on a foggy night, taxied slowly out for take-off.* He could not decide which runway to use. Twice he started a take-off but aborted and stopped. On the third attempt he thought the controls had locked where the aircraft had reached take-off speed. He slammed the throttles shut and braked, but the aircraft crashed into a cabbage field at the end of the runway. There was nothing wrong with the plane.

There is a known co-pilot problem, called the 'Captain God Complex'. Here the man in the right-hand seat, the co-pilot, develops an inferiority complex to the captain on his left. It is entirely at the captain's discretion whether to allow him to fly a take-off or landing. Co-pilots can be airborne for months without getting any real handling experience.

A pattern of errors is established. Co-pilots make particular mistakes when they do fly a sector: they are prone to take-off swing and landing veer, to very bumpy landings and to crashing short of the runway through getting too low on the approach. Captains, on the other hand, handle things wrong when they act as co-pilot. They are responsible for 'premature withdrawal of the undercarriage' (official terminology for pulling up the gear before the plane is airborne) and wrong selection of flaps and undercarriage on landing.

It is difficult to change concentration. A pilot often has to change from flying his aircraft from instruments a few inches in front of him to looking at a rain-soaked runway half a mile away. That runway has to make immediate sense – its distance, its angle relative to the speed and descent of the plane, all judged by eye.

It may be night and raining, gusty with crosswinds on the runway so that he has to crab the aircraft into the wind. On a long-haul route, the pilot may not have seen the ground or flown the aircraft by eye for eight hours or more.

Take a pilot flying into Bombay, when the monsoon is on. The

* CAA 21/63. All on board survived.

controllers talk to him in heavily accented English. His aircraft bumps and swings in the cloud. He scans the instruments for speed, rate of descent, engine power, compass heading, height.

He watches the model on the artificial horizon, trying to anticipate it as it lurches in the turbulence. It is raining in the cloud and the windscreen wipers are going, but nobody is looking out through the windows.

His left hand and his feet control the aircraft with small, co-ordinated movements. His right hand must be free for other tasks such as stroking the throttles back. The other pilot is busy selecting flap, changing radio circuits, flipping the no smoking and seat belt signs on, setting the altimeters, putting the undercarriage down.

His eyes are totally adjusted to the soft red lighting of the cockpit. He has not seen the ground since he left Europe nine hours before.

Slowly the aircraft lets down from the cloud. With 800 feet left on the altimeter, his co-pilot says he can see the airport. He looks up from the artificial horizon. There is no real horizon. Rain is drumming off the windshield and the wipers distort the glass as they clear it. The forward speed is 180 mph, as fast as a Grand Prix car flat out. There is half a mile to go. The wind is gusting off the Indian Ocean.

Touchdown will be in fifteen seconds. He has just fifteen seconds to decide whether he has satisfied the demands of three dimensions for a safe landing, and to set it down, fifteen seconds of sight after hours of instruments. It is asking a good deal. Sometimes it is too much.

Any pilot will opt to fly by sight rather than on instruments when he can. It's easier, he can cut corners and get through more quickly. There has been a fatal tendency for a pilot who has carried out an instrument approach in cloud to go visual as soon as he is below the cloud. He will try to maintain visual flying even if he has to overshoot: instrument overshoots are complicated. But he may well go back into cloud whilst circling, and in the involuntary transition from eyes to instruments while close to the ground there is great danger.

At least sixty major accidents have been caused by pilots trying to fly visually in instrument weather.

A special committee of the British Airline Pilots' Association examined flight fatigue in great detail, producing a lengthy report.* It accepted that 'pilot error' was the biggest single cause of aircraft accidents – but said that fatigue is the most readily rectifiable component of pilot error.

Some of the cases the committee recorded are highly disturbing. A VC10 captain wrote to his flight manager: 'At chocks under (end of flight) at Hong Kong I had been on duty for 14 hours and had been without sleep for 25 hours and 15 minutes. In my opinion the condition of the flight deck crew on arrival at Hong Kong was totally unfitted for duty. Both my first officers fell asleep more than once during the flight from Darwin, and in fact I had to waken one of them to give him the approach briefing.'

Other pilots reported extreme fatigue. 'About an hour after take-off from Manchester, at about 0900 GMT, the navigator stated that he was the only one awake.' 'Two serious errors – flaps called for and not selected – and no one noticed till a dangerously low airspeed. The approach was low.' 'Both the first officer and the engineer were falling asleep during the last two hours prior to descent. The first officer forgot to call final heights from radio altimeter and I was finding difficulty in keeping eyes open on final approach.'

Pilots complain of disorientation through time-zone changes. 'To start with, the four days it takes to get to Tokyo (from Europe) with a time difference of eight hours leaves one with a colossal inability to sleep in Tokyo,' one wrote to BALPA. 'During the forty hours off there, I would say that seventy-five per cent of the crew were snatching the odd few hours' sleep their body would allow them during the rest period.

'Consequently, out of Tokyo, everybody was more than a little disoriented. From here follows the Hong Kong–Delhi–Hong Kong–Delhi shuttle . . . This necessitates a stop at Rangoon for refuelling. Weather at Hong Kong and *en route* was pretty diabolical, coupled with temperatures of 115°F in Delhi (monsoon starting shortly, with similar problems) all combined to produce a very tired crew.

* *Flight Fatigue*, Report of the Special Committee, BALPA, London, 1973.

'Finally the last straw; Delhi, Beirut, Frankfurt, then as passenger home on the same aircraft, was 14 hours 30 minutes' duty time. Thus three night duties and one day duty stretching into night, within the last five days coupled with an eight-hour time change.'

The pilot ended: 'This doesn't make Jack a very safe boy.' This is far from reassuring for any passenger.

The pilots claim that there has been evidence of pilot fatigue in many crashes involving pilot error. The crew of a BAC1–11, which crashed at Milan after they shut down the good engine after an engine failure to the other, had been on duty for 13 hours 53 minutes. A DC4 on a holiday charter from the Mediterranean crashed on Stockport killing seventy-two, the pilot having been on duty for 12 hours 55 minutes. A VC10 crew slammed into the ground near Lagos, killing all eighty-seven aboard, after 10 hours 35 minutes on duty.

Fatigue often leads to tension between pilots and airline management, who consider that demands for shorter hours are sparked off by industrial reasons and not safety. A pilot wrote of his airline doctor: 'He just took my pulse, and said that if I was "having a go" at the management, then the medical people did not want to be involved.'

The worst-affected pilots tend to be those whose day-night-day work patterns are superimposed on the effect of continual time-zone changes as the crews cross and recross the Atlantic or the US.

All of us are prone to regression, particularly when tired: under stress we tend to go back to what we were first taught. Thus pilots can try to fly a jet in an emergency as they would the turboprop or propeller aircraft they learned on. This has serious implications on the approach, where pilots miss the immediate response in power when the throttles are opened that the prop planes had, and the slowing effect of idling propellers. Crashing short of the runway has been an all too common accident for jet pilots trained on props.

Some pilots have 'left-right' problems. Confusion between left and right is not uncommon. For years the British Army would put a piece of straw on a recruit's left foot, and would order 'straw foot forward' so the recruit could look down. One Norwegian fighter pilot flies with his watch clearly visible on his left arm to help him.

Nevertheless crashes occur. A Dove, a twin-engined propeller aircraft, was landing at Heathrow when it suffered falling oil pressure. The pilot stopped the port engine, bringing the pitch control back through the feathering gate. When the propeller had stopped he switched off the port engine switches. It was the starboard engine that had a fractured crankshaft. He had identified it correctly on the radio to the tower, but then he shut down the wrong engine.

Aircraft can survive a wide range of potential disasters. One four-engined passenger jet has even survived a total engine failure, when all four stopped at 37,000 feet. The British Airways Super VC10 was cruising from Hong Kong to Tokyo at 37,000 feet when the number three engine failed and was shut down.*

Almost immediately, the number one, two and four engines ran down. There was a complete electrical failure, since the generators are run off the engines. The crew managed to establish the aircraft in a dive of 3,000 feet a minute at an indicated airspeed of 290 knots. It would take the powerless aircraft twelve minutes to fall into the dark sea beneath it. They were flying on emergency lighting, standby instruments and limited flying controls. There were no yaw dampers to prevent the nose swinging from side to side, and the aircraft started to roll badly.†

The divergent Dutch roll became serious, with bank angles of forty-five degrees as the plane rolled wing up, wing down out of control. The yaw was also considerable. The crew turned the aircraft ninety degrees to get it off the airway: it might otherwise have slammed into aircraft below it as it made its rapid descent.

Partly extended speed brakes were used to assist in controlling the Dutch roll. The transponder was selected to the emergency setting and an attempt was made to transmit a mayday distress call. The crew lowered the electrical ram air turbine, the ELRAT. This is a turbine which is driven by the rush of air when it is

* *AIB Bulletin* 20/74.
† The VC10 is very prone to Dutch roll. Its three-section rudder has a yaw damper on each section. With the yaw dampers inoperative, a VC10 at cruising speed will roll to forty-five degrees of bank within twelve seconds.

lowered under the wing. The airflow of 290 knots was enough to get it spinning and charging power, exactly as a windmill produces electricity. The crew got power back on the flying controls and on the standby yaw damper.

As the aircraft came back under control, the crew established the cause of the engine failures. They restarted all four engines with the help of ELRAT and got the aircraft back to normal at 28,000 feet three minutes after it had first plunged down. They climbed back to 37,000 feet and flew on safely to Tokyo.

The cause of the incident was simple. The number four fuel tank had been allowed to empty at a time when all four engines were being fed from that tank in order to correct an imbalance between left and right wing fuel quantities. The engines stopped because they ran out of fuel, a classic case of crew error.

In August 1980, a British Viscount of Alidair was approaching Exeter airport with a charter load of holidaymakers from Santander when its four engines stopped. The pilot made a thoroughly professional landing in a field and nobody aboard was hurt. The reason for the crash, however, was slightly less professional: the aircraft had run out of fuel.

Pilots have pushed aircraft beyond their limits and broken them up, although fortunately this is restricted to training flights. Thus a Braniff captain was flying a 707 with a Boeing test pilot as instructor. During one of a series of Dutch rolls, which were beyond the maximum bank angles permitted for the aircraft, the aircraft went out of control. The numbers one, two and four jet pods were torn off by loads beyond the design strength. The aircraft, on fire and with only one engine left, was crash-landed along a river.*

Five years later, in 1964, a Lufthansa Boeing was flying in the Winerzburg–Ansbach area.† The three-man crew was on a training flight at 13,000 feet, flying VFR. The aircraft rolled right over once far beyond the design maximum. On the second attempt it went out of control whilst upside down, and it became overstressed and disintegrated.

The crew died. The accident report revealed that 'there were

* CAA 21/59.
† CAA 16/64.

no signs of any technical defect or technical failure of any unusual nature of the aircraft or of weather influences as causative or contributive factors. There is nothing to say that the two rolls were not intentional.'

There can be no training against error, or recklessness. Pilots are symbols of stability and stern sense. They can be frighteningly different from their image, even with the very best airlines.

This is part of the radio communication between ground control and the crew of a DC9 jet landing at Fort Lauderdale in Florida.* The plane is on a flight for Eastern Airlines, Flight 346. A thunderstorm is taking place.

Flight 346: 'Hello, approach man, Eastern 346, maintaining three [thousand feet].'

Miami Approach: 'Roger, Eastern 346, fly heading 300, maintain 3,000 to Runway 9L final approach course, following a Northeast DC9.' [This identical aircraft decided rightly that the weather was below limits and did not attempt to land.]

346: 'OK, how about a 320 heading here? We're just trying to stay clear of some showers.'

Miami: 'Yes, sir; that's good enough . . . Eastern 346 descend and maintain 2,000 [feet altitude].'

346: 'Out of three of 2,000, Eastern 346.'

Miami: 'Roger, new weather at Lauderdale estimated 700 overcast, one half-mile, thunderstorm, heavy rain showers . . . The glide slope is out of service [for the instrument landing system].'

346: 'Ah, f—.'

Miami: 'Eastern 346, what do you need to shoot at it with the glide slope out [what weather minima to attempt a landing]?'

346: 'Ah, moment . . .'

Miami: 'Eastern 346, turn left heading 270.'

346: 'Two-seven-zero, 346. Can we get lower?'

Miami: 'Ah, are you going to make the approach?'

346: 'Four, four-sixty we need [460 feet height of cloud ceiling above the runway]. If we got 700, it's enough.'

Miami: 'OK, sir, ah, descend to 1,700, turn right heading 360.'

346: 'Three-sixty down to seven – to ah, say again.'

Miami: 'Descend to 1,700, reduce to 160 knots now, please.'

346: 'OK.'

Miami: 'Eastern 346, turn right heading 070, cleared straight in, ah, localizer Runway 9 – left approach Ft Lauderdale airport. Glide slope inoperative.'

346: 'Three-forty-six, right.'

* NTSB *AAR* 72–31.

Miami: 'Eastern 346, contact the tower 119.3 [radio frequency].'

346: 'Nineteen-three, and have a happy. Tower man, Eastern 346.'

Fort Lauderdale Tower: 'Eastern 346, Ft Lauderdale tower, report the marker inbound for nine left, wind 180 degrees at ten [knots]. Estimated 700 [feet cloud ceiling], overcast, half-mile [forward visibility], heavy rain shower over the airport.'

[There was to be no more air-to-ground talk, but cockpit talk continued:]

Captain: 'Get it lined up with . . .'

Co-pilot: 'Put the VOR on yours [for an instrument approach].'

Captain: 'Right, you got the localizer on yours?'

Co: 'Yeah.'

Co: 'Gimme 25 [degrees of flap].'

Captain: 'No you'd better get over there, get on the localizer.'

Co: 'That's 460 feet. I haven't heard that marker come in yet . . . see if they can give us a radar fix to find out how far we're out.'

Co: '50 [degrees of] flaps.'

Captain: 'I'd use . . . 25.'

The captain took over the controls.

Co: 'There's the runway, right under us.'

At this point the aircraft crashed. It broke apart at the tail and was destroyed by fire, although nobody was killed. The pilots had begun the approach after another DC9 had turned back because of bad weather. They did not carry out landing checks. They never reported passing the outer marker and never got clearance to land. When they crashed the flaps were fully down and the throttles at idle – a combination giving the plane its maximum rate of sink.

Most chilling, they were both fully qualified pilots flying with a highly respected airline.

25 Mechanical Failure

Mechanical and airframe failure account for most non-pilot-error crashes. A pilot must never exceed his aircraft's specification or disaster will result. The values on modern jets are fine and they must be flown accurately.

Each aircraft type has a limitations book, which the pilot must adhere to, or his machine will be in instant distress. The limitations are broad-ranging, as a look at a 707's book shows.

The machine is sensitive to weight. The maximum taxi weight is 160 tons (a 747 is 358 tons). This weight would be dangerous in flight after the flaps are brought in and wing lift is reduced. The inflight maximum is four tons less with flaps in – the aircraft will have lost weight anyway through burning off fuel on taxiing and take-off. Maximum landing weight is 110 tons, so fifty tons of fuel have to be burnt off or dumped before a fully laden aircraft can land again.

The aircraft must only be operated when ground temperatures are between $-54°C$ ($-65°F$) and $49°C$ ($120°F$). The take-off altitude limits are from 1,000 feet below sea level to 10,000 feet above. Runway slopes must not exceed two degrees, tailwinds must not exceed ten knots. *En route* altitude maximum is 42,000 feet.

The engine exhaust gas temperature reaches a maximum of $555°C$ on take-off for five minutes: the maximum continuous temperature is $490°C$. Oil pressures must keep within 35 and 55 pounds per square inch, with an upper temperature limit of $143°C$.

There are a host of maximum airspeed limitations. With flaps fully extended, the pilot must not exceed 195 knots; with take-off flaps at fourteen degrees he can go up to 223 knots. The undercarriage can be put down at 270 knots. Flaps cannot be extended above 20,000 feet.

Emergency drills are set out on yellow cards. Engine failure on take-off is the most commonly practised. If it occurs before V1 – the computed decision speed at which a take-off can still be abandoned – the pilot immediately applies full brakes and closes the throttles. The speed brakes on the wings are put up at sixty degrees, and reverse thrust is used on the remaining engines.

After V_I the pilot has to continue, building up speed and taking off. As soon as he is climbing, the pilot gets the undercarriage up. V_2 is the lowest safety speed. The flaps come in at $V_2 + 30$ knots at a height of 800 feet. The aircraft is then flown level until the speed builds up to $V_2 + 50$ knots.

At $V_2 + 50$ knots the aircraft can fly up to a safe height to dump fuel, at 8,000 feet and above. The flaps and speed brakes must be in during dumping. The dump chutes, pipes that extend under the aircraft, are lowered at a maximum speed of 240 knots. Once the chutes are down, the aircraft accelerates to 275 knots as the aircraft load is lightened as the fuel is pumped out. Normal dump time is from ten to twenty minutes.

An engine-out landing involves a slightly higher speed to maintain lift. Modern jets can land with two engines out, although speeds are much higher and more dangerous. An aircraft with two engines out is set up in the approach sixty knots above the normal landing speed. The turbo compressors and bleeds are switched off to keep maximum power. Six miles out fourteen degrees of flap are selected.

A speed thirty knots above normal has to be maintained all the way in now. The gear goes down as late as possible. Rudder trim has to be zeroed at 500 feet. The loading on the rudder, caused by the asymmetrical engine thrust, could be trimmed out during the cruise and approach. For landing, the pilots must take all the strain without artificial trim in order to keep the aircraft flying straight.

The commit point is at 300 feet. If the crippled plane is off line and height for the runway, it can go around for another try as long as it stays above 300 feet. The thrust is increased – slowly, because it increases the asymmetric yaw from the engines, which must be controlled with the rudder. The flaps come in, and slowly, very slowly the aircraft will creep back to a safe speed to circle round again.

Below 300 feet, the aircraft is committed to land: if it veers off-course, nothing can be done about it. The speed is very fast, thirty knots above normal, and the crew will be sweating with the exertion of keeping the aircraft straight. Even with the rudder boost, preventing yaw on the rudder will take all the strength in their legs. The throttles have to be played with delicately as the plane drifts crabwise across the runway. When the gear hits, maximum braking is necessary straight away to compensate for the lack of reverse thrust.

A failure of the hydraulic system also causes abnormal landings. Flaps, undercarriage, spoilers, speed brakes and nosewheel steering are all normally hydraulically operated. The pilot first makes sure that he has 'dumped' or turned off the hydraulics on these to prevent them working unintentionally.

The approach is made at fifteen knots above normal speed. The undercarriage has to be extended manually, by turning a cranking handle, a slow and laborious job. Once it is down, it cannot be got up again, so the aircraft cannot divert easily to another airport. The flaps are worked electrically. The aircraft is lined up very carefully on the runway since there is no nosewheel steering and the aircraft has to be running straight when the rudder ceases to steer at eighty mph.

Reverse thrust is put on immediately on touchdown. The reservoir in the brakes should stop the aircraft although emergency pneumatic brakes can be used in the last resort.

A dread of the modern pilot is the stuck, stalled or runaway stabilizer. Most jets have variable incidence tailplanes, where the tail moves up and down to establish the rough angle of climb or descent, and smaller elevators are used for accurate trim.

A runaway stabilizer is very dangerous. It is when the tail starts moving of its own accord, and at high speed it can very easily be fatal. When it happens, the manual trim wheel spins madly in the cockpit and the plane lurches on its nose. The pilot must immediately cut out the stabilizer switch and circuit breakers, and grab the trim wheel with his hand and stop it.

When this terrifying wheelspin, as the aircraft tries to destroy itself, is stopped, the pilot can wind the stabilizer by hand on the wheel or adopt the drill for a stuck stabilizer. With a stuck tailplane, the pilot must keep a constant speed for as long as possible in order to maintain his trim.

He then makes a jammed stabilizer landing. This is again physically exhausting, with constant pulling needed on the control column. The basic nose-up and nose-down pitch of the aircraft is controlled by the flaps and speedbrakes. The flaps put the nose down, since they are under the back of the wings, and the speed-brakes above push it up. Fine trim is maintained with the elevators.

By pulling circuit breakers, the pilot isolates the inboard flaps to use for the landing. He uses the outer flaps to keep the nose down. The inboard flaps go down to fifty degrees at an early stage, and the trim is maintained with the speedbrakes. The aircraft must only bank gently, or the nose will be pulled down too far for recovery. If, as is most likely, the tail jammed whilst cruising, any reduction in speed will tend to put the nose down. Pulling back on the stick could exhaust the pilots. This is checked by moving the aircraft's centre of gravity aft, either by moving the passengers or by transferring fuel to the back.

Stabilizers can also stall, when the load on the tailplane is so great that the motor drive cannot move it. An aircraft can recover from a full nose-down stall or runaway, although it requires great courage and skill from the pilot.

Against all natural inclination, the pilot must not pull back on the stick even though he is hurtling earthwards. This makes things worse since the stabilizer cannot recover whilst the controls are forcing on it. It will recover only when it is relieved of pressure. Neither must the pilot throttle back, even though his speed in the dive will be approaching the design limit. Throttling back simply puts the nose even further down.

The speedbrakes are pulled fully up, and very slowly as the aircraft loses height the nose starts to come up, and the speed drops off. Gradually the forces on the tailplane reduce and the controls are effective again.

The price of new aircraft forces many smaller airlines to buy on the second-hand market. A new 747 costs $60 million, a 727 $16 million, a BAC1–11 $10 million, a Tri-Star $36 million, a DC10 $40 million. Against this, old model 707s sell for $4 million, BAC1–11s for $850,000, DC8s for $2 million. The Convair 880 is a thirsty and expensive machine to run, but it is a four-engined jet and at $150,000 it could seem cheap. There is plenty of evidence to indicate that maintenance and the standard of machinery on financially rocky airlines is substantially worse than on the richer ones.

Two aircraft which suffered structural failure in flight were the Hawker Siddeley Comet and the Lockheed Electra. The Comet suffered from metal fatigue in the fuselage, and was grounded after a series of crashes in 1954. Later it was modified and made fully safe.

An accident report on an Electra which crashed in Indiana in 1960, killing sixty-three, said that there had been an 'inflight separation of the right wing because of flutter induced by oscillation of the outboard nacelles'. In simple English, the wing fell off through strain and vibration. The Electra was also modified safely.*

Structural failure is often associated with a particular type of aircraft. But it can also affect an individual plane. The last message from a British Airways Vanguard *en route* to Salzburg came as the plane cruised over Belgium. 'We're going down, flight 706, we're going down vertically . . . out of control.' The rear pressure bulkhead ruptured, helped by corrosion from the lavatory. It tore off the tailplanes and the aircraft nosedived into the ground.†

If the cabin suddenly depressurizes, the pilot goes through an immediate emergency check: oxygen mask on, communications with crew and passengers established and passenger oxygen switched on. Passengers must put out cigarettes at once and breathe from the oxygen masks that drop down above their heads.

The captain announces the emergency descent to a lower altitude where there is air. He has fifteen seconds to lose height before the passengers start to become unconscious. He closes the throttles, the 'thrust levers' as he calls them. The speedbrakes are extended, the autopilot cancelled. The aircraft banks and turns to lose height more quickly, although the angle of bank must not exceed forty-five degrees.

The undercarriage goes down. The airspeed must not creep above Mach .83 or 320 knots on most aircraft, or there will be structural damage. The pilot levels out at 14,000 feet after the emergency descent.

Depressurization should be survivable. An Aer Lingus 707 was at 25,000 feet with 112 aboard when the main cargo door partially

* CAA 9/60. It cost Lockheed $118 million to strengthen the wings. A worrying factor was that the wing condition became evident after only 132 hours of flight. The test programme should surely have discovered this.
† CAA 20/71.

blew out.* The aircraft at once decompressed. The co-pilot, who was flying the aircraft, flew an immediate emergency descent to 11,000 feet. There was noise and buffeting, but the aircraft landed quite safely with nobody injured.

But tragedy followed when the port rear freight door of a DC10 blew out.† Turkish Airlines THY Flight 981 was a scheduled run from Istanbul to London via Paris. As it climbed through 13,000 feet on take-off from Orly, it disappeared from the radar. It crashed in woods, and all 346 aboard died instantly, making it the world's biggest air disaster at the time.

The freight door, together with a number of bodies, was found nine miles from the main wreckage. When it blew out and the cargo hold decompressed, the cabin floor distorted and disrupted the cables of the main flying controls in the tail. The huge plane went out of control and crashed. There was much bitterness when it was discovered that a similar accident had already crippled another DC10, though not fatally, which should have prevented this repetition. McDonnell Douglas, the DC10 manufacturer, alleged that an employee at Paris Orly had not latched the door by the correct procedure. The manufacturer also alleged that Turkish Airlines might have added unauthorized shims to the lock-limit warning switch, to correct a flickering warning light, and misrigged a lockpin in the mechanism.

McDonnell Douglas had good reason to mitigate its own liability. The original door-lock design was unquestionably poor – though McDonnell Douglas further alleged that this was the fault of its design-and-manufacturing subcontractor responsible for the door lock. And McDonnell Douglas had delivered the aircraft, DC10 ship 29, to Turkish Airlines without some safety modifications that McDonnell Douglas had itself recommended in its Service Bulletin SB 52 37.

The Service Bulletin followed two carbon-copy incidents. The same freight door had blown out on American Airlines DC10 ship 1 above Windsor, Ontario, more than a year before. The pilot managed to land the stricken airliner, but American Airlines was not to be so fortunate during another post-take-off emergency six years later at Chicago.

* CAA 25/70.
† *AIB Bulletin* 5/74.

The Federal Aviation Administration did not emerge unscathed from Paris. The FAA had not made the Windsor-incident modifications mandatory by issuing an Airworthiness Directive. Neither had it ordered floor-venting modifications to prevent the floor from buckling and jamming the controls. Yet modifications had been recommended by the National Transportation Safety Board after the Windsor incident, and would have saved the Turkish airliner.

As for the legal aftermath of the crash, lawyer Lee S. Kreindler, who specializes in this area, said, 'Intelligent laymen can only have contempt for what lawyers, governments and airlines have created.'

There were grotesque differentials in liability limits. This was a Turkish flight from France to England by an American aircraft containing passengers of several nationalities. That is complex, but no more so than any average international flight. Where the airline's limited liability was concerned, some passengers were on a 1929 Warsaw Convention compensation limit of $10,000, others on a 1955 Hague Protocol limit of $20,000, and yet more on the Montreal Agreement limit of $75,000.

Another DC10 crashed shortly after take-off at Chicago in May 1979, killing all 273 aboard. An engine broke away as it was developing full take-off power. As it tore upwards and back, it damaged the leading edge of the wing and cut hydraulic power. The leading-edge droops on the wing withdrew, causing it to stall. The other wing continued to produce high lift, and the aircraft banked and crashed.

The FAA took the unprecedented step of grounding all 138 DC10s operated by American carriers for five weeks. Inspections of DC10s revealed cracks in the pylon mountings that attach the engine to the wing. The ban was ended on condition that maintenance procedures be carried out properly.

McDonnell Douglas was also ordered to redesign parts of the pylon within two years.

The accident also involved instrumentation. Had the pilot known that the wing had stalled, it is possible that an emergency landing could have been made.

The US National Transportation Safety Board found that the crash was the result of maintenance damage that caused the separation of the left engine and pylon. During routine overhauls, mechanics had sometimes detached the pylon and engine together, instead of disassembling them separately.

The NTSB, in its 1980 findings on the accident, said that the DC10 wing pylon met regulatory strength requirements but 'neither the designers nor the certification review team adequately considered the vulnerability of the structure to damage during maintenance. In several places, clearances were unnecessarily small and made maintenance difficult to perform.'

Damage to pylons on Continental Airlines DC10s had been detected and repaired before the Chicago crash. The NTSB was concerned that key engineering and maintenance staff at American Airlines were not aware of this. The board felt that reporting procedures showed a serious deficiency and that the accident 'may be indicative of a climate of complacency'.

Whether it deserves it or not, the DC10 has got a bad name. When the wings fell off the Electra and the tail off the Comet, the manufacturers ultimately took the responsibility and fixed their products so that it did not happen again. The aircraft were restored to confidence.

The DC10 has been different. There was haggling between airline, manufacturer, and safety authorities after Paris, and again after Chicago. The only beneficiaries have been the lawyers, who have seen a fresh cornucopia of fees slide into their grasp as their clients fight to evade responsibility. The cost of the Chicago crash to the insurers has been estimated at $138 million.

The DC10 has raised some serious questions about safety. The Paris crash showed that despite the procedures for the instant notification of faults and incidents between airlines operating the same aircraft, carbon-copy accidents still occur. There were suggestions that McDonnell Douglas had rushed through the design in order to compete with the Lockheed 1011.

Both Paris and Chicago revealed the aircraft to be remarkably vulnerable to the whims of junior airline employees, at least in some reports. A cargo handler allegedly mis-shut a door at Paris; mechanics allegedly used a forklift to remove engine and pylon at Chicago. A great airliner should not easily fall prey to mishandling at this level.

And both incidents showed the failsafe capability of the DC10 in a bad light.* The Paris crash occurred because decompression jammed the control lines under the cabin floor. Had the controls been differently sited, there would have been no accident. The DC10 can be flown on two engines, even if the third has fallen off. But the loss of electrical and hydraulic power that followed the loss of the engine at Chicago doomed the aircraft, since the lift devices on the wing retracted and the pilot had no information that the wing had stalled.

Airline reaction to Chicago was not reassuring either. The grounding was enormously expensive, with twelve per cent of all airline seats in the US being removed from the market and some airlines losing over $20 million in revenue. US airlines honoured the ban. They had little option. But foreign airlines lobbied immediately, powerfully, and often successfully at home to continue flying their DC10s. One might have thought that an aircraft that was banned in its place of manufacture would be banned elsewhere. But restrictions were quickly lifted in Europe, including those on Freddie Laker's famous Skytrain DC10s which were serviced by American Airlines.

Pilots love the DC10. It is, one said, 'an enormously forgiving aircraft'. Perhaps it should be more forgiving to a cargo door and a pylon and to those who either close them, maintain them, or design them.

The DC10 was the result of a particularly bitter marketing war against Lockheed. The development of very powerful fan-jet engines in the 1960s made it obvious that wide-bodied aircraft capable of seating several hundred passengers would dominate the industry in the future.

Boeing scooped the long-range intercontinental market with the 747, which it developed early and well. That left the other two major US manufacturers, Lockheed and McDonnell Douglas, to fight for the medium-range market.

---

* The failsafe standard of the *crew* on American Airlines DC10s has been dramatically upheld on one flight. An FAA flight inspector was carrying out flight checks on an AA DC10. The first officer was flying. Just after take-off rotation, he died of a heart attack. Although the aircraft was in a critical phase of flight, at night, turning over water at low altitude, the captain took the controls and landed safely.

Many in the industry thought it was absurd to develop both the Lockheed 1011 and the McDonnell Douglas DC10. The two aircraft are virtually identical in terms of speed, range and capacity, if not in design detail. To get both manufacturers into profit, five hundred aircraft have to be sold. This means that they must not only compete with each other, but must also penetrate the 747's intercontinental market.

Lockheed and McDonnell Douglas knew that it made more sense for only one aircraft to be developed, but both were adamant that it should be theirs. Thus both proceeded. TWA was so convinced that only the 1011 should be developed that it offered United Airlines some of its delivery positions if United would buy 1011s. United was the last big US airline to decide which airliner to buy.

In April 1968, United decided on the DC10 and thus the DC10 programme got under way. The decision was perhaps inevitable. The DC10 has General Electric engines. General Electric's allied bank is Morgan Guaranty. Morgan Guaranty has one of the largest single shareholdings in United.

McDonnell Douglas had the motto 'Fly before they roll'. This meant getting the DC10 into the air before the 1011 was rolled out of its hangar. They succeeded triumphantly, with a nine-month lead. This gave the DC10 a clear commercial edge, and at the time of the Chicago crash McDonnell Douglas had sold 277 DC10s and was into profit. Lockheed still had a long way to go with the 163 1011s sold.

There is no evidence that McDonnell Douglas developed the DC10 too quickly. Nevertheless, the DC10 has been involved in two total disasters that are directly attributable to the aircraft and not to the pilot. In both, the DC10's failsafe record has been shown to be 'skimpy'.*

★

* The Chicago DC10 had seven emergencies before its final crash. In February 1975, the rear engine overheated in Acapulco. The same month, the right engine burned out after take-off, again at Acapulco, and then the rear engine failed on take-off at Dallas. That August, the airliner made an unscheduled landing at Phoenix after the slats failed. There was only one emergency in 1976, a forced landing after the loss of hydraulic fluid at Dallas. The aircraft made another forced landing the next year in Los Angeles when the right engine overheated. A take-off at Chicago was aborted in 1978 for the same reason.

Cabin ventilation should be able to cope with even severe smoke. Although the crew all go on to oxygen and wear goggles, putting the turbocompressors on maximum and altering the cabin altitude to the rarer atmosphere of 10,000 feet will deal with dense smoke. The aircraft must never be depressurized to get rid of the smoke as the ventilation system is better than any combination of open windows and doors. In the very rare event of flying unpressurized, the co-pilot's window is opened.

Fire in the cargo compartments can spread very quickly. When it is suspected, the flight engineer puts on a smoke mask and takes a 'walkaround' bottle of oxygen and a portable fire extinguisher. He is lowered through the nose compartment on the cockpit escape rope.

The first move with an engine fire is to cut off the warning klaxon. All the crew shout out the number of the engine on fire, since pilots have been known to shut down the good engine by mistake. The throttle is then shut. The aircraft goes on to essential power, since one of the generators will have had its engine stopped. If necessary the pilot can switch off radar, galley heat, window heat, fuel boost pumps and the reserve hydraulic pump to save power.

The engine fire handle is pulled, the boost pumps switched off and the manifold valve closed. If the first warning light stays on, the bottle discharge button is pushed, and the extinguisher is sprayed into the engine. If the warning light is still on after thirty seconds, Phase II starts – another foam bottle sprays the engine.

If that does not work, Phase III begins. This is literally an attempt to blow the fire out. The aircraft has to be flown at a minimum of 250 knots, the faster the better since there is no Phase IV.

The chances of surviving a crash are much reduced on aircraft using JP4 fuel. This is a 'wide-cut' gasoline like petrol, needed by piston engines because it is volatile. However, this makes it ignite readily in a fire. JP1 fuel, as kerosene is known, is much less inflammable.* A study, by A. F. Taylor and Lin Beow Hong,

---

* JP4 can ignite down to −10°F (−23°C). JP1 kerosene has a flash point of around 100°F (38°C). The advantages of JP4 are that it is cheaper and lighter at 7.6 lb to the gallon compared to 8 lb for JP1. Lord Brabazon, when Chairman of the British Air Registration Board,

showed that in 130 JP1 accidents, under thirty per cent of those aboard died, of whom ten per cent died through fire rather than the crash itself. Of 28 JP4 accidents, over half of the forty per cent on board who died were killed by fire. A passenger should not fly with an airline that uses JP4: it is saving money at the greater risk of his life. JP1 is, however, used by all major airlines.

The odds against a two-engine-out landing have been calculated at 1,000,000 to one. But sometimes, in training, it is done on purpose. Ten per cent of all airliner crashes occur on training flights. A Delta Airlines pilot, Jim Morton, with 16,000 hours experience, was being checked out as a captain on a DC8.* During the take-off run from New Orleans International, the instructor, Maurice Watson, chopped one engine. Morton took off and started to climb out. A minute later Watson chopped a second engine. Numbers one and two engines were dead – there was no power on the left wing. The altitude was only 1,200 feet and the speed a meagre 200 knots.

To lose power at this most critical stage in take-off on two engines is so unlikely that it could only happen on a check flight. Even so, Morton might have made it. But Watson cut the rudder boost, the hydraulic aid that was helping Morton keep the nose straight against the asymmetrical thrust of the engines on the starboard wing.

The altitude was down to 800 feet. Speed was deteriorating. 'Don't get below 160 . . .' said Watson.

Watson called the landing checks and looked at the runway lights. It was after midnight. 'OK, looks good. How 'bout that now, we're straightened out.'

The good humour did not last long.

The runway was only a mile away, and coming up fast.

'Call my airspeed for me,' said Morton.

'140.'

---

suggested a 'fuel duel' to JP4 adherents. He would stand in a pool of kerosene lighting matches. They should do the same in JP4. He had no takers.

* CAA 8/67. Quoted at length in *Safety Last*, by Captain Brian Power-Waters, Millington, London, 1974.

Too slow. Power was put on the engines on the right wing. The plane immediately turned left.

'135 is your airspeed . . . see you're getting near . . .' Watson shouted. 'Put the rudder in there . . . you're getting your speed down now . . . You're not going to be able to get it.'

'I can't hold it, Bud.' Morton had no rudder boost. Watson had chopped it to add realism to the check.

Watson shouted: 'Naw, don't. Let it up . . . Let it up! . . . Let it up!'

It exploded into the ground and smashed through three houses and a hotel. Six crew and thirteen on the ground died.

Overloading and overheating of tyres has emerged as a major problem on big jets like the DC10 and 747. The tyres are strained on long taxi ways and by acute corners, sometimes to the point of exploding on take-off. The problem was highlighted in the summer of 1982. Pilots consider that the long taxi-ing necessary at airports like Rome and Denver worsens the problem.

The incident list of a major airline shows what happens short of accidents. Behind the unblemished record of British Airways in 1975 lay 442,904 hours of flight, and 264,324 take-offs and landings. The passengers at the back would be amazed at the dramas they lived through. There were 99 stall warnings and 230 abandoned take-offs and 625 engines were shut down in flight. Lightning struck 127 flights, and birds hit 153. The same airline registered 35 air misses in the first six months of 1976. (Source: *British Airways Air Safety Review*, 2 February 1976.)

These statistics are for a notably safe and large airline. An average airline would have clocked up more incidents. The reader should note that BA shows exceptional frankness in revealing its operational details. The reticence of other airlines to exchange accident information lessens safety standards. The reader should not fall into the trap of regarding BA as dangerous because it is frequently mentioned. The reverse is the truth: a frank airline is generally a safe one.

Appendix One
What Goes Up . . .

World airlines work through emergencies at a fair rate. Take a typical January, this one in 1976, and the accidents notified during it.*

New Year's Day itself saw two. A DC10 of SAS took off from Copenhagen's Kastrup airport into a flock of gulls. The crew heard a loud bang and saw a flash in the big tri-jet's number one engine, which lost power.

The emergency landing was successful, although it was found that fifteen birds had been through the devastated number one engine, and had also damaged the number three. A further twenty-eight gulls were found on the runway.

Later that day, a Boeing 720 of Middle East Airlines took off from war-scarred Beirut for the Gulf of Iran. It disintegrated at 37,000 feet over the Saudi Arabian desert, killing all eighty-one aboard. The cause was a bomb in the forward cargo compartment. The terrorist has not been found.

On 2 January, a DC10 of the big American carrier Overseas National careered off the runway at Istanbul after a heavy landing. The next day an Aeroflot Tu-124 crashed after take-off from Moscow, killing eighty-seven. As with all Russian crashes, no details were given.

On 4 January a Lear 24A jet of Winship Air Service crashed at Anchorage, Alaska, killing six, for the fourth straight day of accidents.

A lull ended on 7 January, when a Viscount prop-jet of Mandala Airlines in Indonesia overshot the runway and ended up in a monsoon ditch. Three days later, an F27 of Burma Airways suffered a collapsed nosewheel on landing. Passengers escaped both these incidents.

On 15 January, nobody survived the crash of a Colombian DC4 into mountains near Bogota. Nor did the passengers escape the crash of a C47 in nearby Bolivia on the 18th, after the right engine failed on take-off.

Again in South America, an HS748 crashed into mountains in Peru, killing thirty-three. A Russian-built An-24 crashed on the approach to Canton on a flight from Shanghai on the 21st, killing all forty aboard. Back in South America, an Emb-110 of Transbrasil crashed fatally on take-off the following day.

The final victim for the month was an L188 of Panarctic which

* CAA *Supplement* No. 28, July 1976.

crashed on landing at Edmonton in Canada. That ended an average month.*

The reasons for crashes of airliners since 1946 have been worked out by the British Civil Aviation Authority. They make interesting reading, although it should be remembered that they include over thirty years of crashes at one go.

Airframe failure, through metal fatigue or turbulence, accounts for 154.

Aquaplaning on wet runways, where the tyres have no bite and braking is useless, has led to fifty-eight crashes, although they are not usually fatal.

Bird strikes have downed thirty-eight aircraft – although nobody has yet been killed on a jet airliner. The cargo has broken loose on twenty flights. 536 aircraft have hit high ground, and 300 water – almost always with fatal results. Crew incapacitation, ranging from food poisoning to death, has affected eighteen flights.

Seven aircraft have crashed after a member of the crew has been shot.

Doors and windows have opened or failed in flight on forty-five aircraft. These accidents can be eerie. The pilot of an Egyptian Viscount on the Luxor to Aswan tourist run reported: 'After take-off from Luxor at an altitude of approximately 9,000 feet a sudden explosion occurred and three quarters of the front entrance door blew out. The aircraft returned to Luxor and on landing one of the stewardesses was found to be missing.'

The main passenger door also blew out on an Aerolineas Argentinas Avro 748. The stewardess was left desperately hanging on to the inside of the lavatory with her left hand, whilst almost the whole of her body was outside the aircraft. The steward caught her blouse, but could not stop her being sucked out and falling 11,000 feet. An Air France passenger was sucked from his seat to the Iranian desert when a window failed.

Electrical faults have contributed to forty-five airliner accidents, and the failure of all engines to 164. Flying controls have jammed or gone wrong on eighty-nine. Dirty or incorrect fuel has affected nineteen flights.

Fuel starvation or mismanagement, and running out of fuel has

* An increase in the accident rate seems to be taking place. An analysis by Dr Shaw, technical director-general of IATA, indicates that the loss rate of jet airliner hulls, having declined up to the mid-1970s, is now creeping up again. Approach and landing crashes, having dropped to almost one per million in the early 1970s, have now returned to the 1960s rate of between two and three per million.

contributed to seventy-nine incidents. The most common error is for pilots to switch to empty tanks.

Hail damage has caused twenty-three accidents, and the build-up of ice and snow eighty-seven. Almost all these are to propeller aircraft. Jets produce huge quantities of hot air which can be piped to places where ice can form.

Hidden bombs have exploded on thirty-four flights. PAL of the Philippines has had three aircraft sabotaged. British Airways lost a Comet into the Mediterranean, killing all sixty-six aboard in a 1967 attempt to kill the Cypriot guerrilla leader General Grivas. A TWA Boeing 707 with eighty-eight aboard also plunged into the Mediterranean after a bomb blast in 1974. Swissair lost a CV990 jet and thirty-nine passengers near Frankfurt in 1970 and Continental a 707 with forty-five aboard over Mississippi in 1962.

Twenty-four aircraft have been shot at by ground fire, or shot or forced down by fighter aircraft. Most incidents were in the Taiwan area and Vietnam, although a Boeing jet of Libyan Arab Airlines was forced down by Israeli fighters and crashed into the Sinai desert. There is an international code for military aircraft to use to airliners. The fighter rocks its wings from a position in front and to the left of the airliner. This means: 'You have been intercepted. Follow me.' The fighter then circles an airport, lowering its undercarriage and overflying the runway in the direction of landing. This means: 'Land at this aerodrome.' Had this procedure been followed, there would have been no tragedy in Sinai.

Inflight fire has a bad record – 316. Many fires start in the toilets, most commonly from cigarette ends. An Alitalia Jumbo, and Pan Am and American Airlines 707s have all been forced to make precautionary landings after fires in the toilets. In one extraordinary incident on a DC10 of National Airlines *en route* to Miami at 39,000 feet, a passenger deliberately burnt himself to death in the right aft 'blue room' or toilet. The toxicity of fires is due to a wide range of materials used in aircraft toilets and cabins – vinyls, honeycomb, a variety of plastics, stainless steel, aluminium and fibreglass.

Instruments, either missed, misread or failed, account for sixty-three incidents. Lightning strikes are held responsible for thirteen accidents.

Major powerplant disruptions and the loss of propellers in flight have caused 184 accidents, marginally above the figure for mid-air collisions, at 137.

The biggest category of all, only to be expected since take-off and landing are the most dangerous parts of flight, is overrunning and veering off the runway, a total of 1,226.

Tyre bursts are low, at eleven. 'Third party' accidents, which means hitting anything from an hotel to a coconut tree, measure 102.*

It is also possible to work out which aircraft have been involved in the most accidents. DC3s, also known as Dakotas, have been involved in some 1,600 accidents. The Curtis C46 Commando has been in 720, and the DC4 in 201.

Of jets, 194 Boeing 707s, 84 Boeing 727s, 15 737s and 23 747s had been listed by the CAA as involved in accidents up to 1976. An accident is defined by ICAO as an occurrence where there is death or injury to those on board, or substantial damage to the aircraft. The DC8 had totted up 85, the DC9 61 and the DC10 19. The Fokker Friendship was on 13. The Comet 4 series has had 43 accidents and the Trident 15. The Lockheed Tri-Star was on 8, the Caravelle 54, Convair 880s and 990s 32, the VC10 has been in 12, and the BAC1–11 30.

The most abused aircraft in the world undoubtedly have been United Arab Airlines' Comets. Things were bad enough with SU-AII and SU-ANI. The former first crashed into snowbanks at Geneva, and then collapsed its undercarriage and went off the runway again at Khartoum. SU-ANI's first off-runway excursion came at Kuwait, after she had landed on her starboard wing-tip, setting it on fire. Her second came in 1970 at Addis Ababa, when she touched down halfway along the runway. This time her port wing tip and fuel pod hit the ground.

But the Egyptian airline managed to crash poor old Comet SU-ALD not twice, but thrice.

On Christmas Eve 1960, whilst landing in Libya, the pilot put SU-ALD straight into a drainage ditch. She was repaired. Less than two months later, on 15 February 1961, she was landed heavily taildown at Damascus. She was again badly damaged and repaired.

For a little while, she led a charmed life, with no incidents. Then on 27 July 1963, whilst trying to land at Bombay in bad weather, the pilot

* A DC8 on a training flight hit a hotel at St Louis. A Garuda F28 hit a coconut tree at Palembang in Indonesia. The impact was severe enough to kill twenty-six, including the crew, although another thirty-six survived. The tree was destroyed. ICAO *Summary* 3/76.

Amongst the odder collisions, a Hughes 500 helicopter suffered tailboom damage when it was hit by a London Transport bus outside the Dorchester Hotel in Park Lane, London. A Tri-Star of All Nippon Airways had two flight-deck windows broken when it hit volcanic rock thrown up by the eruption of Mount Usu. Smoke and ash were reported up to 40,000 feet. The big jet landed safely at Sapporo. And an Ethiopian Airlines DC3 collided with a donkey on 15 November 1977. It was written off in the subsequent crash landing. History does not relate what happened to the donkey.

put her into the sea in severe turbulence – writing off himself, his passengers and poor SU-ALD.

But, to end on a more optimistic note, take the case of a Constellation of F & F Livestock Airlines. As those other aircraft were crashing in 1976, the Connie's number one propeller ran away when she was sixty-five miles east of Belize in Central America. The pilot could not control the RPM or feather the prop and twenty-five miles east of Belize, out over the Caribbean, it flew off. It hit the number two engine, which also stopped. The aircraft was now flying on the starboard engines alone.

The undercarriage was lowered for an emergency landing at Belize. The left main gear failed to extend. The crew couldn't get it down even manually. By now the oil temperatures on the two remaining engines were dangerously high. The pilot decided to put it down at once, without one propeller and two engines, with faulty landing gear and oil temperature well in the red on the now faltering starboard engines.

Not a soul aboard was scratched.

Appendix Two
Pilot Aptitude Test

Devised by the author, based on RAF Pilot Selection at Biggin Hill

General Intelligence Test

Pilots need special skills for their job, with a flair for mathematics, obtaining information from instruments, and physical coordination, applied to a machine rather than a sport. They must also have a reasonable intelligence on a general basis. This IQ test is designed to screen out those whose general intelligence is not up to pilot standards.

There is a strict time limit of twenty minutes.

1. Which one is wrong, if

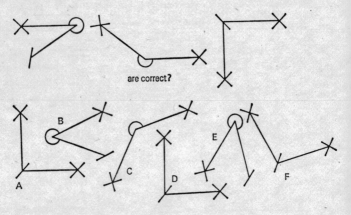

are correct?

2. What should x be?

5   11   23   47   x

3. What number goes into the brackets?

24   (47)   42
35   (52)   14
32   ( )   16

4. What number is missing in this sequence?

6   36   18   324   26244

5. Which is wrong?

6. Which is the odd man out in these anagrams?
DANGLEN YONWAR BIGLEUM NIPAS RECNAF

7. If MDSDQ becomes JAPAN and SRODQG becomes POLAND,
what is WXUNHB?

8. Which piece fits the missing section?

9. Which diagram continues this pattern?

10. What is x?
4 5 16 25 256 x 65536

11. What is the odd man out?
COW DEER SNAKE MAN DOG

12. If these results are in the relationship of the letters to numbers:

	Won	Lost
LIVERPOOL	4	5
BAYERN	2	4
REAL MADRID	4	6

How has HAMBURG done?

13. Which pattern is inconsistent?

14. What should x be?

15. If CHILE = 37 and ITALY = 67 and ZAIRE = 59, what is SPAIN?

Answers

1. F. It is the wrong pattern for an obtuse angle. 2 points.

2. 95. Each number is doubled, and one added. 2 points.

3. 42. In the first line, the numbers outside the brackets are divided by 6, in the second by 7, in the third by 8. 2 points.

4. 162. The first number is squared for the second number, halved for the third and squared again, and so forth. 3 points.

5. D. It has only six horizontal bars. 1 point.

6. FRANCE. All the others are monarchies. 2 points.

7. TURKEY. Each letter moves back three places in the alphabet. 2 points.

8. C. 1 point.

9. A. It turns ¼ of a revolution each time. 1 point.

10. 625. There are two sequences, alternately squaring from 4 and 5. 2 points.

11. SNAKE. All the others are mammals. A snake is a reptile. 1 point.

12. Won 2, Lost 5. Each vowel is a win, each consonant a loss. 1 point.

13. F. One semi-circle has no dot in it. 1 point.

14. 7. Each number triples its opposite lower number and adds one. 2 points.

15. 59, like ZAIRE. Each letter is given its number in the alphabet and the totals are added. Thus A = 1, Z = 26, and so forth. 2 points.

Average score	14
Good score	17
Excellent score	22

The pass mark is 15, just above the average. With jobs hard to get at the moment, many airlines would insist on at least 17. But historically it has been 15 and that, rather than today's intake, is likely to be flying you.

Error Rectification Test

First read the Instrument Explanation (no time limit)

A pilot has to be quick and firm about rectifying errors, whether from his instruments or from mechanical failure such as an engine shut-down. Select the appropriate description.

There is a strict time limit of five minutes.

Instrument Explanation

Altitude. The inner pointer indicates thousands of feet. The outer gives the hundreds. Thus the altitude shown above is 3,800 feet: 3,000 on the inner pointer and 800 on the outer.

Compass. The course is self-explanatory. Here it is north.

Artificial horizon. If the model plane is above the line of the horizon, it is climbing. If below, it is descending. Here it is descending.

Turn and bank. The bubble is to the left, so there is a left turn here.

Rate of climb. The pointer shows how many hundred feet per minute the plane is climbing or descending. Here it points at 400 feet, in the down section. The aircraft is thus descending at 400 feet per minute.

Airspeed. The inner dial shows the hundreds of miles an hour, the outer is in tens. The inner here points to 400, the outer to 35. The airspeed is thus 435 mph.

Simply write down your answers in sequence. The case above would be:

3,800 feet, north, descending, turning to the left, down at 400 feet a minute, at 435 mph.

1. The aircraft above is:
A. Flying at 3,000 feet, heading south, climbing at 400 feet a minute, banking left, and climbing at 300 mph.

B. Climbing at 400 feet a minute, banking right, climbing, flying at 3,400 feet, heading south, at 340 mph.

C. Flying at 350 mph, climbing at 300 feet a minute, banking right, climbing, heading south, at 3,500 feet.

D. Flying at 3,400 feet, at 310 mph, heading south, climbing at 200 feet a minute, climbing, banking left.

E. Flying at 310 mph, heading east, at 3,400 feet, climbing at 200 feet a minute, banking left, climbing.

F. Flying at 320 mph, heading south, at 3,400 feet, climbing at 200 feet a minute, banking left, climbing.

| Altitude | Compass | Artificial horizon | Turn and bank | Rate of climb Feet per minute × 100 | Airspeed (mph) |

2. The aircraft above is:

A. Flying at 540 mph at 6,100 feet, heading north, descending at 400 feet a minute, descending, turning right.

B. Turning right, heading north at 540 mph, descending at 400 feet a minute, turning right, descending, at 10,600 feet.

C. Descending, descending at 400 feet a minute, at 450 mph, turning left, heading south, at 10,600 feet.

D. Flying at 450 mph, at 10,600 feet, heading north, descending at 400 feet a minute, turning right, descending.

E. Flying at 10,600 feet, heading south, descending at 400 feet a minute, at 540 mph, turning right, descending.

F. Flying at 450 mph, at 9,600 feet, heading north, descending at 400 feet a minute, turning right, descending.

| Altitude | Compass | Artificial horizon | Turn and bank | Rate of climb Feet per minute × 100 | Airspeed (mph) |

3. The aircraft above is:

A. Flying at 4,300 feet, at 320 mph, climbing, heading east, climbing at 500 feet a minute, climbing, no turn.

B. Flying at 320 mph, climbing at 500 feet a minute, turning left, climbing, heading east, at 3,000 feet.

C. Climbing at 400 feet a minute, heading south, no turn, altitude 3,400 feet, at 300 mph, descending.

D. Climbing at 500 feet a minute, at 4,300 feet, heading east, climbing, no turn, at 320 mph.

E. No turn, climbing at 500 feet a minute, at 3,400 feet, climbing, at 320 mph, heading east.

F. Flying at 230 mph, climbing at 500 feet a minute, at 3,400 feet, no turn, climbing, heading east.

4. What is wrong with the instruments above?

5. The aircraft above is:

A. Flying at 3,200 feet, at 420 mph, climbing, turning left, climbing at 600 feet a minute, heading east.

B. Climbing, flying at 2,300 feet, at 440 mph, turning right, climbing at 600 feet a minute, heading east.

C. Heading east at 420 mph, climbing, climbing at 600 feet a minute at 420 mph, turning right, at 2,300 feet.

D. Flying at 240 mph, heading east, climbing at 600 feet a minute, at 2,300 feet, turning right, climbing.

E. Heading east at 640 mph, climbing at 600 feet a minute, at 2,300 feet, turning right, climbing.

F. Flying at 420 mph, heading east, climbing at 800 feet a minute, climbing, turning right, at 2,300 feet.

Altitude Compass Artificial horizon Turn and bank Rate of climb Feet per minute x 100 Airspeed (mph)

6. The aircraft above is:

A. Flying at 11,200 feet, descending, at 510 mph, descending at 600 feet a minute, no turn, heading south.

B. Descending at 400 feet a minute, heading south, at 510 mph, descending at 12,100 feet, no turn.

C. Flying at 510 mph, descending at 600 feet a minute, heading east, at 12,200 feet, turning left.

D. Flying at 11,200 feet, descending, at 420 mph, heading south, no turn, descending at 600 feet a minute.

E. Heading south at 510 mph, descending, no turn, at 12,100 feet, descending at 600 feet a minute.

F. Descending at 600 feet a minute, heading south, left turn, descending, at 510 mph and 12,100 feet.

Answers

1. D
2. D
3. E
4. The artificial horizon shows the aircraft is climbing, but the rate-of-climb indicator shows it descending at 400 feet a minute.
5. C
6. E

Score 2 points for each answer that is correct. No points unless it is correct.

Average score   8
Good score   10
Excellent score   12

The pass mark is 8. The rapid grasp of instruments is extremely important for pilots, particularly on short-haul and holiday routes, where traffic is dense, aerial traffic jams common, and ground controllers are issuing frequent orders. Although 8 would be acceptable initially, and for an airline with long routes such as the transatlantic, holiday pilots should score at least 10.

Instrument Comprehension Test

It is a long time since pilots flew by the seat of their pants. They are now taught, in fact, totally to ignore what the seat of their pants or any other part of their bodies is telling them. It is common for a pilot flying in cloud to feel he is upside down when in fact he is the right way up, or to feel he is turning to the left when in fact he is turning to the right.

Unlike birds, which can fly in blinding conditions of fog or cloud with no trouble, man needs an artificial horizon and instruments to tell him what he is doing. Pilots learn to trust their instruments without hesitation. They scan them constantly. The ability to interpret this information from instruments quickly and accurately is vital. After reading the introduction about instruments, start the test. Write down the altitude, course, attitude of the aircraft from the artificial horizon, the turn, the rate of climb and the airspeed for each question.

There is a strict time limit of four minutes.

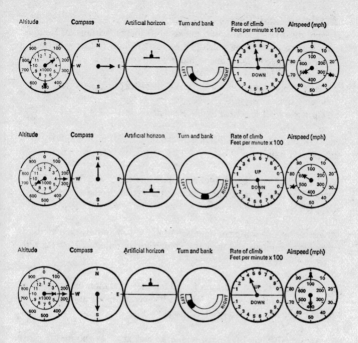

Answers

1. 3,750 feet, south, climbing, left turn, up 200 ft/min, 250 mph
2. 10,250 feet, west, descent, no turn, down 400 ft/min, 565 mph
3. 12,150 feet, north, descent, right turn, down 600 ft/min, 150 mph
4. 3,500 feet, east, climbing, left turn, up 500 ft/min, 530 mph
5. 9,250 feet, north, descent, no turn, down 600 ft/min, 670 mph
6. 4,250 feet, south, climb, left turn, up 400 ft/min, 400 mph.

Score 2 points for each correct answer and deduct one point for each error with a maximum of two errors for each question.

Average score	8
Good score	10
Excellent score	11

The pass mark is 9. The ability to absorb information from instruments whilst under pressure of time is fundamental to flying an airliner on a complex course on the approach to a crowded airport.

Mathematical Test

A pilot must be good at quick and accurate mental arithmetic. He must constantly calculate how much fuel he has left, how fast he is burning it at different speeds, how much time it will take to arrive at an airport or a navigational beacon.

Use a paper and pencil, or a pocket calculator, to answer the following questions.

There is a strict time limit of fifteen minutes.

1. How far will an aircraft flying at 550 mph travel in 25 minutes, to the nearest mile?

2. An aircraft is 90 miles from an airport and flying at 470 mph. How long will it take to reach the airport at this speed, to the nearest half-minute?

3. An aircraft flies at a constant 200 mph for 10 minutes, then at 300 mph for 20 minutes and then at 400 mph for 30 minutes. How far will it fly in this hour?

4. An aircraft flies at 100 mph for 20 minutes, 200 mph for 10 minutes and 250 mph for 30 minutes. What is its average speed in miles per hour, to the nearest two decimal places?

5. An aircraft takes off from London Airport at 12.45 and flies towards Frankfurt at 550 mph. Another aircraft takes off from Frankfurt at 12.50 and flies towards London at 600 mph. The distance between the two cities is taken as 400 miles. Will they be nearer London or Frankfurt when they meet?

6. Your car does 30 miles to the gallon at 50 mph and 25 mpg at 70 mph. You drive 40 miles at 50 mph and 125 miles at 70 mph. How much petrol do you need?

7. How much petrol do you save by driving 90 miles at 50 mph rather than at 70 mph, on the fuel consumption shown in Question 6?

8. How much longer will the journey of 90 miles take if you drive at 50 mph and not 70 mph?

9. The car in front of you is driving at 50 mph. You are moving at 75 mph. It is 5 miles ahead. How many minutes will it take you to catch up?

10. Your car does 35 miles to the gallon. It has 2½ gallons in the tank. How far can you go?

Answers
Score 1 point for each correct answer.

1. 229 miles.
2. 11½ minutes. 11 or 12 minutes acceptable.
3. 333.33 miles. 333 miles acceptable.
4. 191.66 mph. 190 mph acceptable.
5. Nearer Frankfurt.
6. 6.33 gallons or 6⅓.
7. 0.6 or ⅗ gallon.
8. 31 minutes. 30 minutes or ½ hour acceptable.
9. 12 minutes.
10. 87½ miles. 87 acceptable.

Average score	6
Good score	8
Excellent score	10

The pass mark is 8. Pilots have to be above average in mathematics. This is an area where people improve with practice, so do not be too disappointed if you fail it the first time. It can be worked on.

Mechanical Coordination

Coordination is very important. Despite advanced controls and systems, a modern airliner still has to be flown with sensitivity and accuracy. This is particularly true in landing, when the pilot has to bring a 200-ton machine moving at 150 mph out of the sky on to the first 1,000 feet of a narrow runway. He uses his feet and hands for totally different purposes – his feet to yaw left or right, one hand to steer and the other to move throttles and levers – so he must be well coordinated.

With a pencil in each hand, trace a line within the patterns *simultaneously* and *continuously*. Thus, in the first example you must draw a circle between the two existing circles with your left hand, and a square with your right. Your drawing must NOT touch the existing lines. You must move both your hands at the same time and you must not stop and restart. There are penalties for this. This is a high-scoring test.

There is a strict time limit of two minutes.

Make sure the paper is firmly weighted down and cannot move as you draw on it.

1

2

3

4

5

Scoring: Mechanical Coordination

Start with 15 points, and subtract one point each time you have crossed the line to a maximum of three points per problem. Thus you cannot lose more than three points in Problem 1, even if you cross the line four times.

Average score   6
Good score   10
Excellent score   13

The pass mark is 8. Below this, you are unlikely to have the natural aptitude in coordination for flying. (With helicopters, which require a very constant and high standard of coordination to keep them in the air, the pass mark goes up to 10.)

Personality Test

Personality plays as important a role in flying as it does in anything else. The airline pilot needs to be stable, self-confident, extroverted and able to fit easily into a team. Flying can impose considerable emotional strain, particularly on long-haul pilots who are constantly jet-lagged, far from home and close to pretty stewardesses. Pilots have been known to develop a severe fear of flying. Pilots are screened intensively before they are accepted. Stability and team spirit are the qualities which rate high. There is *no time limit* on this test, but the questions should be answered yes or no fairly rapidly. It is impossible to be totally accurate about one's emotions. So settle for what you generally think is the right answer, and not what is precisely right.

1. Do you ever feel exhausted by problems?
2. Do you ever wonder what you're doing with your life?
3. Do you put things down to 'luck' or 'fate'?
4. Would you say you are happy?
5. Do you like planning for the future?
6. Do you always wear a safety belt?
7. Do you always keep your word, even on trivial matters?
8. Were you afraid of ghosts as a child?
9. Are you frightened of failure?
10. Do you believe you are the master of your own destiny?
11. Are you gloomy about the prospects for the world?
12. Do you buy things on impulse?
13. Would you shelter under a tree in a thunderstorm?
14. Do you ever 'switch off' for a bit?
15. Did you sleep with your door open as a child?
16. Were you quite popular at school?
17. On the whole did you obey your parents as a child?
18. Do you feel you are unlucky?
19. Do you weigh things up carefully before making a decision?
20. Do you bet on outsiders in horse races?
21. Do you keep up to date with your personal correspondence?
22. Are you afraid of spiders, grass snakes and other harmless things?
23. Do you ever wish you were as successful as somebody else?
24. Will you stick out for your own ideas even when you are in a tiny minority?
25. Have you been successful in life?
26. Do you often change your hobbies?
27. Do you get bored with dull, if safe routine?
28. Do you have your car regularly serviced?
29. Do you ever get worried about trivial things?
30. Do you stick to a decision once you have made it?
31. Do you do a lot of things just to please other people?
32. Do you feel lonely even when there are other people around?

33. Do you prefer spontaneous events to planned ones?
34. Do you have life insurance?
35. Do you often have to rush to catch a train or bus or plane?
36. Do you get embarrassed if you drop a clanger at a party?
37. Do you hate looking at holiday pictures of yourself?
38. Could you give up smoking or begin a diet if necessary?
39. Does somebody love you?
40. Do you get to know people quickly?
41. Do you think that a good pension is a vital part of a job?
42. Do you consider yourself to be a responsible type?
43. Can you relax and sit without fidgeting?
44. Do you mind your ideas being laughed at?
45. Do you know where you want to end up in life?
46. Do you usually feel calm and satisfied?
47. Do you plan a drive carefully, with maps and so forth?
48. Have you ever done something impulsive for a dare?
49. Are you always forgetting little things to do?
50. Do you ever have to take sleeping pills?
51. Is there any feature of your body – skinny legs, protruding ears – that you would like to change?
52. Would you walk under a ladder?
53. Do you usually drop straight off to sleep?
54. Do you blurt things out without thinking?
55. Would the details of a guarantee influence your choice of car?
56. Do you often keep people waiting?
57. Do you like everything to go exactly according to plan?
58. Are you reasonably attractive to the opposite sex?
59. Do you read horoscopes in the paper?
60. Do you feel the fates are against you?
61. Do you often think it over for a day or two before a decision?
62. Have you ever thought of going into business on your own account?
63. Do you find it difficult to concentrate for long periods?
64. Do you worry about the future a lot?
65. On the whole, are you a useful member of society?
66. Do you decide what to watch on TV, and not the person with you?
67. Do you ever feel like giving it all up?
68. Do you know your birth sign?
69. Do you think that 'better safe than sorry' is a good motto for life?
70. Do you think that the world is basically a serious place?

Answers: Personality

The questions are set so that those who are not suited to flying airliners will score higher than those who are. It is worth noting that the qualities needed by a fighter pilot are often the opposite of those an airline pilot should have: thus a fighter pilot should score fairly high in the impulsive, risk-taker and irresponsible sections. An airline pilot would be rejected if he had a similar score.

In each case you score one point if your answer is the same as those given below. The questions are divided into sections to cover the important aspects of personality as far as flying passenger transports is concerned.

Impulsive to Controlled

Impulsives are inclined to act on the spur of the moment. They make hurried, often premature decisions and are unpredictable. Airline flying is very much a routine business and so systematic and controlled people are necessary, who look before they leap.

5. No.
12. Yes.
19. No.
26. Yes.
33. Yes.
40. Yes.
47. No.
54. Yes.
61. No.
68. Yes.

High scorers are impulsive.

Anxious to Calm

Although many high achievers are anxious types, anxiety is not conducive to good airline pilots. Anxious people are easily upset by things that go wrong and worry unnecessarily.

Flying is littered with delays, alterations and minor technical problems that would wear out an anxious pilot's nerves. Serene types, immune to irrational fears and upsets, are wanted.

1. Yes.
8. Yes.
15. Yes
22. Yes.

340

29. Yes.
36. Yes.
43. No.
50. Yes.
57. Yes.
64. Yes.

High scorers are anxious, worried types. Those with low scores are calm.

Inferiority to Self-esteem
Feelings of inferiority can lead to sloppiness and nervous strain. Self-confidence and self-esteem are positive characteristics for the safe pilot. A pilot with an inferiority complex might be unable to translate his decisions into action for fear of being wrong. This is potentially hazardous.

2. Yes.
9. Yes.
16. No.
23. Yes.
30. No.
37. Yes.
44. Yes.
51. Yes.
58. No.
65. No.

High scorers have a feeling of inferiority. Low scorers are proud of themselves.

Dependent to Independent
Although a pilot must not be too much of an individual, and should blend easily into a team or crew, he should have plenty of self-reliance and independence of thought and action. Pilots must monitor each other continuously to avoid the sort of errors that, unchecked, have caused many disasters – mis-set altimeters, wrongly selected flaps, even forgetting to lower the undercarriage. A pilot who is unquestioningly obedient to authority might sit by whilst his captain flew the aircraft into the ground.

3. Yes.
10. No.

17. Yes.
24. No.
31. Yes.
38. No.
45. No.
52. No.
59. Yes.
66. No.

High scorers are overdependent on others.

Depressed to Happy

If a pilot is overly depressed, his state of alertness and anticipation will be affected. Depression also affects powers of concentration and can induce a state where the pilot's arousal point becomes so suppressed that he ignores safety checks.

4. No.
11. Yes.
18. Yes.
25. No.
32. Yes.
39. No.
46. No.
53. No.
60. Yes.
67. Yes.

High scorers are depressed. However, those who score only 1 or 2 on this section will be just as suspect as the person with 8 or 9. To be that happy suggests complacency and smugness, equally incompatible with good flying.

Risk-Taker to Careful

Those with a gambling instinct, always prepared to chance their arm, make good fighter pilots and very bad airline pilots. Nothing in airliner flying should be taken by chance and the risk-taker should not be in the cockpit of such an aircraft.

6. No.
13. Yes.
20. Yes.
27. Yes.

34. No.
41. No.
48. Yes.
55. No.
62. Yes.
69. No.

High scorers are gamblers who should stick to combat planes.

Irresponsible to Responsible
It is clearly vital for a pilot to be responsible and not to indulge in flying tactics that are unorthodox if fun. Irresponsible people can be expected to be casual, unpredictable, careless of regulations. That is a recipe for a serious crash. Pilots must be conscientious, trustworthy and reasonably serious-minded.

7. No.
14. Yes.
21. No.
28. No.
35. Yes.
42. No.
49. Yes.
56. Yes.
63. Yes.
70. No.

High scorers are irresponsible, though making good passengers.

The following people would be eliminated as unsuitable:
1. Those with 9 or 10 points as impulsive, feeling inferior, dependent, irresponsible.
2. Those with 10 points as depressed, anxious.
3. Those with 8, 9 or 10 points as risk-takers.
4. Those with one point as anxious, feeling inferior, depressed (they are so calm, full of self-esteem and happy that they are so complacent that an engine could drop off without them noticing it).
5. Those whose total is over 58 points, since they tend to instability.
6. Those whose total is less than 15 points, since they tend towards torpor and overweening self-pride.

The average score is 45, and scores up to 58 are unremarkable. Personality testing is still very much in its infancy. Many airlines and air forces are reluctant to use it since it is still controversial. They use interviews and observation of would-be pilots at selection centres. However, the criteria and the qualities they are looking for are similar to the ones in this test.

Index

346

John Hatt
The Tropical Traveller £1.95

an essential guide to travel in hot climates

A book of guidance, good humour and hard-won expertise that will ease the journey on the road to Mandalay or even the Matto Grosso for the hardiest wanderer. Whether you're a back-packing student, a jet-setting journalist, or a businessman hunting for new markets for fridge-freezers, here's the book to read before you go, while you pack and when you're wondering how you'll cope with malaria, mosquitoes, pickpockets, hippopotami . . .

Arthur Eperon
Travellers' Britain £2.95

A guide to twelve routes throughout England, Scotland and Wales, finding the best places to eat, drink and stay in the most attractive towns and villages along the way. A detailed and up-to-the-minute handbook for the motorist holidaying in Britain and seeking the interesting places that the main roads miss. Introduction by Cliff Michelmore.

Travellers' France £2.50

Six major routes across France, taking in the best restaurants and hotels, visiting the most interesting out-of-the-way places. This detailed and up-to-the-minute handbook is for the traveller who wants more out of France than a mad dash down the motorway. Each of the six routes across the country is illustrated with a specially commissioned two-colour map, and includes a host of information on where to eat and drink, where to take the children, where to stay, and how to get the most out of the towns and countryside.

Fiction

☐ **Options**	Freda Bright	£1.50p
☐ **The Thirty-nine Steps**	John Buchan	£1.50p
☐ **Secret of Blackoaks**	Ashley Carter	£1.50p
☐ **The Sittaford Mystery**	Agatha Christie	£1.00p
☐ **Dupe**	Liza Cody	£1.25p
☐ **Lovers and Gamblers**	Jackie Collins	£2.50p
☐ **Sphinx**	Robin Cook	£1.25p
☐ **Ragtime**	E. L. Doctorow	£1.50p
☐ **The Rendezvous**	Daphne du Maurier	£1.50p
☐ **Flashman**	George Macdonald Fraser	£1.50p
☐ **The Moneychangers**	Arthur Hailey	£2.25p
☐ **Secrets**	Unity Hall	£1.50p
☐ **Simon the Coldheart**	Georgette Heyer	95p
☐ **The Eagle Has Landed**	Jack Higgins	£1.95p
☐ **Sins of the Fathers**	Susan Howatch	£2.50p
☐ **The Master Sniper**	Stephen Hunter	£1.50p
☐ **Smiley's People**	John le Carré	£1.95p
☐ **To Kill a Mockingbird**	Harper Lee	£1.75p
☐ **Ghosts**	Ed McBain	£1.25p
☐ **Gone with the Wind**	Margaret Mitchell	£2.95p
☐ **The Totem**	David Morrell	£1.25p
☐ **Platinum Logic**	Tony Parsons	£1.75p
☐ **Wilt**	Tom Sharpe	£1.50p
☐ **Rage of Angels**	Sidney Sheldon	£1.75p
☐ **The Unborn**	David Shobin	£1.50p
☐ **A Town Like Alice**	Nevile Shute	£1.75p
☐ **A Falcon Flies**	Wilbur Smith	£1.95p
☐ **The Deep Well at Noon**	Jessica Stirling	£1.95p
☐ **The Ironmaster**	Jean Stubbs	£1.75p
☐ **The Music Makers**	E. V. Thompson	£1.75p

Non-fiction

☐ **Extraterrestrial Civilizations**	Isaac Asimov	£1.50p
☐ **Pregnancy**	Gordon Bourne	£2.95p
☐ **Jogging from Memory**	Rob Buckman	£1.25p
☐ **The 35mm Photographer's Handbook**	Julian Calder and John Garrett	£5.95p
☐ **Travellers' Britain**	Arthur Eperon	£2.95p
☐ **Travellers' Italy**		£2.50p
☐ **The Complete Calorie Counter**	Eileen Fowler	75p

☐	**The Diary of Anne Frank**	Anne Frank	£1.50p
☐	**Linda Goodman's Sun Signs**	Linda Goodman	£2.50p
☐	**Mountbatten**	Richard Hough	£2.50p
☐	**How to be a Gifted Parent**	David Lewis	£1.95p
☐	**Symptoms**	Sigmund Stephen Miller	£2.50p
☐	**Book of Worries**	Robert Morley	£1.50p
☐	**The Hangover Handbook**	David Outerbridge	£1.25p
☐	**The Alternative Holiday Catalogue**	edited by Harriet Peacock	£1.95p
☐	**The Pan Book of Card Games**	Hubert Phillips	£1.75p
☐	**Food for All the Family**	Magnus Pyke	£1.50p
☐	**Everything Your Doctor Would Tell You If He Had the Time**	Claire Rayner	£4.95p
☐	**Just Off for the Weekend**	John Slater	£2.50p
☐	**An Unfinished History of the World**	Hugh Thomas	£3.95p
☐	**The Third Wave**	Alvin Toffler	£1.95p
☐	**The Flier's Handbook**		£5.95p

All these books are available at your local bookshop or newsagent, or can be ordered direct from the publisher. Indicate the number of copies required and fill in the form below

7

Name_____
(Block letters please)

Address_____

_____

Send to Pan Books (CS Department), Cavaye Place, London SW10 9PG
Please enclose remittance to the value of the cover price plus:
35p for the first book plus 15p per copy for each additional book ordered
to a maximum charge of £1.25 to cover postage and packing
Applicable only in the UK

While every effort is made to keep prices low, it is sometimes
necessary to increase prices at short notice. Pan Books reserve
the right to show on covers and charge new retail prices which
may differ from those advertised in the text or elsewhere